U•X•L Encyclopedia of Weather and Natural Disasters

U•X•L Encyclopedia of Weather and Natural Disasters

Flood to Monsoon VOLUME 3

Anaxos, Inc., Editors

U•X•L
An imprint of Thomson Gale,
a part of The Thomson Corporation

THOMSON
GALE

Detroit • New York • San Francisco • New Haven, Conn. • Waterville, Maine • London

THOMSON
GALE

U•X•L Encyclopedia of Weather and Natural Disasters

Anaxos, Inc., editors

Project Editor
Melissa Hill

Editorial
Julie Carnagie, Paul Lewon, Lemma Shomali

Indexing Services
Factiva, a Dow Jones & Reuters Company

Rights and Acquisitions
Margaret Abendroth, Margaret Chamberlain-Gaston, Tracie Richardson

Imaging and Multimedia
Lezlie Light, Robyn V. Young

Product Design
Pamela A. Galbreath, Jennifer Wahi

Composition
Evi Seoud, Mary Beth Trimper

Manufacturing
Wendy Blurton, Dorothy Maki

For more information, contact
The Gale Group
27500 Drake Rd.
Farmington Hills, MI 48331-3535
Or you can visit our Internet site at
http://www.gale.com

Cover photographs: Tornado, supercell thunderstorm, lightning over city, cirrus and cumulus clouds, all FMA Production. Erupting volcano, photograph by Krafft. National Audubon Society Collection/Photo Researchers, Inc. All reproduced by permission.

LIBRARY OF CONGRESS CATALOGING-IN-PUBLICATION DATA

UXL encyclopedia of weather and natural disasters / Anaxos, Inc., editors.
p. cm.
Includes bibliographical references and index.
ISBN 978-1-4144-1879-7 (set : alk. paper) -- ISBN 978-1-4144-1880-3 (vol. 1 : alk. paper) -- ISBN 978-1-4144-1881-0 (vol. 2 : alk. paper) -- ISBN 978-1-4144-1882-7 (vol. 3 : alk. paper) -- ISBN 978-1-4144-1883-4 (vol. 4 : alk. paper) -- ISBN 978-1-4144-1884-1 (vol. 5 : alk. paper) --
1. Meteorology--Encyclopedias, Juvenile. 2. Natural disasters--Encyclopedias, Juvenile.
I. Anaxos, Inc.
QC854.U95 2008
551.503--dc22

2007011300

ISBN-13:

978-1-4144-1879-7 (set)
978-1-4144-1880-3 (vol. 1)
978-1-4144-1881-0 (vol. 2)
978-1-4144-1882-7 (vol. 3)
978-1-4144-1883-4 (vol. 4)
978-1-4144-1884-1 (vol. 5)

ISBN-10:

1-4144-1879-5 (set)
1-4144-1880-9 (vol. 1)
1-4144-1881-7 (vol. 2)
1-4144-1882-5 (vol. 3)
1-4144-1883-3 (vol. 4)
1-4144-1884-1 (vol. 5)

This title is also available as an e-book.
ISBN-13 978-1-4144-1885-8, ISBN-10 1-4144-1885-X
Contact your Gale sales representative for ordering information.
Printed in China

10 9 8 7 6 5 4 3 2 1

Table of Contents

Reader's Guide

Weather in all its manifestations—from peaceful blankets of mountain fog to ferocious hurricanes—fascinates most humans. Young children wonder why the sky is blue. Busy professionals wonder whether ice storms will cause flight delays. Backyard gardeners wonder whether their plants will survive a hot, dry summer. *The U•X•L Encyclopedia of Weather and Natural Disasters* presents a comprehensive, up-to-date survey of weather, weather-related topics, and natural disasters that gives readers the science behind the weather events that affect us all every day.

Scope and format

Each of the chapters in this five-volume series presents its topic in clear, nontechnical language. The topics are arranged in alphabetical order. The material is enlivened with eyewitness descriptions of recent weather phenomena, historical accounts of famous past weather events and disasters, biographies of famous figures in meteorology, practical information on handling extreme weather situations, relevant book and film recommendations, and hundreds of photographs, illustrations, and charts. Each chapter also presents step-by-step experiments, suitable for home or classroom, that allow students to have hands-on experiences with the foundations of weather and meteorology. Additionally, *The U•X•L Encyclopedia of Weather and Natural Disasters* provides a "Words to Know" section in each chapter, with key terms clearly defined. A cumulative index and a comprehensive "Where to Learn More" section at the back of each volume give readers easy access to material both within the series and in outside resources.

Volume 1 of this series serves as a general introduction to the topic of weather and natural disasters, and includes chapters on climate, clouds, and precipitation.

Volume 2 presents the first six of the alphabetically arranged chapters on weather and natural disaster topics: Avalanche, Blizzard, Drought, Dust Storm, Earthquake, and El Niño.

Volume 3 presents the following seven chapters: Flood, Fog, Hurricane, Landslide, La Niña, Local Winds, and Monsoon.

Volume 4 wraps up the alphabetically arranged chapters with six more chapters: Optical Effects, Thunderstorm, Tornado, Tsunami, Volcano, and Wildfire.

Volume 5 examines human involvement with weather and natural disasters, offering chapters on forecasting, climate change, and the influence of humans on weather.

Acknowledgements

The development of *The U•X•L Encyclopedia of Weather and Natural Disasters* was a collaborative effort by the staff of Anaxos, Inc., but several key members of the team require special acknowledgement and appreciation. Many thanks are owed to Dr. Elliot Richmond for his broad meteorological expertise and good humor. Special thanks also to Emily Baker-Falconer and Russ Falconer, for their organizational vigor and editorial acumen, and to Liza Banks, for her copyediting prowess.

The staff of Anaxos would also like to thank Gale content project editor Melissa Hill and content product manager Debra Kirby for their guidance, insight, and inspiration.

Also, Melissa Hill would like to thank Lou Camp for additional review of the Climate Change and Global Warming entry. His knowledge of the topic and candid insights contribute much to the final product.

Timeline

c. 1650 B.C.E. The Mediterranean island of Thera is destroyed by a volcanic eruption. The event possibly gives rise to the legend of the lost civilization of Atlantis.

218 B.C.E. Carthaginian leader Hannibal's army is decimated by avalanches as he attempts to cross the Alps with tens of thousands of soldiers and a multitude of war elephants.

350 B.C.E Greek philosopher Aristotle writes *Meteorology.*

79 Eruption of Mount Vesuvius destroys Pompeii and Herculaneum in Italy.

1281 A Chinese fleet of around 4,000 warships is destroyed by a typhoon during an attempted invasion of Japan. The relieved Japanese called the typhoon *kamikaze,* or "divine wind," believing it came from the gods for their protection.

1375 An earthquake destroys the famous lighthouse of Alexandria, Egypt, one of two remaining wonders of the ancient world (the other being the great pyramids of Egypt).

1441 Invention of standardized rain gauge by King Sejong and Prince Munjong of Korea.

1450 Leone Battista Alberti invents first anemometer.

1606 Galileo invents the thermometer.

1643 Evangelista Torricelli invents the barometer.

1657 King Ferdinand II of Tuscany establishes the Accademia Del Cimento of Florence, which develops many early meteorological tools.

1686 English astronomer Edmund Halley publishes a ground-breaking study of trade winds and monsoons.

1707 Mount Fuji in Japan erupts for the last time.

1714 Gabriel Fahrenheit invents the first mercury thermometer.

1742 Swedish astronomer Anders Celsius outlines the centrigrade temperature scale. This would lead to what is now the Celsius scale.

1752 Benjamin Franklin performs his famous "kite" experiment, flying a kite that dangled a metal key during a thunderstorm to determine the relationship between lightning and electricity.

1783 Iceland's Mount Laki erupts, spewing massive clouds of ash into the atmosphere and killing up to one fifth of the population of Iceland.

1784 Benjamin Franklin theorizes that the abnormally cold European winter of 1783–1784 was due to the eruption of Mount Laki, becoming one of the first scientists to note the relationship between volcanic eruptions and climate cooling.

1786 Benjamin Franklin publishes an accurate map of the Gulf Stream.

1820 The U.S. Army begins making and recording formal weather observations.

1841 Elias Loomis creates the first synoptic weather map.

1842 James P. Espy is appointed first official U.S. government meteorologist.

1846 Irish astronomer and physicist John Thomas Romney Robinson invents the cup anemometer.

1849 The Smithsonian Institution establishes a national weather observation network using information relayed via telegraph from 150 observers across the country.

1860 As head of the newly established British Meteorological Office, Robert FitzRoy uses the new telegraph system to gather daily observations from across England to make "weather forecasts," a term he coined.

1863 Robert FitzRoy publishes *Weather Book*, an important meteorological text.

1870 President Ulysses S. Grant establishes a national weather warning service under the Secretary of War.

1873 International Meteorological Organization founded.

1875 Benito Vines, the director of the Meteorological Observatory at Belen in Havana, Cuba, issues an accurate hurricane warning two days before a hurricane hits Cuba. His warning saves many lives.

1876 A cyclone in Bangladesh kills more than 200,000.

1883 Eruption of Krakatau causes massive tsunamis that kill 36,000 in Java and Sumatra.

1887 The Yellow River in China floods, killing an estimated one million people.

1889 A dam bursts in Johnstown, Pennsylvania, causing a flood that kills 2,000 people.

1890 U.S. Weather Bureau is founded.

1892 Captain Camilo Carrilo tells the Geographical Society of Lima, Peru, of "El Niño," his term for a warm northerly current and associated climate noticeable around Christmas.

1897 Belgian Adrien de Gerlache sets off for the Antarctic (with a crew that included first-mate Roald Amundsen) to make geographical and meteorological observations of Antarctica. It is the first expedition to spend an entire winter in the Antarctic.

1898 U.S. Weather Bureau establishes a hurricane warning network at Kingston, Jamaica.

1900 A hurricane strikes Galveston, Texas, killing more than 6,000 people.

1902 Stratosphere is discovered. Two scientists, working independently, share credit for the discovery: Richard Assmann and Léon Teisserenc de Bort.

1906 Earthquake in San Francisco kills approximately 3,000.

1919 Introduction of the Norwegian Cyclone Model, a revolutionary method of weather map analysis and interpretation.

1921 Sakuhei Fujiwara publishes a paper on the "Fujiwara Effect," the rotation of two cyclones around each other.

1924 Sir Gilbert Walker coins the term "Southern Oscillation" to describe the current and climate shifts popularly known as El Niño.

1925 The so-called Tri-State Tornado ravages Missouri, Illinois, and Indiana, killing nearly 700 people.

1930 Russian scientist Pavel Mochanov successfully launches his radiosonde, a balloon-borne device that can take weather measurements and relay them by radio, into the stratosphere.

1934 The "Dust Bowl," a severe drought in southern plains states that lasted several years, begins.

1938 Guy Steward Callendar publishes "The Artificial Production of Carbon Dioxide and Its Influence on Temperature," considered the first description of global warming caused by carbon dioxide emissions.

1943 Pilot J. B. Duckworth intentionally flies into a hurricane off the coast of Texas for the purpose of weather reconnaissance.

1948 First correct tornado prediction made in Oklahoma.

1948 Pacific Tsunami Warning System is established in Honolulu, Hawaii.

1951 The World Meteorological Association, operating as a specialized agency of the United Nations, replaces the International Meteorological Association.

1954 The U.S. National Weather Service begins naming each season's hurricanes alphabetically using female names.

1956 F. K. Ball publishes his theory of the generation of Antarctic katabatic winds.

1959 World's first weather satellite, Vanguard 2, is launched.

1969 The Saffir-Simpson Hurricane Scale is created. The scale rates the strength of hurricanes on a scale of 1 to 5.

1969 Hurricane Camille hits the Gulf Coast of the U.S., killing several hundred people.

1970 The National Oceanic and Atmospheric Administration (NOAA) is established.

1971 Ted Fujita introduces the Fujita scales for rating tornadoes.

1978 Record-breaking blizzard hits northeastern U.S.

1980 Mount St. Helens in Washington State explodes.

1985 Discovery of the Antarctic ozone hole.

2004 Massive tsunami kills nearly 300,000 people in Thailand, India, and Indonesia.

2005 Hurricane Katrina pummels New Orleans and the Mississippi Gulf Coast, killing nearly 2,000 people and forcing millions of people from their homes.

2006 The U.S. experiences a record-breaking wildfire season, with nearly ten million acres burned.

2007 The Enhanced Fujita Scale replaces the Fujita scale as a system for rating tornadoes.

Words to Know

A

absolute humidity: the amount of water vapor in the air, expressed as a ratio of the amount of water per unit of air.

accretion: the process by which a hailstone grows larger, by gradually accumulating cloud droplets as it travels through a cloud.

acid precipitation: rain and snow that are made more acidic when carbon, sulfur, and/or nitrogen oxides in the air dissolve into water. Also known as acid rain.

acid rain: rain that is made more acidic when carbon, sulfur, and/or nitrogen oxides in the air dissolve into water. Also known as acid precipitation.

active solar collector: system for gathering and storing the Sun's heat that uses pumps and motors. Often used for heating water.

active volcano: a volcano that continues to erupt regularly.

adiabatic process: a process by which the temperature of a moving air parcel changes, even though no heat is exchanged between the air parcel and the surrounding air.

advection: the horizontal movement of a mass such as air or an ocean current.

aftershock: ground shaking that occurs after the main shock of an earthquake.

agricultural report: a specialized weather report tailored to the needs of farmers that includes current temperature, precipitation, and wind speed and direction, as well as frost warnings and predictions of temperature and precipitation for the days to come.

air mass: a large quantity of air throughout which temperature and moisture content is fairly constant.

air pollutant: any harmful substance that exists in the atmosphere at concentrations great enough to endanger the health of living organisms.

air pressure: the pressure exerted by the weight of air over a given area of Earth's surface. Also called atmospheric pressure or barometric pressure.

Air Quality Index (AQI): measurement of air quality, based on concentrations of surface ozone averaged over an eight-hour period for specific locations.

Alps: mountain system composed of more than fifteen principle mountain ranges that extends in an arc for almost 660 miles (1,060 kilometers) across south-central Europe.

anabatic wind: winds caused by warm air close to Earth's surface. The air is less dense than the surrounding air and travels upward along a slope.

Andes: mountain range extending more than 5,000 miles (8,045 kilometers) along the western coast of South America.

anemometer: an instrument that measures wind speed.

aneroid barometer: a type of barometer that consists of a vacuum-sealed metal capsule, within which a spring expands or contracts with changing air pressure.

anvil: the flattened formation at the top of a mature cumulonimbus cloud.

aquifer: an underground layer of spongy rock, gravel, or sand in which water collects.

arid: describes a climate in which almost no rain or snow falls.

ash: very small, fine fragments of lava or rock that are blasted into the air during volcanic explosions.

asthenosphere: region of the mantle below the lithosphere, composed of partially melted rock.

aurora: a bright, colorful display of light in the night sky, produced when charged particles from the Sun enter Earth's atmosphere.

avalanche: a large mass of snow, ice, rocks, soil, or a combination of these elements that moves suddenly and swiftly down a mountain slope, pulled by the force of gravity.

avalanche path: the course an avalanche takes down a slope, composed of a starting zone, a track, and a runout zone.

avalanche wind: a cloudlike mixture of snow particles and air pushed ahead of a slab avalanche as it races downward.

aviation report: a specialized weather report tailored to the needs of pilots that provides information on the height of the clouds, visibility, and storm systems.

B

backfire: a small fire set by firefighters in the path of an oncoming wildfire to burn up the fuel before the main fire arrives, thus blocking it.

backing wind: a wind that shifts direction, rotating counterclockwise higher in the atmosphere.

barchan dune: a sand dune that, when viewed from above, resembles a crescent moon, with the tips of the crescent pointing downwind. Also called barchane dune, barkhan dune, or crescentic dune.

barograph: an aneroid barometer that records changes in air pressure over time on a rotating drum.

barometer: an instrument used to measure air pressure.

basalt: a type of rock that forms from hardened lava.

blizzard: the most severe type of winter storm, characterized by winds of 35 miles (56 kilometers) per hour or greater, large quantities of falling or blowing snow, and low temperatures.

blocking system: a whirling air mass containing either a high-pressure system (a blocking high) or a low-pressure system (a blocking low), that gets cut off from the main flow of upper-air westerlies.

C

caldera: a large depression, usually circular or oval shaped, left behind when a volcano's summit collapses.

calvus: "bald"; describes when the upper part of a cloud is losing its rounded, cauliflower-like outline and becoming diffuse and fibrous.

capillatus: "having hair"; a cloud with a cirriform, streaky structure on its upper edges.

castellanus: "castlelike"; used to describe clouds with vertical extensions.

Cenozoic era: the historical period from sixty-five million years ago to the present.

chaos theory: the theory that the weather, by its very nature, is unpredictable. Every time one atmospheric variable (such as heat, air pressure, or water) changes, every other variable also changes—but in ways that are out of proportion with the first variable's change.

chinook: a dry, warm katabatic wind in North America that blows down the eastern side of the Rocky Mountains, from New Mexico to Canada in winter or early spring.

chinook wall cloud: a solid bank of wispy, white clouds that appears over the eastern edge of the Rocky Mountains in advance of a chinook wind.

chlorofluorocarbons (CFCs): compounds similar to hydrocarbons in which one or more of the hydrogen atoms are replaced by fluorine or chlorine.

cinder: a small piece of material thrown from a volcano during an eruption.

cinder cone: a volcanic cone made of lava fragments.

cirriform: a wispy, feathery fair weather cloud formation that exists at high levels of the troposphere.

cirrostratus: a thin layer of high-altitude clouds that cover most of the sky, but are semitransparent.

cirrus: clouds at high levels of the troposphere, created by wind-blown ice crystals, that are so thin as to be nearly transparent.

Clean Air Act: set of environmental regulations limiting pollutants emitted by cars, factories, and other sources. First enacted by the U.S. Congress in 1970 and updated several times since then.

clear-cutting: the logging practice of harvesting all trees from vast forest tracts.

climate: the weather experienced by a given location, averaged over several decades.

coalescence: the process by which an ice crystal grows larger. The ice crystal collides and sticks together with water droplets as the ice crystal travels down through a cloud.

coastal flood: an overflow of water onto a coastal area caused by a storm surge, strong winds, or tsunami.

cold front: the leading edge of a moving mass of cold air.

cold-phase ENSO (El Niño/Southern Oscillation): another name for La Niña; colder-than-normal eastern Pacific waters.

composite volcano: a volcano with steep sides made of layers of lava and ash.

compressional warming: an adiabatic process by which an air parcel warms as it descends. The descending parcel is compressed by the increasing pressure of the surrounding air, which adds kinetic energy to the molecules. Also called compressional heating.

condensation: the process by which water changes from a gas to a liquid.

condensation nucleus: a tiny solid particle around which condensation of water vapor occurs.

conduction: the transfer of heat by collisions between moving molecules or atoms.

cone: the sloping outer sides of a volcano (not all volcanoes have cones).

conelet: a small cone on the side of a large volcano.

congestus: "congested"; describes clouds with upper parts that are piled up and sharply defined; resembles a head of cauliflower.

conservation tillage: the practice of leaving vegetation on fields during idle periods to protect the soil from erosion and trap moisture.

continental drift: geologic theory that all continents were part of a single, original landmass before they slowly separated and gradually drifted apart.

convection: the upward motion of an air mass or air parcel that has been heated.

convection current: circular movement of a gas or liquid between hot and cold areas.

convective cell: a unit within a thunderstorm cloud that contains updrafts and downdrafts.

convective zone: the region of warm tropical water over which thunderstorms form; the ocean under the Intertropical Convergence Zone.

conventional radar: instrument that detects the location, movement, and intensity of precipitation, and gives indications about the type of precipitation. It operates by emitting microwaves, which are reflected by precipitation. Also called radar.

convergence: the movement of air inward toward a central point, such as the trade winds blowing from the north and south near the equator.

Coriolis effect: the apparent curvature of large-scale winds, ocean currents, and anything else that moves freely across Earth, due to the rotation of Earth around its axis.

corona: a circle of light centered on the Moon or Sun that is usually bounded by a colorful ring or set of rings.

cosmic rays: invisible, high-energy particles that bombard Earth from space.

crater: the bowl-shaped area around the opening at the top of a volcano.

crepuscular rays: bright beams of light that radiate from the Sun and cross the sky.

crest: the highest point of a wave.

critical angle: the angle at which sunlight must strike the back of the raindrop in order to be reflected back to the front of the drop.

crown fire: a fire that spreads through the treetops, or crown, of a forest.

crust: the outermost layer of Earth, varying in thickness from 3.5 miles (5 kilometers) under the ocean to 50 miles (80 kilometers) thick under the continents.

cumuliform: a puffy, heaped up cloud formation.

cumulonimbus: a tall, vertically developed cloud reaching to the top of the troposphere or above, and capable of producing heavy rain, high winds, and lightning.

cumulus: fluffy, white, mid level clouds that look like white or light-gray cotton balls of various shapes.

cyclone: a weather system characterized by air that flows inward and circulates around a low-pressure area.

D

dart leaders: the series of dim lightning strokes that occur immediately after the original lightning stroke, that serve to discharge the remaining buildup of electrons near the base of the cloud.

debris avalanche: a downward slide of loose, earthen material (soil, mud, and small rocks) that begins suddenly and travels at great speeds;

similar to a snow avalanche. It builds into a fearsome mass of mud, trees, and rocks that can cause much damage.

debris slide: a slide of small rocks and shallow layers of loose soil that commonly follows volcanic eruptions.

deforestation: the removal of all or most of the trees from an area.

dendrochronology: the study of the annual growth of rings of trees.

deposition: the process by which water changes directly from a gas to a solid, without first going through the liquid phase.

derecho: a destructive, straight-line wind, which travels faster than 58 mph (93 kph) and has a path of damage at least 280 miles (450 kilometers) long. Also called plow wind.

desert climate: the world's driest climate type, with less than 10 inches (25 centimeters) of rainfall annually.

desert pavement: hard, flat, dry ground and gravel that remain after all sand and dust has been eroded from a surface.

desertification: the process by which semiarid lands turn to desert (also called land degradation). It is caused by prolonged drought, during which time the top layers of soil dry out and blow away.

dew point: the temperature at which a given parcel of air reaches its saturation point and can no longer hold water in the vapor state.

diffraction: the slight bending of sunlight or moonlight around water droplets or other tiny particles.

dispersion: the selective refraction of light that results in the separation of light into the spectrum of colors.

divergence: the movement of air outward, away from a central point.

Doppler radar: a sophisticated type of radar that relies on the Doppler effect, the change in frequency of waves emitted from a moving source, to determine wind speed and direction as well as the direction in which precipitation is moving.

dormant volcano: a volcano that has not erupted for many years.

downburst: an extremely strong, localized downdraft beneath a thunderstorm that spreads horizontally when it hits the ground, destroying objects in its path.

downdraft: a downward blast of air from a thunderstorm cloud, felt at the surface as a cool wind gust.

drizzle: precipitation formed by raindrops between 0.008 inches and 0.02 inches in diameter.

drought: an extended period when the amount of rain or snow that falls on an area is much lower than usual.

dry adiabatic lapse rate: the constant rate at which the temperature of an unsaturated air parcel changes as it ascends or descends through the atmosphere. Specifically, air cools by 5.5°F for every 1,000 feet (1.0°C for every 100 meters) it ascends and warms by 5.5°F for every 1,000 feet (1.0°C for every 100 meters) it descends.

Dust Bowl: the popular name for the approximately 150,000 square-mile-area (400,000-square-kilometer-area) in the southern portion of the Great Plains region of the United States. It is characterized by low annual rainfall, a shallow layer of topsoil, and high winds.

dust devil: a spinning vortex of sand and dust that is usually harmless but may grow quite large. Also called a whirlwind.

dust storm: a large cloud of dust blown by a strong wind.

E

earthflow: a landslide that consists of material that is moist and full of clay, yet drier than the material in mudflows.

earthquake: a sudden shifting of masses of rock beneath Earth's surface, which releases enormous amounts of energy and sends out shock waves that cause the ground to shake.

eccentricity: the alternating change in shape of Earth's orbit between a circle and an ellipse.

ecosystem: a community of plants and animals, including humans, and their physical surroundings.

effusive eruption: the type of eruption in which lava spills over the side of a crater.

El Niño: Spanish for "the Christ child;" an extraordinarily strong episode (occurring every two to seven years) of the annual warming of the Pacific waters off the coast of Peru and Ecuador.

El Niño/Southern Oscillation (ENSO): the simultaneous warming of the waters of the eastern Pacific and the accompanying shifts in air pressure over the eastern and western Pacific.

electromagnetic spectrum: the array of electromagnetic radiation, which includes radio waves, infrared radiation, visible light, ultraviolet radiation, x rays, and gamma rays.

ENSO: stands for El Niño/Southern Oscillation. It describes the simultaneous warming of the waters in the eastern Pacific Ocean and the shifting pattern of air pressure between the eastern and western edges of the Pacific.

entrainment: the process by which cool, unsaturated air next to a thunderstorm cloud gets pulled into the cloud during the mature stage of a thunderstorm.

Environmental Protection Agency (EPA): government agency charged with implementing the provisions of the Clean Air Act.

epicenter: the point on Earth's surface directly above the focus of an earthquake, where seismic waves first appear.

equinoxes: the days marking the start of spring and fall. Also the two days of the year in which day and night are most similar in length and the Sun appears to cross Earth's equator in its yearly motion.

erosion: the wearing away of a surface by the action of wind, water, or ice.

eruption: the release of pressure that sends lava, rocks, ash, and gases out of a volcano.

evaporation: the process by which water changes from a liquid to a gas.

evaporation fog: fog that is formed when water vapor evaporates into cool air and brings the air to its saturation point.

extinct volcano: a volcano that is never expected to erupt again.

extratropical cyclones: a storm system that forms outside of the tropics and involves contrasting warm and cold air masses.

eye: an area of clear sky and warm, dry, descending air at the center of a hurricane.

eye wall: a vertical area of thick clouds, intense rain, and strong winds marking the outer boundary of the eye.

F

fair-weather waterspout: relatively harmless waterspout that forms over water and arises either in conjunction with, or independently of, a severe thunderstorm. Also called nontornadic waterspout.

fall: the downward motion of rock or soil through the air or along the surface of a steep slope.

Fata Morgana: a special type of superior mirage that takes the form of spectacular castles, buildings, or cliffs rising above cold land or water.

fault: crack in Earth's surface where two plates or sections of the crust push and slide in opposite directions against one another.

fault creep: slow, continuous movement of plates along a fault, allowing pressure to be released.

fibratus: "fibrous"; describes clouds with hairlike strands with no hooks or curls at the end.

fire line: a strip of ground, cleared of all combustible material, that is dug by firefighters to stop the advance of a wildfire. Also called control line.

fire triangle: the combination of three elements required for any fire: fuel, oxygen, and heat.

firestorm: also called a blowup, it is the most explosive and violent type of wildfire.

fissure: a crack in Earth's surface through which volcanic materials can escape.

flash flood: a sudden, intense, localized flooding caused by persistent heavy rainfall or the failure of a levee or dam.

floccus: "flock of wool"; describes clouds with small tufts with ragged undersides.

flood: an overflow of water on land that is normally dry.

flood basalt: high temperature basaltic lava that flows from a fissure in Earth's crust and covers large areas of the landscape. Also known as plateau basalt.

focus: the underground starting place of an earthquake, also called the hypocenter.

fog: a cloud that forms near or on the ground.

food chain: the transfer of food energy from one organism to another. It begins with a plant species, which is eaten by an animal species; it continues with a second animal species, which eats the first, and so on.

foreshock: ground shaking that occurs before the main shock of an earthquake.

fossil fuels: coal, oil, and natural gas—materials composed of the remains of plants or animals that covered Earth millions of years ago and are today burned for fuel.

fractus: "fractured"; describes clouds with broken up, ragged edges.

freezing nuclei: a tiny particle of ice or other solid onto which super-cooled water droplets can freeze.

front: the dividing line between two air masses of different temperatures.

frontal system: a weather pattern that accompanies an advancing front.

frostbite: the freezing of the skin.

fuel cell: device that generates electricity by combining hydrogen and oxygen; it emits water vapor as a by-product.

Fujita Intensity scale: scale that measures tornado intensity, based on wind speed and the damage created.

fumarole: a vent in Earth's surface that releases steam and other gases, but generally no lava.

funnel cloud: cone-shaped spinning column of air that hangs well below the base of a thunderstorm cloud.

G

gale-force wind: any wind whose sustained speed is between 39 and 54 mph (63 and 87 kph).

geologist: a scientist who studies the origin, history, and structure of Earth.

geostationary satellite: weather satellite that remains above a given point on Earth's equator, traveling at the same speed as Earth's rotation about 22,300 miles (35,900 kilometers) above the surface.

geyser: a regular spray of hot water and steam from underground into the air.

glacier: slowly flowing masses of ice created by years of snowfall and cold temperatures.

global warming: the theory that average temperatures around the world have begun to rise, and will continue to rise, due to an increase of certain gases, called greenhouse gases, in the atmosphere. Also called enhanced greenhouse effect and global climate change.

global water budget: the balance of the volume of water coming and going between the oceans, atmosphere, and continental landmasses.

glory: a set of colored rings that appears on the top surface of a cloud, directly beneath the observer. A glory is formed by the interaction of sunlight with tiny cloud droplets and is most often viewed from an airplane.

Great Depression: the worst economic collapse in the history of the modern world. It began with the stock market crash of 1929 and lasted through the late 1930s.

green flash: a very brief flash of green light that appears near the top edge of a rising or setting Sun.

greenhouse effect: the warming of Earth due to the presence of greenhouse gases, which trap upwardly radiating heat and return it to Earth's surface.

greenhouse gases: gases that trap heat in the atmosphere. The most abundant greenhouse gases are water vapor and carbon dioxide. Others include methane, nitrous oxide, and chlorofluorocarbons.

ground blizzard: the drifting and blowing of snow that occurs after a snowfall has ended.

ground fire: a fire that burns beneath the layer of dead plant material on the forest floor.

gust front: the dividing line between cold downdrafts and warm air at the surface, characterized by strong, cold, shifting winds.

H

haboob: a tumbling black wall of sand that has been stirred up by cold downdrafts along the leading edge of a thunderstorm or cold front. It occurs in north-central Africa and the southwestern United States.

hail: precipitation comprised of hailstones.

hailstone: frozen precipitation that is either round or has a jagged surface, is either totally or partially transparent and ranges in size from that of a pea to that of a softball.

hair hygrometer: an instrument that measures relative humidity. It uses hairs (human or horse) that grow longer and shorter in response to changing humidity.

halo: a thin ring of light that appears around the Sun or Moon, caused by the refraction of light by ice crystals.

harmattan: a mild, dry, and dusty wind that originates in the Sahara Desert.

haze: the uniform, milky-white appearance of the sky that results when humidity is high and there are a large number of particles in the air.

heat cramps: muscle cramps or spasms, usually afflicting the abdomen or legs, that may occur during exercise in hot weather.

heat exhaustion: a form of mild shock that results when fluid and salt are lost through heavy perspiration.

heat stroke: a life-threatening condition that sets in when heat exhaustion is left untreated and the body has spent all its efforts to cool itself. Also called sunstroke.

heat wave: an extended period of high heat and humidity.

heating-degree-days: the number of degrees difference between the day's mean (average) temperature and the temperature at which most people set their thermostats. The total number of heating-degree-days in a season is an indicator of how much heating fuel has been consumed.

heavy snow: snowfall that reduces visibility to 0.31 mile (0.5 kilometer) and yields, on average, 4 inches (10 centimeters) or more in a twelve-hour period or 6 inches (15 centimeters) or more in a twenty-four-hour period.

hollow column: a snowflake in the shape of a long, six-sided column.

Holocene: the most recent part of the Cenozoic era, from ten thousand years ago to the present.

horse latitudes: a high-pressure belt that exists at around 30° latitude, north and south, where air from the equatorial region descends and brings clear skies.

hot spot: an area beneath Earth's crust where magma currents rise.

hotshot: a specialized firefighter who ventures into hazardous areas and spends long hours battling blazes.

humilis: "humble" or "lowly"; describes clouds with a small, flattened appearance.

humiture index: an index that combines temperature and relative humidity to determine how hot it actually feels and, consequently, how stressful outdoor activity will be. Also called temperature-humidity index or heat index.

hurricane: the most intense form of tropical cyclone. A hurricane is a storm that forms in the northern Atlantic Ocean or in the eastern Pacific Ocean. It is made up of a series of tightly coiled bands of thunderstorm clouds, with a well-defined pattern of rotating winds and maximum sustained winds greater than 74 mph (119 kph).

hurricane warning: hurricane landfall is imminent.

hurricane watch: hurricane landfall is possible.

hurricane-force wind: sustained winds greater than 74 mph (119 kph).

hygrometer: an instrument used to measure relative humidity. It consists of a dry-bulb thermometer and a wet-bulb thermometer. Also called psychrometer.

hypothermia: a condition characterized by a drop in core body temperature from the normal 98.6°F (37°C) to 95°F (35°C) or lower.

I

ice age: a period during which significant portions of Earth's surface are covered with ice.

igneous rock: rock made of solidified molten material that made its way from the interior of the planet to the surface.

incus: "anvil" or "fan-shaped"; describes a cloud with a spreading, smooth or fibrous mass at the top.

induction: the process whereby excess electrical charges in one object cause the accumulation by displacement of electrical charges with the opposite charge in another nearby object.

inferior mirage: a mirage that appears as an inverted, lowered image of a distant object. It typically forms in hot weather.

insulator: a substance through which electricity does not readily flow.

intensity: description of the physical damage caused by an earthquake.

interglacial period: a relatively warm period that exists between two ice ages.

Intertropical Convergence Zone: a belt of warm, rising, unstable air formed from the inward-flowing trade winds from north and south of the equator.

intortis: "intertwined"; describes clouds with entangled, fibrous strands.

inversion, atmospheric: a stable reversal of the normal pattern of atmospheric temperature, formed when a warm air mass sits over a cold air mass near the surface.

ion: an atom that has lost or gained an electron, thereby acquiring a positive or negative electrical charge.

iridescence: an irregular patch of colored light on a cloud.

isobar: an imaginary line that connects areas of equal air pressure, after the air pressure measurements have been adjusted to sea level.

isotherm: an imaginary line connecting areas of similar temperature.

J

jet stream: the world's fastest upper-air winds. Jet streams travel in a west-to-east direction, at speeds of 80 to 190 miles (130 to 300 kilometers) per hour, around 30,000 feet (9,150 meters) above the ground. Jet streams occur where the largest differences in air temperature and air pressure exist. In North America, jet streams are typically found over southern Canada and the northern United States, as well as over the southern United States and Mexico. The northern jet stream is called the polar jet stream, and the southern jet stream is called the subtropical jet stream.

K

katabatic wind: a strong wind that travels down a mountain under the force of gravity, and is stronger than a valley breeze.

khamsin: a hot, dry, southerly wind that originates on the Sahara and produces large sand and dust storms.

kinetic energy: the energy of motion.

L

La Niña: Spanish for little girl, a period of cooler-than-normal water temperatures in the eastern Pacific near the coast of Peru and Ecuador. It often follows an El Niño.

lahar: a mudflow of volcanic ash and water that sometimes occurs after a volcanic eruption.

lake breeze: a wind similar to a sea breeze that can be felt at the edge of a large lake.

landfall: the point on a coast where the center of a hurricane first crosses.

landslide: the movement of large amounts of soil, rocks, mud, and other debris downward and outward along a slope.

latent heat: the heat that must be removed from a quantity of water vapor to cause it to turn into a liquid, or that must be added to a quantity of liquid water to cause it to turn into a vapor; called latent because the temperature of the quantity of water or water vapor does not change.

latitude: an imaginary line encircling Earth, parallel to the equator, that tells one's position north or south on the globe.

lava: molten rock that erupts from a fissure or a vent (*see* magma).

lava domes: volcanic formations built up from layers of viscous lava that does not flow far from its source.

lava tube: a tube formed when an outer layer of lava is cooled by the air and hardens and molten lava then flows out of the middle of the tube, leaving it hollow.

leeward: the opposite direction from which the wind is blowing. Also the slope of a mountain opposite to the direction of local or prevailing winds down which cold air descends, producing dry conditions.

lenticularis: "lens-shaped"; describes clouds that are elongated, or almond-shaped with well-defined outlines.

lightning: a short-lived, bright flash of light during a thunderstorm that is produced by a 100-million-volt electrical discharge in the atmosphere.

liquefaction: the transformation of water-saturated soil into a liquidlike mass, usually by the action of seismic waves.

lithosphere: the rigid outermost region of Earth, composed of the crust and the upper part of the mantle.

local winds: winds that blow across surface areas ranging from a few miles to about 100 miles (about 160 kilometers) in width. Also known as mesoscale winds or regional winds.

loose-snow avalanche: avalanche composed of loosely packed snow that begins at a single point and slides down a slope, fanning out in the shape of an inverted V.

M

magma: molten rock containing dissolved gas and crystals that originates deep within Earth. When it reaches the surface it is called lava.

magma chamber: a reservoir of magma beneath Earth's surface.

magnitude: the power of an earthquake, as recorded by a seismograph, or seismometer.

mammatus: round, pouchlike cloud formations that appear in clusters and hang from the underside of a larger cloud.

mantle: the thick, dense layer of rock that lies beneath Earth's crust. The mantle is about 1,800 miles (2,900 kilometers) thick and accounts for about 84 percent of Earth's volume.

marine forecast: a specialized weather forecast of interest to coastal residents and mariners, which gives projections of the times of high and low tide, wave height, wind speed and direction, and visibility.

Maunder minimum: a period of time from 1645 to 1715, during which sunspot activity was almost nonexistent.

mediocris: "mediocre"; describes clouds of moderate vertical development with lumpy tops.

mesocyclone: region of rotating updrafts created by wind shear within a supercell storm; it may be the beginnings of a tornado.

mesoscale winds: winds that blow across surface areas ranging from a few miles to about 100 miles (about 160 kilometers) in width. Also known as local winds or regional winds.

Mesozoic era: the historical period from 225 million years ago to 65 million years ago, best known as the age of the dinosaurs.

meteorologist: a scientist who studies weather and climate.

meteorology: the scientific study of the atmosphere and atmospheric processes, namely weather and climate.

middle latitudes: the regions of the world that lie between the latitudes of 30° and 60° north and south. Also called temperate regions.

Milankovitch theory: the theory stating that the three types of variation in Earth's orbit, taken together, can be linked with warm and cold periods throughout history. These variations include: the shape of Earth's orbit, the direction of tilt of its axis, and the degree of tilt of its axis.

mirage: an optical illusion in which an object appears in a position that differs from its true position, or a nonexistent object (such as a body of water) appears.

modified Mercalli scale: scale developed by Italian seismologist Giuseppe Mercalli to measure the intensity of an earthquake based on the amount of vibration felt by people and the extent of damage to buildings.

moist adiabatic lapse rate: the variable rate at which the temperature of a saturated air parcel changes as it ascends or descends through the atmosphere.

monsoon: a name for seasonal winds that result in a rainy season occurring in the summer on tropical continents, when the land becomes warmer than the sea beside it.

monsoon climate: a climate that is warm year-round with very rainy (flood-prone) summers and relatively dry winters. It encompasses much of southern and southeastern Asia, the Philippines, coastal regions of northern South America, and slices of central Africa.

mountain breeze: a gentle downhill wind that forms at night as cold, dense, surface air travels down a mountainside and sinks into the valley. Also called gravity wind or drainage wind.

mud slide: a landslide of mostly mud mixed with debris, often caused by heavy rains on steep land with sparse vegetation.

mudflow: a landslide consisting of soil mixed with water. It is wetter than the material in an earthflow.

multi-cell thunderstorm: a thunderstorm system that contains several convective cells.

multi-vortex tornado: tornado in which the vortex divides into several smaller vortices called suction vortices.

N

nebulosus: "nebulous"; describes clouds that are a thin, hazy veil.

NEXRAD: acronym for Next Generation Weather Radar, the network of high-powered Doppler radar units that cover the continental United States, Alaska, Hawaii, Guam, and South Korea.

nor'easter: a strong, northeasterly wind that brings cold air, often accompanied by heavy rain, snow, or sleet, to the coastal areas of New England and the mid-Atlantic states. Also called northeaster.

Northern Hemisphere: the half of the Earth that lies north of the equator.

numerical prediction model: a computer program that mathematically duplicates conditions in nature. It is often used to predict the weather.

O

obliquity: the angle of the tilt of Earth's axis in relation to the plane of its orbit.

occluded front: a front formed by the interaction of three air masses: one cold, one cool, and one warm. The result is a multi-tiered air system, with cold air wedged on the bottom, cool air resting partially on top of the cold air, and warm air on the very top.

ocean currents: the major routes through which ocean water is circulated around the globe.

oceanography: the study and exploration of the ocean.

Organized Convection Theory: a widely accepted model of hurricane formation.

orographic lifting: the upward motion of warm air that occurs when a warm air mass travels up the side of a mountain.

orographic thunderstorm: a type of air mass thunderstorm that's initiated by the flow of warm air up a mountainside. Also called mountain thunderstorm.

orographic uplift: the forcing of air upward, caused by the movement of air masses over mountains.

oxidation: a chemical reaction involving the combination of a material with oxygen.

ozone days: days on which the smog threshold is surpassed.

ozone hole: the region above Antarctica where the ozone concentration in the upper atmosphere gets very low at the end of each winter.

ozone layer: the layer of Earth's atmosphere, between 25 and 40 miles (40 and 65 kilometers) above ground, that filters out the Sun's harmful rays. It contains a higher concentration of ozone, which is a form of oxygen that has three atoms per molecule.

P

paleoclimatologist: a scientist who studies climates of the past.

Paleozoic era: the historical period from 570 million years ago to 225 million years ago.

particulates: small particles suspended in the air and responsible for most atmospheric haze. Particulates can irritate the lungs and cause lung disease with long exposure.

passive solar collector: system for collecting and storing the Sun's heat that has no moving parts and is generally used for home heating.

period: the time between two successive waves.

permafrost: a layer of subterranean soil that remains frozen year-round.

photochemical smog: a hazy layer containing ozone and other gases that sometimes appears brown. It is produced when pollutants that are released by car exhaust fumes react with strong sunlight.

photovoltaic cell: light-sensitive device containing semiconductor crystals (materials that conduct an electric current under certain conditions) that convert sunlight to electricity. Also called solar cells.

phytoplankton: tiny marine plants that occupy the lowest level of the food chain.

pileus: "felt cap"; small cap- or hood-shaped formation perched above or attached to the top of a cloud.

pipe: a narrow passageway that leads from a magma reservoir to a vent.

plate: a large section of Earth's crust.

plate tectonics: the geologic theory that Earth's crust is composed of rigid plates that are in constant motion with respect to each other, creating the major geologic features on the planet's surface.

Plinian eruption: a volcanic eruption that releases a deadly cloud of gas, dust, and ash.

polar easterlies: cold, global winds that travel across the polar regions, from the northeast to the southwest in the Northern Hemisphere and from the southeast to the northwest in the Southern Hemisphere.

polar front: the region or boundary separating air masses of polar origin from those of tropical or subtropical origin.

polar jet stream: a North American jet stream, typically found over southern Canada or the northern United States.

polar orbiting satellite: a weather satellite that travels in a north-south path, crossing over both poles just 500 to 625 miles (800 to 1,000 kilometers) above Earth's surface.

precession of the equinoxes: the reversal of the seasons every thirteen thousand years. This occurs because Earth spins about its axis like a top in slow motion and wobbles its way through one complete revolution every twenty-six thousand years.

precipitation: water particles that originate in the atmosphere (usually referring to water particles that form in clouds) and fall to the ground as rain, snow, ice pellets, or hail.

prescribed burn: a planned, controlled fire that clears flammable debris from the forest floor.

pressure gradient: the difference in air pressure between a high and low pressure area relative to the distance separating them.

psychrometer: an instrument used to measure relative humidity. It consists of a dry-bulb thermometer and a wet-bulb thermometer. Also called hygrometer.

Pulaski: a combination ax and hoe that is used by firefighters to clear brush and create a fire line. It was invented by forest ranger Edward Pulaski in 1903.

pumice: volcanic rock formed during the explosive eruption of magma; it has numerous gas bubbles and may float on water.

pyroclastic flow: a rapid flow of hot material consisting of ash, pumice, other rock fragments, and gas ejected by an explosive eruption.

R

radar: an instrument that detects the location, movement, and intensity of precipitation, and gives indications about the type of precipitation. It operates by emitting microwaves, which are reflected by precipitation. It is an abbreviation for **Ra**dio **D**etection **a**nd **R**anging. Radar may be called conventional radar to distinguish it from Doppler radar.

radiational cooling: the loss of heat from the ground upward into the atmosphere.

radioactive dating: a technique used to determine the age of rocks that contain radioactive elements, which works on the principle that radioactive nuclei emit high-energy particles over time.

radiosonde: an instrument package carried aloft on a small helium- or hydrogen-filled balloon. It measures temperature, air pressure, and relative humidity from the ground to a maximum height of 19 miles (30 kilometers).

rain band: a band of heavy thunderstorms forming a tightly coiled spiral around the center of a tropical storm.

rain gauge: a container that catches rain and measures the amount of rainfall.

rain shadow effect: the uneven distribution of precipitation across a mountain, with most of the precipitation falling on the windward side and very little falling on the leeward side.

rainbow: an arc of light, separated into its constituent colors, that stretches across the sky.

research buoy: a tethered or drifting buoy placed in the open ocean capable of recording atmospheric and ocean conditions and transmitting them to a satellite.

reflection: the process by which light both strikes a surface, and bounces off that surface, at the same angle.

refraction: the bending of light as it is transmitted between two transparent media of different densities.

regeneration: the process of making or starting anew.

relative humidity: a measure of humidity as a percentage of the total moisture a given volume of air, at a particular temperature, can hold.

Richter scale: the scale developed by American seismologist Charles Richter that describes the amount of energy released by an earthquake on a scale from 1 to 10. Each whole number increase in value on the scale indicates a ten-fold increase in the energy released. Earthquakes measuring 7 to 7.9 are major and those measuring 8 or above cause widespread destruction.

ridge: a northward crest in the wavelike flow of upper-air westerlies, within which exists a high pressure area.

Ring of Fire: the name given to the geologically active belt that surrounds the Pacific Ocean and is home to more than 75 percent of the world's volcanoes.

river flood: a flood caused when a river spills over its banks.

rock slide: a cascade of rocks (of any size) down a steep slope at high speeds.

roll cloud: a cloud that looks like a giant, elongated cylinder lying on its side, that is rolling forward. It follows in the wake of a gust front.

S

Saffir-Simpson Hurricane Damage Potential scale: a scale devised by Herbert Saffir and Robert Simpson intended to be used to predict a hurricane's destructive potential.

saltation: the wind-driven movement of particles along the ground and through the air.

saturated: air that contains all of the water vapor it can hold at a given temperature; 100 percent relative humidity.

saturation point: the point at which a given volume of air contains the maximum possible amount of water vapor.

scattering: multidirectional reflection of light by minute particles in the air.

sea breeze: the gentle wind that blows from over the sea to the shore during the day, due to differences in air pressure above each surface.

season: a period of the year characterized by certain weather conditions, such as temperature and precipitation, as well as the number of hours of sunlight each day.

sector plate: a star-shaped snowflake.

seismic waves: vibrations that move outward from the focus of an earthquake, causing the ground to shake.

seismograph: instrument used to detect and measure seismic waves. Also known as a seismometer.

semiarid: a climate in which very little rain or snow falls.

semipermanent highs and lows: the four large pressure areas (two high-pressure and two low-pressure), situated throughout the Northern Hemisphere, that undergo slight shifts in position, and major changes in strength, throughout the year.

severe blizzard: a blizzard in which wind speeds exceed 45 miles (72 kilometers) per hour, snowfall is heavy, and the temperature is 10°F (–12°C) or lower.

severe thunderstorm: a thunderstorm with wind gusts of at least 58 mph (93 kph); hailstones at least 3/4 inch (2 centimeters) in diameter; or tornadoes or funnel clouds.

shamal: a hot, dry, dusty wind that blows for one to five days at a time, producing great dust storms throughout the Persian Gulf.

shelf cloud: a fan-shaped cloud with a flat base that forms along the edge of a gust front.

shield volcano: a volcano with long, gentle slopes, built primarily by lava flows.

shower: a brief spell of localized rainfall, possibly heavy, that only occurs in warm weather.

simoom: a hot, dry, blustery, dust-laden wind that blows across the Sahara and the deserts of Israel, Syria, and the Arabian peninsula.

sinkhole: a natural, steep depression in a land surface caused by collapse of a cavern roof.

skin cancer: a disease of the skin caused primarily by exposure to the ultraviolet rays in sunlight.

slab avalanche: avalanche that begins when fracture lines develop in a snowpack and a large surface plate breaks away, then crumbles into blocks as it falls down a slope.

sling psychrometer: an instrument that measures relative humidity. It consists of a dry-bulb thermometer and a wet-bulb thermometer mounted side by side on a metal strip, which rotates on a handle at one end.

slump: the slow downhill movement of large portions (called blocks) of a slope. Each block rotates backward toward the slope in a series of curving movements.

smog: common name for photochemical smog—a layer of hazy, brown air pollution at Earth's surface comprised of ozone and other chemicals.

smog threshold: the level of smog allowed by law and set by the Environmental Protection Agency at 80 parts per billion (ppb) of surface ozone.

smokejumper: a specialized firefighter who parachutes to strategic locations from airplanes to battle wildfires.

snow fence: a device placed in fields and along highways that slows the wind and reduces the blowing and drifting of snow.

solifluction: the most rapid type of earthflow, occurring when snow or ice thaws or when earthquakes produce shocks that turn the soil into a fluid-like mass.

Southern Oscillation: shifting patterns of air pressure at sea level, between the eastern and western edges of the Pacific Ocean.

spissatus: "tightly packed"; describes icy formations at the top of a vertical cloud that are dense enough to block out the Sun.

spotting: the starting of new fires, called spot fires, by sparks and embers that drift ahead of an advancing wildfire.

squall line: a moving band of strong thunderstorms.

stable air layer: an atmospheric layer through which an air parcel cannot rise or descend.

stationary front: a boundary between two air masses at different temperatures which are not moving or are moving slowly.

steam eruption: a violent eruption that occurs when water comes in contact with magma, rapidly turns to steam, and causes the mixture to explode.

stepped leader: an invisible stream of electrons that initiates a lightning stroke. A stepped leader surges from the negatively charged region of a cloud, down through the base of the cloud, and travels in a stepwise fashion toward the ground.

storm surge: an abnormal rise of the sea over and above normal tides and due to strong winds and low pressure accompanying a storm or hurricane.

stratiformis: "covering" or "blanket"; describes clouds that form a thick layer.

stratosphere: the second-lowest layer of Earth's atmosphere, from about 9 to 40 miles (15 to 65 kilometers) above ground.

stratus: gloomy, gray, featureless sheets of clouds that cover the entire sky, at low levels of the atmosphere.

subduction zone: a region where two plates come together and the edge of one plate slides beneath the other.

subsidence: a gradual sinking of the land surface relative to its previous level.

subtropical jet stream: a North American jet stream, typically found over the southern United States or northern Mexico.

suction vortices: small vortices within a single tornado that continually form and dissipate as the tornado moves along, creating the tornado's strongest surface winds.

sunspot: an area of magnetic disturbance on the surface of the Sun, sometimes referred to as a sun storm.

supercell storm: the most destructive and long-lasting form of a severe thunderstorm, arising from a single, powerful convective cell. It is characterized by strong tornadoes, heavy rain, and hail the size of golf balls or larger.

supercooled water: water that remains in the liquid state below the freezing point.

superior mirage: a cold-weather mirage that appears as a taller and closer, and sometimes inverted, image of a distant object.

surface fire: a fire with a visible flame that consumes plant material and debris on the forest floor.

T

thermal: a pocket of rising, warm air that is produced by uneven heating of the ground.

thermograph: an instrument consisting of a thermometer and a needle that etches on a rotating drum, continually recording the temperature.

thermometer: an instrument used to measure temperature. It consists of a vacuum-sealed narrow glass tube with a bulb in the bottom containing mercury or red-dyed alcohol. Also called dry-bulb thermometer.

thunderstorm: a relatively small but intense storm system resulting from strong rising air currents; characterized by heavy rain or hail along with thunder, lightning, and sometimes tornadoes.

tidal station: a floating instrument center in the ocean that records water levels.

topography: the shape and height of Earth's surface features.

tornadic waterspout: tornado that forms over land and travels over water. Tornadic waterspouts are relatively rare and are the most intense form of waterspouts.

tornado: rapidly spinning column of air that extends from a thunderstorm cloud to the ground. Also called a twister.

tornado cyclone: spinning column of air that protrudes through the base of a thunderstorm cloud.

tornado family: a group of tornadoes that develop from a single thunderstorm.

tornado outbreak: emergence of a tornado family. Tornado outbreaks are responsible for the greatest amount of tornado-related damage.

trade winds: dominant surface winds near the equator, generally blowing from east to west and toward the equator.

translucidus: "translucent"; describes clouds that form a transparent layer covering a large part of the sky, through which the Sun or Moon shines.

transpiration: the process by which plants emit water through tiny pores in the underside of their leaves.

transverse dune: a series of connected barchan dunes, which appear as tall, elongated crescents of sand running perpendicular to the prevailing wind.

tropical cyclone: any rotating weather system that forms over tropical waters.

tropical depression: a storm with rotating bands of clouds and thunderstorms and maximum sustained winds of less than 38 miles (61 kilometers) per hour.

tropical disturbance: a cluster of thunderstorms that is beginning to demonstrate a cyclonic circulation pattern.

tropical storm: a tropical cyclone weaker than a hurricane, with organized bands of rotating thunderstorms and maximum sustained winds of 39 to 73 mph (63 to 117 kph).

tropical wave: an elongated area of low air pressure, oriented north to south, causing areas of cloudiness and thunderstorms.

tropics: the region of Earth between 23.5° north latitude and 23.5° south latitude.

tropopause: the boundary between the troposphere and the stratosphere, between 30,000 and 40,000 feet (9,000 and 12,000 meters) above ground.

troposphere: the lowest atmospheric layer, where clouds exist and virtually all weather occurs.

trough: a southward dip in the wavelike flow of upper-air westerlies, within which exists a low-pressure area. Also, the lowest point of a wave.

tsunami: a huge ocean wave that can travel at speeds up to 600 mph (965 kph) for hundreds of miles over open ocean before it hits land; caused by an earthquake, underwater volcanic eruption, or underwater landslide.

tsunami warning: an alert stating that a tsunami has been detected and is approaching the designated area. People are instructed to move to higher ground immediately.

tsunami watch: an alert stating that an earthquake has occurred with sufficient magnitude to trigger a tsunami. People are instructed to listen for further news.

typhoon: tropical cyclone that form in the China Sea or in the western North Pacific Ocean.

U

uncinus: "hook-shaped"; describes clouds with fibers creating the pattern called "mare's tail."

undulatus: "undulating"; describes clouds with wavelike formation within patches, layers, or sheets.

unhealthy air days: days on which surface ozone levels reach 80 parts per billion—a concentration considered unhealthy to children, people with respiratory problems, and adults who exercise or work vigorously outdoors.

unsaturated air: air that has less than 100 percent relative humidity.

updraft: a column of air blowing upward inside a vertical cloud.

upper-air westerlies: global-scale, upper-air winds that flow in waves heading west to east (but also shifting north and south) through the middle latitudes of the Northern Hemisphere.

upwelling: the rising up of cold waters from the depths of the ocean, replacing the warm surface water that has moved away horizontally.

wind wave: a wave caused by the action of wind on the water surface.

windbreak: row of trees or shrubs placed in a farm field to slow the wind and keep it from blowing away the soil.

windchill equivalent temperature: the temperature at which the body would lose an equivalent amount of heat, if there were no wind. Also called windchill index.

windchill factor: the cooling effect on the body due to a combination of wind and temperature.

windward: the direction from which the wind is blowing. Also the slope of a mountain on the side of local or prevailing winds, up which the air cools as it ascends producing moist, cloudy, or rainy conditions.

Flood

A flood is the overflow of water onto normally dry land. Flooding results when the water level rises and overflows the banks of a river or some other low-lying channel, or when high ocean waters wash over the coast. Floods occur frequently in some parts of the world. While for some areas flooding spells disaster, for other areas yearly flooding is necessary to sustain crops.

Floods kill more people than any other weather phenomenon. Flash floods, which are sudden, intense, localized floods, are especially deadly. Worldwide, 40 percent of all deaths from natural disasters are due to floods.

There are two main types of floods: coastal floods and river floods.

Coastal floods

Coastal floods are floods that occur along the coasts of lakes and oceans. This type of flooding is of great concern in many countries because of the high population density along their coastlines. In the United States, for example, almost two-thirds of the U.S. population lives in states along the three major coasts—38 percent along the Atlantic Ocean, 16 percent along the Pacific Ocean coast, and 12 percent along the Gulf of Mexico. According to the National Oceanic and Atmospheric Administration, 53 percent of the U.S. population (153 million people) live in one of the 673 counties bordering the Great Lakes, the Atlantic, the Pacific, or the Gulf of Mexico.

There are two main causes of coastal flooding: high waters and the subsidence, or lowering, of coastal lands.

Hurricanes and tsunamis Most coastal flooding is produced by high waters associated with hurricanes. As a hurricane crosses over land, it produces a storm surge. A storm surge is a several-foot-high wall of water that results in the flooding of 40 to 100 miles (65 to 160 kilometers) of coastline.

WORDS TO KNOW

coastal flood: an overflow of water onto a coastal area caused by a storm surge, strong winds, or tsunami.

flash flood: a sudden rush of water in a low-lying area brought on by heavy rain or a dam break; flash floods can occur when the ground is so saturated with water that no more can soak in, or in desert regions where hard rocky soil is unable to absorb or hold water.

flood: an overflow of water on land that is normally dry.

precipitation: water in any form, such as rain, snow, ice pellets, or hail, that falls to Earth's surface.

river flood: a flood caused when a river spills over its banks.

sinkhole: a natural, steep depression in a land surface caused by collapse of a cavern roof.

stationary front: a boundary between two air masses at different temperatures which are not moving or are moving slowly.

storm surge: an abnormal rise of the sea over and above normal tides and due to strong winds and low pressure accompanying a storm or hurricane.

subsidence: a gradual sinking of the land surface relative to its previous level.

thunderstorm: a storm resulting from strong rising air currents; characterized by heavy rain or hail along with thunder and lightning.

tornado: a violent windstorm characterized by a twisting, funnel-shaped cloud.

tsunami: a huge ocean wave that can travel at speeds up to 600 mph (965 kph) for hundreds of miles over open ocean before it hits land; caused by an earthquake, underwater volcanic eruption, or underwater landslide.

wind wave: a wave caused by the action of wind on the water surface.

Large waves can also cause flooding. The most common type of waves, those driven by the wind, are called wind waves. The largest wind waves are generated by large, stationary storm systems. Wind waves tend to be largest in the open ocean and diminish in height as they approach land. Large wind waves have the greatest potential for flooding when accompanied by high tide.

The largest waves, however, are generated not by the wind but by submarine earthquakes, landslides, and volcanic eruptions. Waves produced by these forces are called tsunamis (tsoo-NAH-meez). Tsunamis start out small and grow larger as they near land. They travel at speeds of up to 600 mph (965 kph). It is typical for a tsunami to measure 60 to 100 feet (18 to 30 meters) in height by the time it reaches the shore.

Tsunamis occur most often in the Pacific Ocean. Several tsunamis have affected Alaska and Hawaii. In 1958, a tsunami over 200 feet (60 meters) in height, generated by a minor earthquake and resultant rock fall into the sea, crashed into Lituya Bay, Alaska. It destroyed great tracts of forest land as far as 1,700 feet (520 meters) above sea level. In December 2004, the deadliest tsunami in recorded history occured not in the Pacific, but in the Indian Ocean. A powerful earthquake triggered a series of tsunamis in Indonesia, Malaysia, and Thailand, killing nearly a quarter million people. Because tsunamis are not common in the Indian Ocean, there was little advance warning for the people of southeast Asia.

On the shelves: *The Epic of Gilgamesh*

The Epic of Gilgamesh is a four-thousand-year-old story about a king from the region that is now Iraq. The story includes a controversial episode concerning a great flood that some historians and theologians say compares to the worldwide flood mentioned in the Bible.

Subsidence Subsidence is the lowering of land in coastal areas. Subsidence may be caused by the gradual settling of subterranean rocks or sediments or by the removal of ground water by excessive pumping. Subsidence may also be rapid. For example, if the roof of a cave collapses, the result is a large depression called a sinkhole. Whatever the cause, subsidence in coastal areas makes them more susceptible to flooding.

Flooded Ohio River snaking through Cincinnati, Ohio, in 1997. AP IMAGES.

The Mississippi River in flood in St. Louis, Missouri, 1993. © LES STONE/SYGMA/CORBIS.

River floods and flash floods

The banks of rivers and streams overflow due to many causes, including excessive rain, the springtime melting of snow, and blockage of water flow by ice. The failure of a dam or aqueduct is another source of flooding. The primary cause of flooding in large rivers is prolonged heavy precipitation over a large area. Large rivers such as the Mississippi, the Ohio, and the Missouri sometimes flood due to precipitation covering hundreds of square miles. In some areas, flooding occurs nearly every spring when the winter snow melts.

The most dangerous form of river flood is a flash flood. Flash floods are the number one weather-related killer in the United States. Throughout the 1980s, each year flash floods killed an average of 110 people and were responsible for an average of $3 billion in property damage. In the first half of the 1990s, the number of deaths due to flash floods rose to an annual average of 140.

A flash flood can be caused by persistent, torrential rain that falls from a slow-moving or stationary severe thunderstorm, which is itself a result of strong, rising air currents and characterized by thunder and lightning. A flash flood may also be caused by the failure of a dam or levee. A dam is a structure that controls the rate of water flow while a levee is a structure built to prevent water from overflowing the banks of a river.

Watch this: *River Voices: A Portrait of an American River Community.*

In this 2002 documentary, written and directed by Nathan Lorentz, survivors recall both the devastation and the outpouring of community strength caused by the great 1937 Ohio River flood in Portsmouth, Ohio.

Flash floods rise and recede much more quickly than other types of river floods. They are the most dangerous because they come on so fast that people are often unable to reach higher ground in advance of the floodwaters. A series of flash floods in the streams that feed into a large river may result in the flooding of the large river.

Flash floods can be caused by thunderstorms that are either slow-moving or stationary. The reason for their lack of movement is that the high-altitude winds that drive weather systems winds are nearly calm. These storms unleash large quantities of rain over a single area. Thunderstorms that move more quickly spread their rain across larger areas and typically don't produce flash floods.

Boating through a flooded street in Des Moines, Iowa, in 1993. © REUTERS/BETTMANN/CORBIS.

Weather report: Flash flood alerts and safety procedures

A flash flood watch means that heavy rains may cause flash flooding within the designated area. This is the time to prepare to evacuate to higher ground.

A flash flood warning means that a flash flood has been reported and is imminent for the designated area. In some areas, a warning signal sounds when waters reach critical levels. When a warning is issued, it is imperative to move to safe ground immediately. You may only have seconds or minutes before waters become dangerously high.

If you live in an area that's prone to flash flooding, it's wise to take the following precautions:

- Learn the evacuation routes to higher ground.
- Keep your car's gas tank filled.
- Put together a supply kit for your home containing first aid materials, a battery-powered flashlight, a battery-powered radio, extra batteries, rubber boots, rubber gloves, nonperishable food, a non-electric can opener, and bottled water.
- Install check valves in your home's sewer traps to prevent flood water from backing up and coming in through your drains.
- Once a flash flood watch has been issued, fill your bathtub and large containers with water for drinking and cooking in case your local water source becomes contaminated.

If you encounter a flash flood, the most important thing to remember is to avoid the water. If you are driving, turn around and go the other way. If you are on foot, climb to higher ground. Do not try to walk, swim, or drive through flood water. The water is moving rapidly and carries dangerous debris. You can be knocked over by as little as 6 inches of rushing water. Deeper water can have an undertow that drags you beneath the surface.

If you are in a car during a storm, watch for flooding where the road dips down, under bridges, and in low areas. These are the places that fill with water first. If you see a flooded area, turn the vehicle around and go the other way. Be especially careful at night, when the beginnings of flash floods are harder to recognize.

If your car stalls or becomes blocked, abandon the car and seek higher ground. A car will float away in just 2 feet of water. Then it is at the mercy of the current, which may carry it into deeper water or overturn it in a ditch. Sixty percent of people who die in flash floods are either in a car or are attempting to leave a car that has been stranded in high water.

A flash flood happens when the amount of rainfall exceeds the capacity of the ground to absorb it. In that case, the rainwater runs over the surface, rather than sinking into the ground. The water flows to the lowest point, which is generally a river, stream, or storm sewer. If the quantity of water is greater than the capacity of the drainage channel, the channel overflows within a few minutes and a flash flood occurs.

As the banks overflow, water rushes forward at speeds of up to 20 mph (35 kph). It takes the form of a sediment-laden wall that can surge as high as 30 feet (10 meters). The floodwaters are capable of dislodging large objects weighing several tons, such as boulders, cars, and even locomotives. These objects may be carried several miles downstream. Flash floods are also known to tear out bridges in their path.

Flash floods are more common in mountainous areas. Rain runs down mountainsides and becomes concentrated in canyons and valleys. Arid and urban regions are also prone to flash floods, since very little rain can soak into hard desert surfaces or concrete. Most cities have storm sewer systems that direct water underground to nearby rivers. If the storm sewers become clogged or overwhelmed by the volume of water, the streets quickly become flooded.

Flash flooding may also result from rains associated with a hurricane, a break in a dam or levee, or the springtime melting of large quantities of snow and ice. Flooding may even be caused by a small amount of rain that falls on a blanket of snow. If the ground beneath the snow is frozen, the melting snow and rain will not soak into the ground, but will run off and drain into a river. The likelihood of flooding is increased if ice blocks water from flowing in the river.

Rising flash flood waters in Los Angeles, California, trapped this driver in an intersection, causing him to bail out of his car and jump from hood to hood to reach safety.

Did you know? Floods and the spread of disease

Cholera, dysentery, and typhoid are diseases that typically spread during floods, when sewage treatment systems become overloaded and drinking water supplies become contaminated. An abundance of standing water also promotes the breeding of mosquitoes, which may carry malaria, dengue fever, yellow fever, and encephalitis (pronounced en-cef-a-LIE-tis).

In 1982, flooding in Ecuador, Bolivia, Colombia, Peru, India, and Sri Lanka resulted in epidemics of malaria. In early 1998, a malaria outbreak hit Peru because of flooding. In the Piura region of northwest Peru, home to 1.5 million people, there were some thirty thousand cases of the disease.

Historically significant floods

In 1889, a dam break in Johnstown, Pennsylvania, resulted in the worst flash flood in the history of the United States. A wall of water 36 to 40 feet (11 to 12 meters) tall overwhelmed the town, killing over 2,200 people. A second flash flood hit Johnstown in 1977, in which seventy-seven people lost their lives.

The Great Mississippi River Flood of 1927 caused widespread damage over a large area, extending from southern Illinois to the Gulf of Mexico. Flooding began after a year of above-normal precipitation. Water levels along the Mississippi, and rivers flowing into the Mississippi, were already high when 9 inches (22 centimeters) of rain fell on southern Missouri and most of Arkansas in April.

Beginning in April, the river flooded over hundreds of square miles. Levees failed in more than 120 places on the Mississippi and its tributaries. Over twenty-six thousand square miles (seven thousand square kilometers) were flooded

Flash flooding caused the Big Thompson River to swell onto Highway #34 in Loveland, Colorado, in 1976.

across seven states. Six hundred thousand people were forced from their homes and, despite advance warnings, 246 people were killed.

In the summer of 1993, excessive rains caused what is called "The Great Flood of 1993," one of the largest floods in the history of the United States. Water overflowed the banks of the Mississippi and Missouri Rivers, inundating 16,000 square miles (41,000 square kilometers) of land in Iowa, Illinois, Minnesota, Missouri, Wisconsin, South Dakota, Nebraska, and Kansas. The Mississippi River swelled to over 7 miles (11 kilometers) wide in some places. Fifty-six small towns along the river were completely submerged in water.

The flooding was preceded by heavy snowfalls throughout the Midwest in December 1992. The snow melted in March, and then 16 inches (41 centimeters) of rain fell in the upper Mississippi Valley in April. The rains continued through July. In mid-June, a stationary front, which is a slow-moving boundary between two air masses at different temperatures, formed across the upper Midwest and began producing daily thunderstorms.

The water reached record heights at many points along the Mississippi River and more than 60 percent of levees on the river were destroyed. Forty-eight people died. There was $6.5 billion in crop damage, out of a total property damage of $15–20 billion. Eighty-five thousand people were evacuated from their homes. Forty-five thousand homes were damaged or destroyed and 404 counties were declared disaster areas. Counties that are designated "federal disaster areas" are eligible to receive federal disaster aid including low-interest loans.

Another of the worst floods in U.S. history ravaged parts of the Midwest and Southeast in March 1997. The disaster was touched off when a series of severe thunderstorms and tornadoes, violent funnel-shaped windstorms, swept through Arkansas, Tennessee, and Mississippi

Extreme weather: Killer flash floods

One of the most destructive flash floods in recent history occurred in Colorado's Big Thompson Canyon, in the mountains west of Denver, in July 1976. Ten to twelve inches (25 to 30 centimeters) of rain, over half the yearly average rainfall for that location, caused the overflow of the river running through the narrow canyon floor. A wall of water 20 feet (6 meters) high rushed forward, killing at least 139 people. More than 400 houses were destroyed, many roads were washed away, and 197 vehicles were lost in the flood. Approximately one thousand people were rescued by helicopter.

In June 1990, a flash flood occurred in Shadyside, Ohio, when 4 inches (10 centimeters) of rain fell in less than two hours. The resultant 30-foot (9-meter) wall of water killed twenty-six people and caused around $7 million in damages.

Cheyenne, Wyoming, was beset by a flash flood in August 1985, after 6 inches (15 centimeters) of rain fell in three hours. The streets were filled with more than 6 feet (about 2 meters) of water. The flood caused the deaths of twelve people and more than $65 million in damage.

Watch this: *The Johnstown Flood.*

Using archival film and photographs, this documentary recreates the story of the Johnstown flood of 1889. The South Fork Dam burst due to very heavy rains and poor maintenance, sending a wall of water and debris downstream to flood the industrial city of Johnstown, Pennsylvania. The film, written and directed by Charles Guggenheim and released in 1989, won an Academy Award for best documentary, short subject.

and killed at least twenty-five people. Flash floods and gusting winds killed thirty-six more people in Kentucky, Ohio, West Virginia, and Tennessee, bringing the death toll to sixty-one.

Due to the tornadoes, eleven counties in Arkansas were declared federal disaster areas. Due to floods, sixteen counties in Ohio and sixty-three counties in Kentucky were also declared federal disaster areas.

During the floods, occasional heavy rains continued to fall throughout the region, accompanied by melting snow. On a single day, March 1, nearly a foot of rain fell on north-central Kentucky, southern Ohio, and West Virginia. New rainfall records were set in Louisville, Kentucky, on that day. Two days later, up to 9 more inches (23 centimeters) of rain fell on the same area.

As a result, flooding occurred along the Ohio, Missouri, and Mississippi Rivers, as well as on numerous tributaries. Rivers throughout Kentucky rose to record levels. Many river towns in Ohio, Kentucky, Tennessee, and West Virginia were swamped. Thousands of people from

Drawing by W. A. Rogers of the flood at Johnstown, Pennsylvania, 1889. © BETTMANN/CORBIS.

for food, for transportation, for reliable sources of drinking water, and for water used in agriculture. Similarly, the oceans have long been an important food source. While many people do need to live and work near the water, the continued building of homes and recreational housing in flood-prone areas will only make the problems of damage and loss of life more difficult to control.

[*See Also* **Climate Change and Global Warming; Human Influences on Weather and Climate; Hurricane; Local Winds; Thunderstorm; Tsunami; Weather: An Introduction**]

For More Information

BOOKS

Drohan, Michele Ingber. *Floods.* New York: Rosen Publishing and PowerKids Press, 1999.

Miller, E. Willard and Ruby M. Miller. *Natural Disaster: Floods.* Santa Barbara, CA: ABC-Clio, 2000.

Waterlow, Julia. *Violent Earth: Flood.* New York: Hodder Children's Books, 1994.

WEB SITES

"Flood." *Federal Emergency Management Agency.* <http://www.fema.gov/hazard/flood/index.shtm> (accessed March 8, 2007).

"Flood Safety." *National Weather Service Flood Safety.* <http://www.floodsafety.noaa.gov/> (accessed March 9, 2007).

Fog

Fog is a cloud that forms near the ground. Like clouds at higher altitudes, fog is formed when water vapor condenses in the air so that the moisture becomes visible. The process of water turning from vapor into liquid is called condensation. In temperate regions, fog is composed of water droplets. In polar and arctic regions, fog may be composed of ice crystals. Technically, fog is defined as condensation in the air that restricts visibility to a bit more than 0.5 mile (1.0 kilometer). If water has condensed in the low-lying air, yet visibility is greater than 0.5 mile (1.0 kilometer), the condition is defined as mist.

Fog production differs from cloud production in one significant way: While a cloud is usually formed as air rises and cools to the dew point (the temperature at which a parcel of air can no longer hold water in its vapor state), fog is formed within surface-level air. This happens in one of two ways. The air may be cooled to the dew point by contact with a cold surface. Or it is brought to the saturation point, the point at which it contains the maximum amount of water, when water vapor is added to the air by evaporation, the process by which water changes from a liquid to a gas.

On clear nights, surfaces that are open to the sky often cool faster than the air above them. When condensation takes place directly on these cooler surfaces due to contact between warmer air and the cooler surface, it is called dew or frost. Fog, on the other hand, is condensation in the air due to the air cooling below the dew point.

Radiation fog

Radiation fog is the fog that forms after sunset on clear summer nights when the air is almost, but not quite, still. The ground loses heat to space by radiation and cools to below air temperature. The cooler ground then conducts heat away from the layer of air just above the ground. This layer

A northern Ohio highway is partially immersed in a thin layer of radiation fog just after sunrise. FMA, INC.

of air is cooled to below the dew point and fog forms. The fog layer can be anywhere from a few feet (around 1 meter) to a thousand feet (around 300 meters) thick. The layer of air above the fog layer is warmer, so the fog layer is stable, at least until the sun rises and warms the ground again.

A light wind of less than 5 miles (8 kilometers) per hour promotes the circulation of the lowest layer of air, bringing all of it in contact with the cold surface. In this way the entire layer of air loses heat and cools to the dew point. If the winds are completely calm, only the very bottom of the surface air layer will come in contact with the ground. In that case, rather than producing radiation fog, moisture will either condense in a very shallow (less than 2 feet, or .6 meter) layer of air, forming ground fog, or it will condense only on the ground and form dew or frost.

Winds also hinder the formation of radiation fog. Winds stronger than 5 miles (8 kilometers) per hour will cause mixing of surface air with warmer, drier layers of air above it. This either prevents the surface air from cooling to the dew point or, if the air does reach the dew point and fog develops, the wind rapidly disperses the fog.

Valley fog is radiation fog that forms in valleys. It may develop into a layer over 1,500 feet (450 meters) thick. Radiation fog forms in low-lying areas because of two factors. In the first place, cold air (in this case, air that has undergone radiational cooling) is heavier than warm air and flows

Ground fog in the early evening hours. FMA, INC.

downward into the valley. In addition, valleys often contain rivers which increase the amount of moisture in low-lying air.

In most cases, radiation fog evaporates within a few hours after sunrise, after the air and ground have warmed up. It typically reveals clear skies, since the absence of clouds was required for the formation of fog. Sometimes, however, the fog is so thick that it effectively blocks the sunlight from reaching the ground, and the ground remains cold. In such cases, which usually occur in winter, the fog may persist all day.

Radiation fog is most likely to form during long nights, when the surface air has more time to cool to its dew point. Thus, this type of fog is seen most often during winter, late fall, and early spring. Visibility in thick radiation fog may be reduced to as little as 10 feet (3 meters).

Advection fog

In contrast to radiation fog, in which a layer of air is cooled as the ground loses heat, advection fog is formed when there is horizontal movement of a warm, moist layer of air over a cold surface. The newly arrived air loses heat to the cold surface below by conduction, the process by which energy is transferred through contact between substances. Conduction lowers the air temperature. Once the air cools to the dew point, fog is formed. While it bears a resemblance to radiation fog, advection fog moves with the wind-blown warm air mass whereas radiation fog is stationary. In

Experiment: Make fog in a jar

This simple experiment allows you to create fog conditions inside a glass jar. All you need for this experiment are:

- a glass jar
- strainer
- hot water
- ice cubes

First, fill up the jar with hot water and let it sit for about a minute. Then pour most of the water out, leaving about a finger's width at the bottom. Put the strainer over the top of the jar and place ice cubes on the strainer. In a little while, you will see fog in the jar. This is caused by the cold air from the ice cubes hitting the warm, moist air in the jar causing the water to condense into fog.

addition, while radiation fog usually forms at night, advection fog may form at any time.

In the spring, advection fog results when a mild breeze passes over ground that has not yet thawed. Throughout the summer, advection fog is produced by warm, moist air blowing across a lake that remains cold, such as one of the Great Lakes.

Another kind of advection fog happens in the winter, when warm air is carried northward. When this warm air encounters cold ground, it cools to the dew point and advection fog results. For instance, warm air from over the Gulf of Mexico may travel as far as the central United States before encountering a sufficiently cold surface for advection fog to form.

Advection fog is the thickest and most persistent type of fog. It sometimes reduces visibility to 650 feet (200 meters), the point at which airports are forced to close. Advection fog can form in layers that range anywhere from very shallow to 1,000 feet (300 meters) deep.

Valley fog in the rolling terrain of western Wisconsin. FMA, INC.

WORDS TO KNOW

advection: the horizontal movement of a mass such as air or an ocean current.

condensation: the process by which water changes from a gas to a liquid.

conduction: the transfer of heat from one molecule to another.

dew point: the temperature at which a given parcel of air reaches its saturation point and can no longer hold water in the vapor state.

evaporation: the process by which water changes from a liquid to a gas.

radiational cooling: the loss of heat from the ground upward into the atmosphere.

relative humidity: a measure of humidity as a percentage of the total moisture a given volume of air, at a particular temparature, can hold.

saturation point: the point at which a given volume of air contains the maximum possible amount of water vapor.

supercooled water: water that remains in a liquid state below the freezing point.

Sea fog

Sea fog is a special form of advection fog that only occurs at sea and in coastal areas. It is produced by the interaction of two adjacent ocean currents, the major routes through which ocean water travels, of different temperatures. A prime example of sea fog occurs in the Atlantic Ocean off the coast of Newfoundland, in Canada. There the warm Gulf Stream flows northward, parallel to the cold, southward-flowing Labrador Current. When the air that is warmed by the Gulf Stream travels over the iceberg-filled Labrador Current, it is cooled and moisture condenses, forming fog. For two out of every three summer days, the coastal region off Newfoundland is shrouded by the famous "Grand Banks fog."

This process is also responsible for the thick fog that is common in parts of the British Isles. In that case, the warm air comes from above the Gulf Stream and blows across cooler British coastal waters.

Sea fog is also well-known to the residents of San Francisco, California, and other West Coast communities. It forms in the summer when warm air from over the Pacific Ocean is carried shoreward by westerly winds. As the air moves over the colder, coastal surface water, the air cools and fog forms. The fog is then blown inland by a sea breeze. This explains the fog that can often be seen rolling in past the Golden Gate Bridge on a

Weather report: Smothered by sea fog

The town of Argentia, situated on the Avalon Peninsula of southeastern Newfoundland, averages 206 days per year of thick fog. This makes it the foggiest place in Canada and among the foggiest places in the world. Argentia's fog is sea fog, generated by the passage of warm air over cold North Atlantic ocean water.

A similar process produces the fog at Cape Disappointment, Washington, one of the foggiest places in the United States. Cape Disappointment is situated at the point where the Columbia River flows into the Pacific Ocean. It is blanketed by sea fog 29 percent of the time, or about 106 days each year.

breezy summer day. Conversely, if a land breeze is blowing out to sea, it will take the fog out with it.

As sea fog moves farther inland, it crosses over warmer ground and dissipates. The bottom of the fog layer evaporates first, revealing a low layer of gray clouds. As the surface temperature increases, ever-higher layers of the fog evaporate until it has completely disappeared. Fog also dissipates at a given location as the air becomes progressively warmer throughout the day. For this reason, coastal areas often have fog in the morning and at night, with clear skies in the afternoon.

Sea fog is extremely important to the vegetation of northern coastal California. Throughout the dry summers, the fog condenses on objects in its path. It provides moisture to the redwood trees; the redwoods absorb moisture through their needles. Some water drips off the trees and onto the ground, where it is absorbed by the trees' shallow roots.

Evaporation fog

Evaporation fog is formed in a completely different manner than the other types of fog discussed so far. Rather than being formed when warm air cools to the dew point, evaporation fog is formed when water evaporates into cool air and brings that cool air to its saturation point. The water may evaporate from a wide range of sources, such as a puddle, a lake, a river, an ocean, or even exhaled breath.

The reason why water molecules evaporate into unsaturated air (air which has less than 100 percent relative humidity) has to do with equilibrium. Water molecules are continually entering and leaving the surface of a body of water. If the relative humidity is less than 100 percent, water molecules will leave the surface faster than they enter. Thus the number of water molecules in the air will increase. At 100 percent relative humidity, the rates of entering and leaving are equal. The water vapor in the air is at equilibrium with the liquid water.

Steam fog rises from Lake Michigan on a sub-zero January morning. FMA, INC.

There are two main types of evaporation fog: steam fog, which occurs over a body of water, and frontal fog, which accompanies the passage of a cold or a warm front (the line behind which a cold or a warm air mass is advancing).

Steam fog The production of steam fog requires cold air to travel over a warmer body of water. Steam fog can often be seen over inland lakes and rivers in the fall, when the air is cool but the water is still warm. Water evaporates from the lake or river, saturates the cold air, and condenses into a shallow (less than 2 feet, or .6 meter) layer of steam fog.

Steam fog occurs all year long over the thermal ponds (hot springs) in Yellowstone National Park. The reason for this pattern is that the temperature of the water is always greater than that of the air. In the winter, it is common to see steam fog over large bodies of water, such as the Great Lakes, which can take several weeks to cool to air temperature. The fog there sometimes forms in dense, rising, swirling columns known as steam devils, because of their similarity to dust devils in the American Southwest.

In arctic regions, where the air is always extremely cold and dry, steam fog occurs over unfrozen waters on a large scale. Commonly called arctic sea smoke, this form of steam fog is patchy and wispy in appearance.

Did you know? Driving in fog

Most people, when driving along poorly lit roads at night or in other conditions of reduced visibility, instinctively turn on their high-beam headlights. However, this is not a wise strategy for driving in fog. Light is scattered by fog droplets and is reflected into the driver's eyes. High-beam lights merely illuminate the fog directly ahead of the vehicle and make it difficult to see anything beyond. Close to the ground, the fog is usually less dense. Low-beam headlights point lower toward the ground than do high-beam headlights and are thus more appropriate for foggy, nighttime driving. Fog lamps are often installed just above or below the front bumper. This low mounting position reduces the amount of light scattered back to the driver's eyes.

Frontal fog Frontal fog, sometimes called precipitation fog, is a type of evaporation fog that forms when a layer of warm air rises over a shallow layer of colder surface air. The uplift of warm air forms clouds that often yield precipitation, or falling water particles. The precipitation, usually rain, is warmer than the cold air beneath it and evaporates into the air. This raises the cold air to its saturation point and fog is produced.

This type of fog is called frontal fog because the conditions that give rise to it occur just before the arrival of a warm front or just after the passage of a cold front.

Upslope fog

Upslope fog is formed by the slow passage of a moist parcel of air up the side of a hill or mountain. As the air rises, it expands adiabatically; that is, with no heat transfer. When air expands, it cools. Once the air cools to the dew point, condensation occurs. Upslope fog generally covers a large area, sometimes hundreds of miles, and may persist for days.

Ragged patches of upslope fog form as moist air moves up a forested mountain slope. FMA, INC.

Rime ice covers fence wires after a cold fog. COURTESY WALTER A. LYONS.

Upslope fog is common in all mountain ranges. It is prevalent on the eastern slopes of the Rocky Mountains in the winter and spring. It occurs when cold air, following in the wake of a cold front, drifts westward from the Great Plains and rides up the gentle slopes. A similar phenomenon occurs in eastern Australia. There, moist air from the Tasman Sea is blown to shore and travels along the eastern slopes of the Great Dividing Range to a level where fog forms.

Freezing fog

Freezing fog is the term used to describe fog that develops in air that has a temperature below freezing. In most cases, freezing fog is comprised of supercooled water droplets. Supercooled water is water that exists in the liquid state below its freezing point. Freezing fog freezes onto any solid surface it comes in contact with, such as trees, telephone poles, cars, and roadways.

When freezing fog encounters a surface, it deposits a layer of frost called rime. Rime is not crystalline like true frost, which is called hoar frost. Rather, it is ice that contains trapped air, giving it a whitish appearance. Rime often persists long after the fog has cleared. It creates extremely hazardous driving conditions and is nearly impossible to walk on without slipping.

Hurricane

When Katrina struck the coasts of Louisiana and Mississippi on August 20, 2005, it reminded us that hurricanes certainly deserve the title "greatest storms on Earth." No other storm system has the power of a hurricane. To get a sense of the power contained in a hurricane, consider the following: 1) Just 1 percent of the energy in an average hurricane could supply the entire United States with electric power for one year; and 2) the energy unleashed by a hurricane in one day is equal to the energy of four hundred 20-megaton hydrogen bombs.

Hurricanes that strike populated areas are among the deadliest and most destructive of all natural disasters. A single strong hurricane can kill hundreds or thousands of people. Fortunately, the number of deaths caused by hurricanes has declined greatly in recent years (particularly in the United States) due to the development of early detection systems. Historically, hurricanes have been directly responsible for an average of 162 deaths per year. However, this includes the Galveston, Texas, hurri cane of 1900 in which 6,000 people lost their lives. Since 1965, hurricanes have accounted for about 20 to 30 deaths per year in the United States.

Population growth and the construction of vacation and retirement homes in hurricane-prone areas raise the risk of increased losses from property damage. However, the cost of property damage from hurricanes has not shown a steady increase. According to information from the National Oceanic and Atmospheric Administration (NOAA) the increase is very slight in inflation-adjusted dollars from 1971 to 2000. In 1992, there was a loss of nearly forty billion in inflation-adjusted dollars. If this spike is not included, the cost of property damage would show a slight decrease. On the other hand there were huge property losses in 2004 and 2005. When these numbers are included, property damage losses from 1971 to 2006 show a slight but definite upward trend. However, it is not a steady increase, since some years are high and some are low.

The word "hurricane" is used to refer to tropical cyclones that form in the northern Atlantic Ocean or in the eastern Pacific Ocean off the coasts of Mexico and Central America. A tropical cyclone is any rotating weather system that forms over tropical waters, which are within the area of 23.5° north latitude and 23.5° south latitude. Hurricanes that occur in the western North Pacific and China Sea region are called "typhoons" (pronounced TIE-foons). The word "typhoon" may come from *taaîfung*, which is Cantonese for "great wind." It is also possible that the word comes from the ancient Greek word *tuphon*, which means whirlwind. Hurricanes that form over the Indian Ocean are called "cyclones" (pronounced SIGH-clones).

Hurricane Katrina devastates New Orleans, Gulf Coast

Hurricane Katrina shocked the world after hitting the U.S. Gulf Coast on August 29, 2005. Katrina was the third most powerful hurricane ever to make landfall, or come across a land mass, in the United States. Until this disaster, recent advances in early detection systems had helped to decrease the disastrous effects of hurricanes. From 1965 to 2005, deaths from hurricanes in the United States were around twenty to thirty people per year. In contrast, Katrina alone claimed over eighteen hundred lives and caused up to $100 billion in damage. This storm, which displaced at least a half-million people, will be remembered as one of the deadliest and costliest natural disasters in U.S. history.

Katrina first made landfall on August 25 in Florida as a Category 1 storm according to the Saffir-Simpson intensity scale. The storm caused some damage and loss of life across the state before exiting land and beginning a path through the Gulf of Mexico toward Louisiana. In the warm waters of the gulf, Katrina intensified to a Category 5 storm. The Gulf Coast braced itself for the oncoming hurricane.

Katrina lost momentum as it moved toward the Gulf Coast. The storm gradually reduced to a Category 3 on its path toward landfall. However, since the storm was a Category 4 just before the eye of the storm made landfall, the area experienced sustained winds of more than 130 miles (209 kilometers) per hour. Katrina made landfall near New Orleans, Louisiana, setting off a disastrous chain of events.

Katrina hit Louisiana just after 6 AM on a Monday. Within hours, low-lying parts of New Orleans and surrounding parishes stood under water of up to 10 feet (3 meters) deep. The city of New Orleans, which

WORDS TO KNOW

air mass: a large body of air with approximately the same temperature and humidity throughout.

air pressure: barometric pressure; the force exerted on a surface due to the weight of air.

anemometer: an instrument that measures wind speed.

cirrostratus cloud: a thin layer of high-altitude clouds that cover most of the sky, but are semitransparent.

cirrus cloud: a wispy, high-level cloud.

cold front: the leading edge of a moving cold air mass.

condensation: the process by which water changes from a gas to a liquid.

convergence: where things come together, such as the trade winds blowing from the north and south near the equator.

Coriolis effect: the deflection of a moving object such as an air mass due to the rotation of Earth.

cumulonimbus cloud: a tall, vertically developed cloud reaching to the top of the troposphere or above and capable of producing heavy rain, high winds, and lightning.

cumulus cloud: fluffy, white, mid-level cloud.

cyclone: a weather system characterized by air that flows inward and circulates around a low pressure area.

eye: an area of clear sky and warm, dry, descending air at the center of a hurricane.

eye wall: a vertical area of thick clouds, intense rain, and strong winds marking the outer boundary of the eye.

flood: inundation by water of normally dry land.

front: the boundary between two air masses of different temperatures.

hurricane: a tropical cyclone that forms in the northern Atlantic Ocean or in the eastern Pacific Ocean.

hurricane warning: hurricane landfall is imminent.

hurricane watch: hurricane landfall is possible.

Intertropical Convergence Zone: the area of rising air near Earth's equator where the trade winds converge.

inversion, atmospheric: a stable reversal of the normal pattern of atmospheric temperature, formed when a warm air mass sits over a cold air mass near the surface.

jet stream: a fast-flowing, relatively narrow air stream found at an altitude of approximately 36,000 feet (11,000 meters).

landfall: the point on a coast the center of a hurricane first crosses.

latent heat: the heat that must be removed from a quantity of water vapor to cause it to turn into a liquid, or that must be added to a quantity of liquid water to cause it to turn into a vapor; called latent because the temperature of the quantity of water or water vapor does not change.

lies below sea level, is protected from the waters of Lake Ponchartrain and the Mississippi River by a 350-mile-long (563-kilometer-long) series of levees. Soon after the storm hit, three of these protective levees failed, and

Hurricane Katrina slams Gulfport, Mississippi, 2005.
©JIM REED/CORBIS.

water poured in, filling the city like a bathtub. By the end of the first day, entire neighborhoods were completely underwater. At the disaster's height, 80 percent of the city was submerged.

Calls for evacuation of New Orleans began on Friday and Saturday, a few days before the storm hit the Gulf Coast. However, thousands of people were still in New Orleans when the storm hit. Many people had no access to transportation—by some estimates, one-third of New Orleans' population did not own a car. Some were elderly or in poor health, some had small children, and some simply did not want to leave their homes. Around the time the storm hit, citizens who remained in New Orleans were advised to head for the Louisiana Superdome or the convention center, which were being used as temporary shelters for evacuees. Many found refuge in these shelters, but thousands were left behind in homes, hospitals, jails, and the streets.

The rest of the world watched in horror as tragedy unfolded. Parts of the city remained submerged for weeks. Fires raged as the floodwaters became increasingly polluted with gasoline, landfill contents, industrial waste, snakes, and rats. Many people were stranded in the hardest-hit areas, which were mostly poor neighborhoods. Rescue workers used helicopters and boats to navigate the floodwaters in order to rescue people from trees and rooftops. Hundreds waited on highway overpasses to be rescued as the water rose. The region lacked electricity and drinkable water. Civil unrest mounted as military and police forces tried to keep the peace.

Weather extremes: The Galveston disaster

Before Hurricane Katrina, the worst hurricane disaster and the worst weather disaster in the United States occurred on September 8, 1900, in Galveston, Texas. It was the worst storm of the twentieth century in terms of lost lives. Initial estimates were that more than six thousand people died when a storm surge 20 feet (6 meters) in height swept across the low-lying barrier island. Modern estimates put the death toll closer to seventy-two hundred.

Galveston's residents had received warning from the U.S. Weather Bureau on September 6 that a tropical storm was detected near Cuba. However, they did not pay much notice. After all, other tropical storms had come their way but had inflicted only minor damage. Galveston residents had no way of knowing the power of the storm that was about to strike them.

It was not until the morning of September 8 that the higher-than-usual tides and strong winds hinted at the severity of the approaching storm. However, rather than evacuating the island, most residents merely took shelter in brick houses at higher elevations. The problem with that strategy was the highest point on the island, at that time, was only 9 feet (about 3 meters) above sea level. That meant that no place on the island was safe from the storm's rushing waters.

The hurricane's assault on Galveston lasted for several hours, starting at about 4 PM. Winds gusting to 100 miles (160 kilometers) per hour were recorded before the island's anemometer, an instrument that measures wind speed, was destroyed. A 20-foot (6-meter) storm surge crashed onto shore and entirely submerged the island. The storm leveled almost every structure within three blocks of the south shore and severely damaged many others. As buildings collapsed, the wreckage was carried inland to smash into other buildings. Many people were thrown into the water, where high winds and surging water battered them with the debris. To add to the misery of the survivors, 10 inches (25 centimeters) of rain fell during the night. Once the storm had passed and flood waters subsided, very few structures were left standing in the town.

Since that time, Galveston has been rebuilt and extensive measures have been taken to prevent future disasters. The residents have constructed a seawall facing the Gulf of Mexico that is 17 feet (5 meters) tall and 3 miles (5 kilometers) long. They also brought in sand and raised the elevation of the island, at some points as high as 17 feet (5 meters) above sea level.

Though much of the public focus on Hurricane Katrina was on the New Orleans tragedy, the storm pulverized a long stretch of the Gulf Coast region, including Florida, Mississippi, Tennessee, and Alabama. Storm surges, or abnormal sea rises, occurred as far away as Mobile, Alabama. Hundreds of people died, and thousands upon thousands lost their homes and livelihoods.

The tragedy of Hurricane Katrina reminded the United States and the world of the complicated social and political aspects of natural

Hurricane Katrina hits Mobile, Alabama, 2005. © WARREN FAIDLEY/CORBIS.

disasters. Residents of the hardest-hit areas in the Gulf Coast region were among the nation's poorest people. Two-thirds of New Orleans residents were African American, a fact that caused a number of leaders to speculate that the government's botched relief efforts reflected a lack of concern for minorities.

Recent events: Catastrophic hurricanes since 2000

Hurricane Katrina is not the only recent hurricane to have caused substantial destruction and economic loss in the United States. The years since the turn of the twenty-first century have been very active in the formation of hurricanes. With the exception of Hurricane Katrina, most of these storms did not cause extensive loss of life. However, they have been extremely costly. Hurricanes that have made landfall in the United States since 2000 have caused more than $148 billion in damage.

Hurricane Isabel Hurricane Isabel was the only Category 5 storm of the 2003 Atlantic hurricane season. It made landfall as a Category 2 storm on September 18, 2003, just south of Cape Hatteras, North Carolina. It produced storm surges as high as 10 feet (3 meters) above normal tide levels and spun off a number of tornadoes, violently rotating winds capable of great destruction, in the days following its landfall.

Isabel caused damage from South Carolina all the way to Ontario, Canada. The official damage estimate was $3.37 billion. As with many hurricanes, the majority of that damage resulted from flooding, which affected more than sixty million people in the mid-Atlantic region. The flooding also caused extensive crop damage in several states. All told, fifty people died: sixteen as a direct result of the storm and thirty-four indirectly.

Hurricanes Charley, Frances, Ivan, and Jeanne In 2004, four separate hurricanes bombarded the state of Florida over a six week period, causing more than $30 billion in damage and claiming more than sixty lives in Florida alone. Hurricane Charley was the first to hit, a Category 4 storm that made landfall in southwest Florida on August 14. It was the strongest hurricane to hit the United States since Hurricane Andrew in 1992. Because Charley was predicted to make landfall further north, near Tampa Bay, many residents in the affected parts of Florida were caught off guard. The storm claimed ten lives and caused $15 billion in losses, making it the third-costliest hurricane in U.S. history.

Just weeks later, on September 4 and 5, Hurricane Frances battered both the east and west coasts of Florida. After initially making landfall on the eastern seaboard near West Palm Beach, Frances traveled across the Florida peninsula and into the Gulf of Mexico. It once again hit Florida, this time in the panhandle in the northwest portion of the state. Frances caused forty-two deaths in the United States and about $9 billion in losses.

Hurricane Ivan was the strongest storm of the 2004 Atlantic hurricane season. After causing major damage in Grenada, Jamaica, and the Cayman Islands, Ivan made landfall as a Category 3 storm in Alabama on September 16. On September 20 it looped back across the Florida peninsula, doing most of its damage in the state's panhandle near the Alabama border. Ivan killed sixty-four people in the Caribbean and fifty-seven people in the United States, including fourteen in Florida, and caused $13 billion in damage.

Less than two weeks later, on September 25, Hurricane Jeanne made landfall on Florida's east coast, just two miles north of Frances. Where Frances traveled west after making landfall, Jeanne turned north and headed up the coastline to Georgia. Jeanne killed five people and caused about $6.9 billion in damage in the United States, but the worst of its damage came in Haiti, where more than three thousand people died in flooding and mud slides caused by the storm.

Hurricane Isabel seen from space via NASA's Aqua satellite in 2003. © CNP/CORBIS.

The 2005 Atlantic hurricane season Charley, Frances, Ivan, and Jeanne combined to make the 2004 Atlantic hurricane season one of the deadliest and costliest ever, with losses of more than three thousand lives and $42 billion. The 2005 Atlantic hurricane season was even more severe. It was the most active hurricane season to date. Tropical storms, which are storms that have sustained winds of 39 to 73 miles (63 to 117 kilometers) per hour, are given names from a pre-determined list. During the 2005 Atlantic hurricane season, there were twenty-seven named tropical storms. This number included fourteen hurricanes and seven major hurricanes.

Three of the six most powerful hurricanes ever recorded in the Atlantic basin formed in 2005, including Wilma, the most powerful in history. In addition to Hurricane Katrina, the most destructive hurricane in U.S. history, hurricanes Dennis, Rita, and Wilma all caused significant damage. All told, damage from the 2005 Atlantic hurricane season topped $100 billion.

Hurricane Dennis made landfall as a Category 3 storm in the Florida panhandle in July, less than a year after Hurricane Ivan struck the same area. Dennis claimed eighty-nine lives, including fifteen in the United States, and did more than $2.2 billion in damage.

Hurricane Rita, a Category 5 storm, was the first hurricane to make landfall in the United States after Hurricane Katrina, hitting near the Texas-Louisiana border on September 24. Rita had been projected to make landfall near Houston, Texas, prompting nearly three million residents of the greater Houston area to evacuate. The evacuation created an enormous gridlock, with the trip from Houston to Dallas, normally three or four hours, taking between twenty-four and thirty-six hours to complete. After it made landfall, Rita caused $10 billion in damage. Though only seven direct deaths were recorded, 113 people died from indirect causes, many in the evacuations that preceded the storm.

With the formation of Hurricane Wilma in October, the 2005 Atlantic hurricane season surpassed the 1933 season as the most active in history. After setting the record as the most powerful hurricane in Atlantic basin history, Wilma devastated the Yucatán peninsula in Mexico and then traveled east and made landfall in southwest Florida on October 24. Wilma caused more than $12 billion in damage and killed thirty-five people in Florida.

The year 2005 saw so many hurricanes that, for the first time since the practice of naming hurricanes began in 1950, all of the allotted names

Motorists clog a Houston, Texas, highway as they evacuate before the arrival of Hurricane Rita in 2005. © CJ GUNTHER/ EPA/CORBIS.

were used, and the later storms of the season were named using letters of the Greek alphabet. Tropical Storm Zeta, the sixth storm to be named with a Greek letter, was the final storm of the 2005 season.

The components and causes of a hurricane

A hurricane is the most intense form of tropical cyclone, which is any rotating weather system that forms over tropical waters. Winds blow inwards toward, and rotate around, an area of low pressure. Cyclones rotate counterclockwise in the Northern Hemisphere and clockwise in the Southern Hemisphere. To qualify as a hurricane, a storm must have a well-defined pattern of rotating winds with maximum sustained winds greater than 74 miles (119 kilometers) per hour. Sustained winds are winds that blow continuously for at least one minute.

A hurricane is made up of a series of tightly coiled bands of thunderstorm clouds. These bands spiral around an almost totally calm region, called the eye, at the center of the hurricane. A hurricane may have within it hundreds of strong thunderstorms, which have the very tall cumulonimbus clouds producing rain and thunder. The diameter of an average hurricane is about 350 miles (560 kilometers) while the diameter of the largest hurricanes approaches 900 miles (1500 kilometers).

Is global warming producing more hurricanes?

Atmospheric scientists have determined that Earth's temperature is increasing. This phenomenon is called global warming. Since one of the effects of global warming is to heat up tropical ocean water, many scientists expect hurricanes to become more frequent. Warmer water also contains more energy for hurricanes, so global warming may give rise to storms more powerful than ever witnessed before. The world's hurricane breeding regions are expected to expand as well, as a larger area of water warms to 80°F (27°C)—the minimum water temperature necessary for hurricane formation.

Recently, hurricanes have been forming more frequently and with greater ferocity. Hurricanes' duration and strength have increased by about 50 percent over the last thirty years. The 2005 Atlantic hurricane season was the most active season on record. In the eleven years between 1995 and 2005, twenty-nine Atlantic hurricanes were so destructive and costly that their names were permanently retired from the National Hurricane Center's list of available storm names. In the thirty-three years preceding, only twenty-eight storms had been retired.

It is not yet clear whether this increase in hurricane activity is attributable to global warming. Historically, hurricane activity has been cyclical, with several decades of high activity followed by several decades of fewer storms. For instance, the 1920s–30s and 1950s–60s were very active periods, while the 1970s–80s were relatively calm. Whether the frequent hurricanes of the 1990s and early twenty-first century are part of a long-term trend toward more hurricanes or simply another cycle of high activity is an ongoing scientific debate. While there is a near consensus in the scientific community that one of the effects of global warming will be more frequent and powerful hurricanes, some scientists caution against attributing any particular hurricane or weather phenomena to global climate change.

Less intense forms of tropical cyclones are referred to as tropical storms, tropical depressions, or tropical disturbances. A tropical storm is similar to a hurricane in that it has organized bands of rotating strong thunderstorms, yet its maximum sustained winds are only 39 to 73 miles (63 to 117 kilometers) per hour. A tropical depression, the weakest form of tropical cyclone, consists of rotating bands of clouds and thunderstorms with maximum sustained winds of 38 miles (61 kilometers) per hour or less. A tropical disturbance is a cluster of thunderstorms that is beginning to demonstrate a cyclonic circulation pattern. Tropical disturbances frequently occur over tropical waters. Only a small percentage of these disturbances, however, become hurricanes.

A hurricane starts out as a tropical disturbance and passes through the stages of tropical depression and tropical storm on its way to maturity. A hurricane will continue to grow as long as there is a fresh supply of warm,

Hurricane Wilma over the Florida Peninsula as seen from space, 2005. © NOAA/HANDOUT/REUTERS/CORBIS.

humid air. Once the hurricane crosses over colder waters or land, its supply of warm, humid air is cut off and it weakens. A typical hurricane lasts about thirteen days. A hurricane may pass back through those weaker stages, in reverse order, as it dissipates.

Over the ocean, a hurricane generates waves 50 feet (15 meters) or greater in height. When a hurricane reaches land, it may pound the shore with a wall of water up to 20 feet (6 meters) high. This wall can produce severe flooding across 100 miles (160 kilometers) of coastline. Hurricanes also bring fierce winds and intense downpours of rain. It is not unusual for coastal and inland communities to receive 6 to 12 inches (15 to 30 centimeters) of rain when a hurricane comes onshore. For its onshore finale, a dissipating hurricane may spin off numerous tornadoes.

What is the structure of a hurricane? A hurricane consists of spiraling bands of clouds called rain bands, around a calm, low-pressure center, the eye. The rain bands, which are tightly coiled around the eye, produce

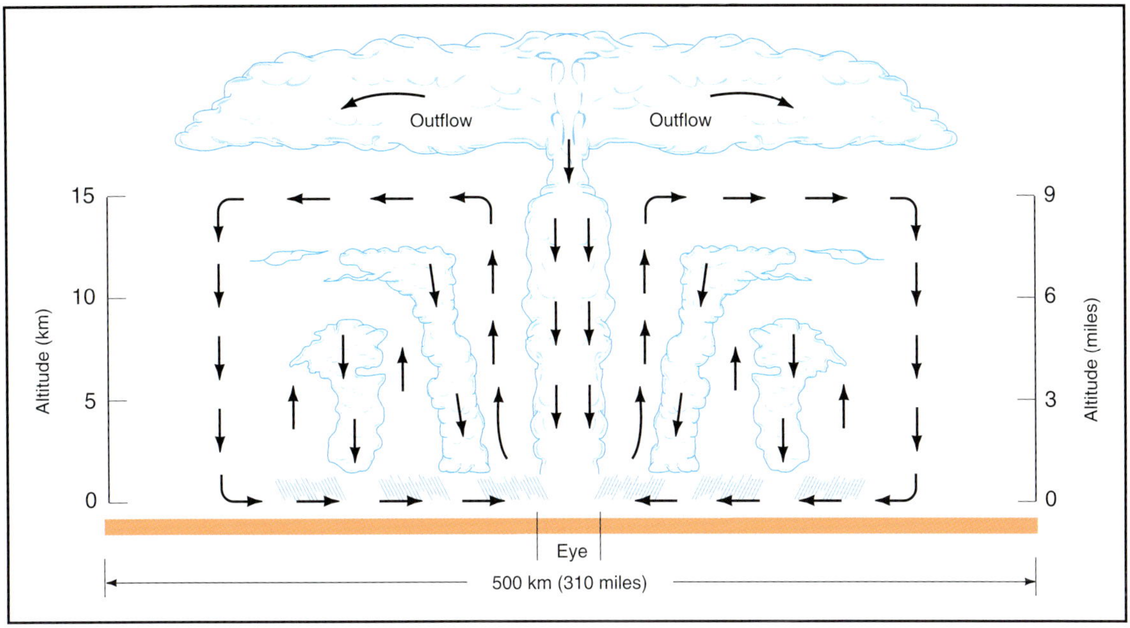

Air flow within a hurricane.

heavy rains and forceful winds. Surrounding the outer edge of the rain bands is a region of wispy, high-level cirrus or cirrostratus clouds.

The hurricane's eye has an average diameter of 12 to 40 miles (20 to 65 kilometers). Within the eye, winds are light and skies are partly cloudy or clear. The reason that clouds break up in the eye of a storm is that air sinks in that region. Air warms as it falls and the water droplets within it evaporate.

The lowest pressure of the storm exists in the eye. Typically, pressure there dips to 950 millibars (28 inches, or 71 cm), although measurements as low as 900 millibars (26.5 inches, or 67.3 cm) have been recorded. By way of comparison, the average pressure at sea level is 1013.25 millibars (29.92 inches, or 76.00 cm).

It may take an hour or more for the eye of the hurricane to pass over an area. The calm weather associated with the eye sometimes fools the residents of that area into thinking the storm is over when, in fact, the heavy winds and rain will soon resume.

The region immediately surrounding the eye, called the eye wall, is the strongest part of the storm. The eye wall is a loop of thunderstorm clouds that produce torrential rains and forceful winds. The closer one

Weather report: Comparing hurricanes and extratropical storms

Hurricanes are tropical cyclones. An extratropical cyclone is a large-scale storm that forms in the middle latitudes. Extratropical cyclones are produced by interactions between contrasting warm and cold fronts.

Tropical and extratropical storms have different mechanisms of energy supply. An extratropical cyclone gets its energy from temperature contrasts between the air masses found on either side of a front, while a hurricane gets energy from warm ocean waters and the latent heat released as the moist surface air rises.

Both extratropical cyclones and hurricanes are centered around an area of low pressure, a hurricane has a much steeper pressure gradient. The air pressure at the center of a hurricane is typically much lower than it is at the center of an extratropical cyclone.

Other differences between the two types of cyclones include:

- The diameter of the typical extratropical cyclone is three times the size of the diameter of the typical hurricane.
- Hurricanes weaken with height while extratropical cyclones intensify with height.
- Air sinks in the center of a hurricane while it rises in the center of an extratropical cyclone.
- Air at the center of a hurricane is warmer than the surrounding air while the air at the center of an extratropical cyclone is colder than the surrounding air.
- The winds of a hurricane are strongest at the surface while the winds of an extratropical cyclone are strongest at upper levels, in the jet stream.

Despite all these differences, it is possible for hurricanes to transform into extratropical cyclones. This happens when a hurricane moves across a front and draws in air of different temperatures. Then the hurricane, which was weakening as it traveled over land, intensifies as it becomes linked with a low-pressure area aloft.

An example of a hurricane that became linked with an extratropical storm is Hurricane Agnes of 1972. After combining with a low-pressure system in the Northeast, Agnes produced heavy rains and extensive flooding. Harrisburg, Pennsylvania, for instance, received 12.5 inches (32 centimeters) of rain in twenty-four hours. The rising waters in central Pennsylvania forced the evacuation of more than 250,000 people. Agnes caused a total of 122 deaths and $6.4 billion in property damage. The floods were responsible for around half of the deaths and about two-thirds of the property damage.

gets to the center of the storm without actually entering the eye, the faster the winds blow. Within a radius of 6 to 60 miles (10 to 100 kilometers) of the eye, winds may reach speeds of 100 to 180 miles (160 to 300 kilometers) per hour.

The winds are a result of the pressure gradient, which is the difference in air pressure between high- and low-pressure areas relative to their distance apart. The pressure gradient between the edge of the storm and the eye drives the winds of a hurricane. The closer in to the eye, the steeper the pressure gradient becomes and the faster the winds blow. At points farther away from the eye of the storm, the pressure gradient becomes more gradual and the winds become weaker.

The most violent part of the hurricane is the side of the eye wall in which the wind blows the same direction that the storm is progressing. In that region, the hurricane's winds combine with the winds that are steering the hurricane, to create the storm's fastest winds.

The cyclonic wind circulation of the hurricane weakens with height, starting at about 9,800 feet (3,000 meters). The airflow actually reverses direction at heights greater than approximately 50,000 feet (15,000 meters). That means that while the eye of the storm and the surface beneath it are intensely low pressure areas, a high pressure area exists above.

The fact that a hurricane has a ceiling below the top of the troposphere, the lowermost portion of Earth's atmosphere, makes it possible to fly above a hurricane in an aircraft and take aerial photographs of the entire system. It is not possible to do this in a middle-latitude thunderstorm since the mature cumulonimbus clouds in that system, the clouds that produce the lightning, extend to the top of the troposphere and sometimes beyond.

Interesting facts: "Hurricane Huron"

In September 1996 an extratropical cyclone formed over the Great Lakes. It formed from what meteorologists call a cut-off low-pressure area (a low-pressure area that has become separated from other weather systems and may remain stationary). This was a particularly intense low. It started out as a typical "cold-core" extratropical cyclone, but over time it evolved into a "warm-core" system, similar to a hurricane, with an eye and spiral bands of gusty rain squalls.

The storm likely formed because the low pressure area stalled over Lake Huron. At the time, the lake waters were at their maximum seasonal high temperature, 70°F (21°C). This would be too low under normal conditions for tropical storm development. But over time, the water warmed the air enough that the storm developed its warm core. From a satellite, it strongly resembled a tropical storm, and researchers at Pennsylvania State University dubbed it "Hurricane Huron." This incident is thought to be the only such storm ever documented over the Great Lakes.

Where do hurricanes form? Hurricanes are tropical phenomena. The tropics are defined as the region of Earth bounded by 23.5° latitude, north and south. The tropics receive the most direct sunlight of anywhere on the planet, making that region the world's warmest.

The heating of Earth's surface leads to the daily formation of cumulus clouds and afternoon thunderstorms. While these thunderstorms are generally not severe individually, they sometimes become organized in

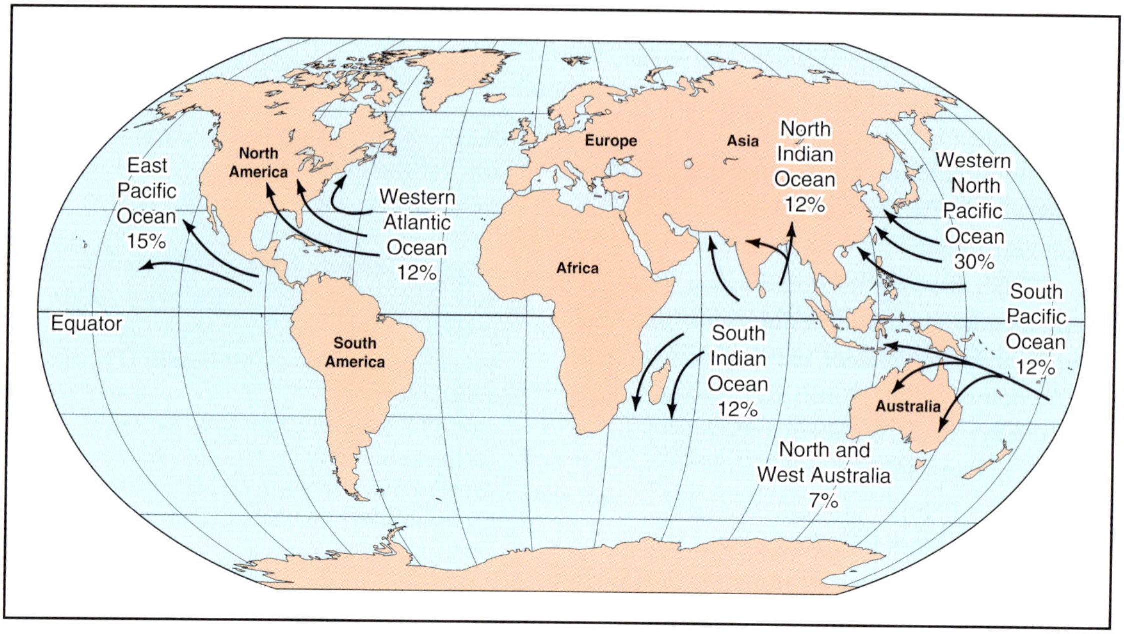

The world's hurricane breeding regions.

and the moisture within it condenses, or turns into water. When moisture condenses, it releases latent heat, the heat removed from a quantity of water vapor to cause it to turn into a liquid, and that heat provides additional energy to the storm system.

Another necessary ingredient for the formation of a hurricane is surface winds that are converging, or blowing toward a common point. Where winds converge at the surface, air rises. A number of events can trigger surface air convergence. One is that a front, a leading edge of an air mass of warm or cold air, moves into the tropics from the middle latitudes. By the time the front reaches the tropics, the temperatures on either side of the front have equalized. However, the front still has an associated low pressure area aloft. The winds at the surface converge to a point beneath that low pressure area and rise.

Another source of convergence of surface winds is the meeting of the trade winds from the north and the south, along the intertropical convergence zone, or ITCZ. Convergence at the ITCZ promotes hurricane development only during the of winter and summer when the ITCZ is located furthest from the equator. At other times of year, when the sun is directly over the equator, the ITCZ also sits very close to the equator. At those times the ITCZ does not experience the Coriolis effect. Once the ITCZ shifts to a point 4 or 5 degrees from the equator, however, the Coriolis effect is apparent.

A third possible source of converging winds is an easterly trade wind that flows in a wavelike fashion from Africa. As the trade wind proceeds westward, a low pressure trough may flow over the tropical waters, triggering surface winds to converge beneath it.

Hurricane formation also requires ideal conditions in the winds aloft. Namely, the winds at all altitudes need to be light and blowing in approximately the same direction and speed, so as not to scatter the moisture and dissipate the developing storm. Hurricane formation is most likely to occur when the upper air is cold, a factor that contributes to the low pressure.

Most often, there is some condition in the winds aloft that prohibits hurricane development. For instance, in some latitudes, particularly between 20 and 30 degrees, the upper-level air sinks. It warms as it falls, creating an inversion, or reversal of the normal temperature pattern, that prevents the upward development of thunderstorms.

Another condition that works against hurricane formation is a relatively dry middle layer of air. The amount of latent heat necessary to generate a hurricane requires condensation to occur at all heights throughout the system. Moisture will not condense until the relative humidity of the air, which is the amount of water vapor in an air mass for a particular temperature, has reached 100 percent.

How do hurricanes unfold? Let's assume that the following atmospheric conditions exist: warm, humid surface air; cold air and low pressure aloft; converging surface winds; and light winds and high humidity at all altitudes. The stage has been set for the development of a hurricane.

The most widely accepted model of how a hurricane forms is called the Organized Convection Theory. According to this theory, the first step in the development of a hurricane is the formation of large thunderstorm clouds. That proceeds as follows: As warm air rises to the region of low pressure above, condensation occurs. Latent heat released during condensation warms the air at greater and greater heights. Eventually, the cold layer of upper air also becomes warm. As a result, its air pressure increases.

When the low pressure region aloft becomes transformed into a high pressure region, the thunderstorm ceases to develop upward. Rather, at that height air diverges outward, away from the high pressure area at the

Extreme weather: Sea Islands storm

On the night of August 27, 1893, a fierce hurricane laid waste to the South Carolina Sea Islands off the coast of Beaufort, South Carolina. Some two thousand (some sources claim as many as five thousand) islanders perished in the storm. Virtually all survivors on the islands were left homeless and penniless.

The primary reason the hurricane took so many lives was not that it was an unusually large storm, but because the islanders had no advance warning and no way to escape. The National Weather Service, which had issued a hurricane warning to mainlanders, could not get word to the islanders for lack of telegraph or telephone links.

Most of the island's thirty thousand residents were former slaves. Prior to the Civil War (1861–1865), the slaves had worked on plantations on the islands. Near the start of the war, the plantation owners had fled, leaving behind their former slaves. The plantations were then divided, and the newly freed slaves were given small pieces of land. In the years since the end of slavery, the islanders had built thriving communities.

The hurricane generated tides nearly 20 feet (6.1 meters) above average sea level and winds of 120 miles (193 kilometers) per hour. After the storm passed, survivors found a grisly scene of death and destruction. Bodies littered the beaches and marshes. The destruction of buildings and crops was near total. Most sources of fresh water had been contaminated with sea water. Virtually all animal life on the island had died.

News of the islanders' plight reached the mainland some two days after the hurricane. It took nearly a month for a large-scale assistance campaign to begin. Until that time, island residents survived mainly by eating berries. The American Red Cross coordinated the relief effort under the direction of its founder, Clara Barton. Arriving in the area on September 30, Barton organized deliveries of food, clothing, medicine, and supplies to the islands. Many African American Civil War veterans also volunteered their services in the relief effort. By the following July, reconstruction of the Sea Islands communities was nearly complete.

center of the cloud. The air flows to the edge of the cloud and then sinks back to the surface.

As the same time that the pressure aloft rises, the pressure at the surface falls. It is the formation of the surface low, at the center of the storm, that is the most essential factor in hurricane development. The winds begin to circulate in a counterclockwise pattern (in the Northern Hemisphere) around the center of, but not directly into, this surface low. At the center of the storm, the air sinks directly from the high pressure area above to the low pressure, below.

The winds increase in speed the closer they get to the center. In the process, they generate large ocean waves. These waves create friction on the wind, interrupting the air flow and causing the air to converge. Where the air converges, it rises, carrying moisture and warmth upward to form new thunderstorms.

WORDS TO KNOW

Organized Convection Theory: a widely accepted model of hurricane formation.

pressure gradient: the difference in air pressure between a high and low pressure area relative to the distance separating them.

rain band: a band of heavy thunderstorms forming a tightly coiled spiral around the center of a tropical storm.

relative humidity: the amount of water vapor in an air mass relative to the amount of water in a saturated air mass of the same temperature.

Saffir-Simpson Hurricane Damage Potential Scale: a scale devised by Herbert Saffir and Robert Simpson intended to be used to predict a hurricane's destructive potential.

squall line: a moving band of strong thunderstorms.

storm surge: an abnormal rise of the sea over and above normal tides due to strong winds and low pressure accompanying a storm or hurricane.

thunderstorm: a rainstorm accompanied by thunder and lightning and produced from a cumulonimbus cloud.

tornado: a violently rotating column of air that reaches the ground and is attached to a cumulonimbus cloud; it is nearly always observable as a "funnel cloud."

trade winds: an area near the equator of prevailing winds that blow from the northeast north of the equator and the southeast south of the equator.

tropical cyclone: any rotating weather system that forms over tropical waters.

tropical depression: a storm with rotating bands of clouds and thunderstorms and maximum sustained winds of less than 38 miles (61 kilometers) per hour.

tropical disturbance: a cluster of thunderstorms that is beginning to demonstrate a cyclonic circulation pattern.

tropical storm: a storm with organized rotating bands of strong thunderstorms and maximum sustained winds between 39 to 73 miles (63 to 117 kilometers) per hour.

tropical wave: an elongated area of low air pressure, oriented north to south, causing areas of cloudiness and thunderstorms.

tropics: the region of Earth between 23.5° north latitude and 23.5° south latitude.

troposphere: the lowest atmospheric layer, where clouds exist and virtually all weather occurs.

typhoon: tropical cyclone that form in the China Sea or in the western North Pacific Ocean.

warm front: the leading edge of a moving warm air mass.

westerlies: an area at middle latitudes of prevailing winds that blow toward the northeast in the Northern Hemisphere.

The rising air increases the air pressure aloft. As a result, the surface air pressure becomes even lower. A chain reaction is set in motion: new thunderstorms are formed, the upper-level high pressure area becomes

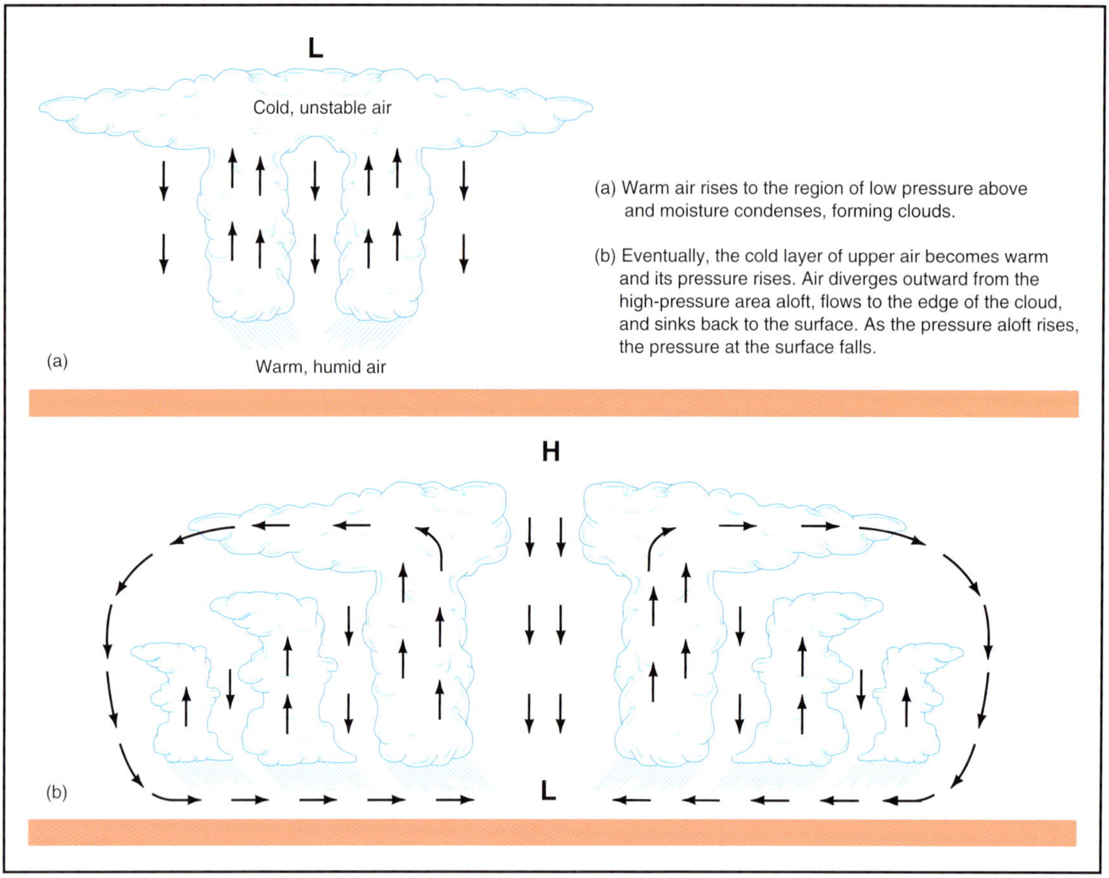

Formation of a hurricane according to the organized convection theory.

higher, and the surface low pressure area becomes lower. Each process drives the other as the storm grows into a mature hurricane.

A hurricane continues to grow as long as a fresh supply of warm, humid air is available. Once the hurricane crosses over colder waters or land, its source of energy is cut off, and it begins to dissipate.

As long as more air flows out from the top of the storm center than flows into the storm from the surface, the hurricane continues to intensify. The point at which that trend reverses the hurricane begins to die.

The level of air flow is a indication of air pressure. A rapid outflow at the top of the hurricane indicates that pressure is high at upper levels and, consequently, low at the surface. However, when the outflow slows, the pressures at the top and bottom of the storm center begin to equalize. In the absence of a strong surface low, the winds weaken. Then there is nothing to support the coiled organization of thunderstorms. The system unwinds and individual thunderstorms dissipate.

How long do hurricanes last? The life cycle of a typical hurricane is about thirteen days. It starts out on day one as a cluster of thunderstorms, a condition that meteorologists call a tropical disturbance. By day three, the thunderstorms have become organized into bands that swirl about a low-pressure center. The system, at this point, is called a tropical depression.

The surface air pressure drops, the winds intensify, and the storm continues to grow. By day five, winds are blowing faster than 39 miles (63 kilometers) per hour. At this stage, the system is upgraded to a tropical storm. By day seven winds are blowing faster than 74 miles (118 kilometers) per hour. The storm is now classified as a hurricane.

For the next few days, as the hurricane moves across the warm water, it maintains its strength and integrity. About day twelve it crosses onto land and weakens. By day thirteen it has dissipated.

How do hurricanes move across the world? Hurricanes that form over the northern Pacific and northern Atlantic oceans are guided to the west-northwest by easterly trade winds. These winds blow a hurricane along at about 10 miles (16 kilometers) per hour. Once a hurricane encounters the Azores-Bermuda High, the semipermanent high pressure system in the eastern Atlantic, it is directed to the northwest, through the Caribbean and toward the East Coast of the United States.

If the hurricane travels so far northward that it reaches the middle latitudes, it will be steered to the northeast by the westerlies, which are prevailing winds in the middle latitudes that blow towards the northeast in the Northern hemisphere. The westerly winds blow the hurricane along at about 55 miles (88 kilometers) per hour, which is significantly faster than the trade winds. This faster movement at higher latitudes makes it more challenging to get advance warning to communities in the hurricane's path.

While the trade winds, Azores-Bermuda High, and westerlies establish a general hurricane route, the specific path taken by a hurricane is much more difficult to predict. The specific path depends on the structure of the hurricane and how it interacts with its environment. Exactly how these factors influence hurricane movement is not well understood.

Tracking Katrina

Hurricane Katrina formed over the southeastern Bahamas as Tropical Depression Twelve on August 23, 2005. It formed from a combination of a tropical wave (a north-south trending low-pressure area) and the remnants of Tropical Depression Ten. The system strengthened to a tropical storm on August 24 and was given the name Katrina. The tropical storm headed towards Florida and became a hurricane only two hours before its first landfall between Hallandale Beach and Aventura, Florida, on the morning of August 25.

Like most storms, Katrina weakened as it passed over land, but quickly regained hurricane status after entering the warm waters of the Gulf of Mexico. On August 27, the storm reached Category 3 intensity on the Saffir-Simpson Hurricane Scale, becoming the third major hurricane of the 2005 season. Katrina continued to intensify and reached Category 5 status on the morning of August 28. It attained its maximum intensity at 1 PM Central Daylight Time on August 28, with maximum sustained winds of 175 miles (280 kilometers) per hour and a minimum central pressure of 902 millibars. The pressure measurement made Katrina the fourth most intense Atlantic hurricane on record at the time and the most intense storm ever recorded in the Gulf of Mexico. However, it held these records for only a short time. Both records were broken by Hurricane Rita a few weeks later.

Katrina weakened in intensity as it approached land but remained a dangerous storm. It made its second landfall on the Louisiana coast southeast of New Orleans at 6:10 AM CDT on August 29 as a Category 3 hurricane with sustained winds of 125 miles (205 kilometers) per hour. At landfall, hurricane-force winds extended outward 120 miles (190 kilometers) from the center and the storm's central pressure was 920 millibars After moving across the Mississippi Delta and over Breton Sound, Katrina made its third landfall near the Louisiana-Mississippi border with sustained winds of 120 miles (195 kilometers) per hour—still a Category 3 storm.

Katrina maintained its status as a hurricane until it moved over 150 miles (240 kilometers) inland. It was finally downgraded to a tropical storm as it passed near Jackson, Mississippi, and to a tropical depression near Clarksville, Tennessee. The remnants of Katrina were still recognizable as it entered the Great Lakes region on August 31. It was then absorbed by a frontal boundary and became an extratropical cyclone. This storm then moved into Ontario and Quebec where it caused additional flooding and isolated several small villages.

The path also depends on the size and location of the Azores-Bermuda High, which varies over the course of the year.

Some hurricanes follow a smooth course, while others move erratically, shifting direction suddenly and inexplicably. For instance, some hurricanes that seem certain to spare the U.S. Atlantic Coast will turn to the west and crash onto shore. On the other hand, coastal communities may brace for a hurricane's onslaught only to be spared at the last minute as the storm turns back to sea.

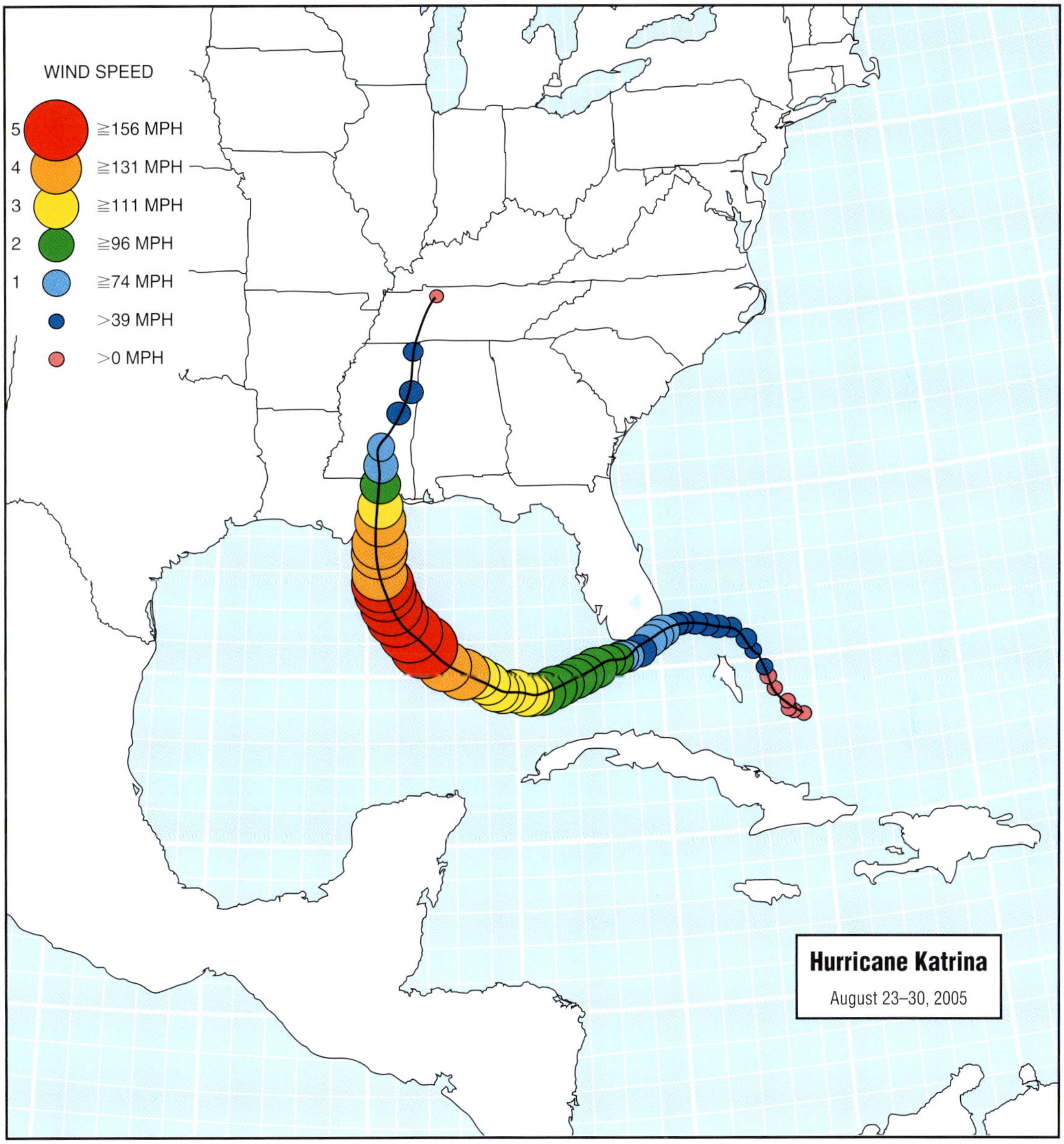

Path of Hurricane Katrina, August 2005.

Hurricanes that form over the eastern Pacific, off the west coast of Mexico, generally move to the west or northwest and travel over the ocean until they dissipate. That is the reason we hear so little about those hurricanes. Occasionally, however, a Pacific hurricane will turn to the north or northeast and strike the west coast of Mexico. A handful of such hurricanes have devastated Mexican coastal communities over the past several decades. The remnants of those hurricanes have brought heavy rains and flooding to the U.S. Southwest and West Coast.

One would expect Hawaii to suffer from a large number of hurricanes, given that Hawaii lies in the path of hurricanes formed off the west coast of Mexico. But that is not the case. As it turns out, Hawaii is located far enough to the west that by the time most hurricanes reach it, they have been significantly weakened.

There have been exceptions to this rule, however. About once a decade, Hawaii is struck by a major hurricane. A notable hurricane in recent history is Hurricane Iniki, which hit the island of Kauai on September 11, 1992. Iniki caused $1.8 billion worth of damage and seven deaths.

The hurricanes that directly affect the United States are typically those formed over the tropical North Atlantic, the Caribbean, or the Gulf of Mexico. On average, six hurricanes form over those waters during each hurricane season, two or three of which strike the U.S. Atlantic or Gulf coasts. The primary factor that determines whether a hurricane hits the United States is the location at which the hurricane moves to the northeast. If a hurricane is still over the ocean when it changes course from northwest to northeast, it will miss the coast. However, some hurricanes move over land before they change direction.

The U.S. West Coast is rarely struck by hurricanes, because storms that form in the eastern Pacific are normally blocked by cold ocean currents. In September of 1932 a hurricane moved up the Gulf of California, producing gusty winds and heavy rainfall in the Arizona desert. In September of 1939, a tropical storm slammed into San Diego with winds of 52 miles (84 kilometers) per hour. In September 1976, a hurricane gusted to 76 miles (122 kilometers) per hour at Yuma, Arizona.

The effects of hurricanes

When a hurricane moves onto land, it is capable of causing tremendous damage. A hurricane's winds are assumed by most people to be its most destructive element, but this is often not the case. The winds do cause a great deal of damage, but floods caused by ocean swells and torrential rains cause the most hurricane damage. Floodwaters, both in coastal and inland areas, account for about 90 percent of hurricane fatalities. Another

Buildings in downtown Kapaa, Hawaii, rest with their roofs split open in the aftermath of Hurricane Iniki. © REUTERS/ CORBIS.

destructive force of hurricanes is the tornadoes that hurricanes spawn in their final stages.

Storm surges In coastal areas, most of the property damage, as well as about 90 percent of deaths, are due to the hurricane's storm surge. A storm surge is a wall of water that sweeps on shore when the eye of a hurricane passes overhead. Storm surges range from 3 to 6.5 feet (1 to 2 meters) in a weak hurricane, to over 16 feet (5 meters) in a strong hurricane. A storm surge affects a stretch of coastline between 40 to 100 miles (65 to 160 kilometers) long. It levels any structure in its path. When squeezed into narrow channels, a storm surge produces flooding of inland bays and rivers.

The abnormal swelling of the ocean that produces a storm surge is caused by the combined effects of a storm's pressure gradient and high winds. In the open ocean, strong winds and high pressure around the edges of the hurricane push down on water, lowering its level. The displaced water flows toward the center of the storm, where pressure is lowest. The water at the center rises and then spirals downward to about 200 feet (60 meters) beneath the surface, where it flows outward.

When the storm moves into shallow waters, there is no place for the mound of water beneath the storm center to descend. Thus, the water there is forced to pile upward. The mound of water reaches its greatest

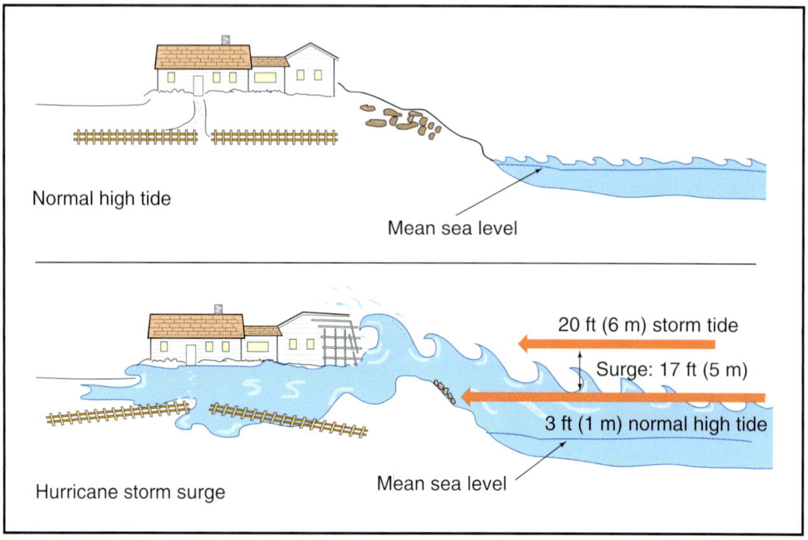

A hurricane storm surge.

height where it crashes onto shore. The storm surge is highest in strong hurricanes, especially where the ocean floor slopes gradually to the shore.

The largest storm tide in recent U.S. history was 25 feet (8 meters). It was caused by Hurricane Camille in August 1969, which made landfall in Pass Christian, Mississippi. The storm tide destroyed more than 5,500 homes. In addition, it damaged around 12,500 homes and 700 businesses. The area of greatest destruction was along a 60 mile (97 kilometer) stretch of coastline in Mississippi, Alabama, and Louisiana. As far as 125 miles (201 kilometers) away, the water level was 3 feet (.9 meters) higher than usual.

The largest recorded storm surges have occurred in other parts of the world. In 1737, a storm surge estimated to be 40 feet (12 meters) tall struck the Bay of Bengal, killing more than three hundred thousand people. A storm surge of 42 feet (13 meters) inundated Bathurst Bay, Australia, in 1899.

The destructive capabilities of a storm surge are the result of two factors: the density of the sea water, which is about 64 pounds per cubic foot (1030 kilograms per cubic meter); and the debris that the water sweeps along. Debris may include boats that were ripped from their moorings by the waves, pieces of destroyed buildings, trees, and sand. As the water plus this debris moves farther onshore, it batters and flattens

Ten Deadliest Hurricanes to Strike the United States Since 1900

Hurricane	Year	Category	Deaths
Texas (Galveston)	1900	4	8,000–12,000
Florida (Lake Okeechobee)	1928	4	2,500–3,000
Katrina (Lousiana, Mississippi)	2005	3	1,836
Florida (Keys and S. Texas)	1919	4	600
New England	1938	3	600
Florida (Keys)	1935	5	408
Audrey (Louisiana and Texas)	1957	4	390
Northeast U.S.	1944	3	390
Louisiana (Grand Isle)	1909	3	350
Louisiana (New Orleans)	1915	4	275

anything in its path. A storm surge also destroys structures such as buildings, roads, and sea walls by eroding the sand and soil beneath them, causing them to buckle or collapse.

A storm surge may also have the secondary effect of causing flooding of inland bays and rivers. This flooding results when storm surge water is squeezed into narrow channels. Sometimes inland waters rise even higher above normal levels than coastal waters in the wake of a storm surge.

Winds The winds of a hurricane also cause a significant amount of damage to coastal areas. Hurricane winds range between 75 and 180 miles (120 and 290 kilometers) per hour. Winds of this strength can damage buildings and homes and knock down trees and telephone poles, as well as cause beach erosion. A hurricane's winds can totally demolish lightweight structures such as mobile homes and poorly constructed buildings.

Part of wind damage is due to objects that are picked up and hurled through the air. Shingles, metal siding, road signs, and any items left outdoors become deadly missiles during a hurricane.

Most wind damage from a hurricane occurs within 125 miles (200 kilometers) of the coast. Once a hurricane travels farther inland, it generally begins to weaken. Occasionally a hurricane will retain its strength for greater distances. In 1989, for example, Hurricane Hugo ripped through Charlotte, North Carolina, with winds gusting to 100 miles (160 kilometers) per hour. Charlotte is about 175 miles (280 kilometers) inland.

Heavy rain and flooding A hurricane's destruction is certainly not limited to coastal areas. To the contrary, for hundreds of miles inland,

The winds of Hurricane Beulah topple shrimp boats in Brownsville, Texas, in 1967. © BETTMANN/CORBIS.

and for several days after the hurricane-strength winds have died down, the storm may continue to produce torrential rains and flooding. When an area receives more than 6 inches (15 centimeters) of rain, flooding is likely. Hurricanes typically drop 5 to 10 inches (13 to 25 centimeters) on the land in their path. Some hurricanes have produced more than 25 inches (63 centimeters) of rain in a period of twenty-four hours.

Inland flooding is the most destructive element of some hurricanes. Examples of this include:

- Hurricane Diane in 1955 brought rains and flooding to Pennsylvania, New York, and New England. The flooding caused nearly 200 deaths and $4.2 billion in damage.
- Hurricane Camille in 1969 brought 9.8 inches (25 centimeters) of rain to Virginia's Blue Ridge Mountains. The storm resulted in 150 deaths.
- Tropical storm Claudette in 1979 dumped 45 inches (114 centimeters) of rain outside of Alvin, Texas, resulting in over $600 million in damage.

Heavy rains due to hurricanes are not always harmful. These rains may spell relief for regions with parched soil and withering crops. In some cases, the value of saved crops in one region is greater than the value of property destroyed by the flooding in another region. In some areas of the world, particularly in the Far East, farmers are dependent on annual hurricane rains for their economic survival.

Tornadoes Tornadoes are another hazard of hurricanes. About one-quarter of all hurricanes that come on shore in the United States produce tornadoes. A single hurricane, on average, spawns ten tornadoes.

The thunderstorms embedded in the outer regions of a hurricane are the most likely to spawn tornadoes, although tornadoes also form in thunderstorms close to the eye wall. The greatest number of tornadoes are produced in the portion of the hurricane that is northeast of the eye.

Theodore Fujita, a tornado specialist from the University of Chicago, is the author of a recent theory that the greatest damage from hurricane-induced tornadoes is caused by small funnels called spin-up vortices. These vortices are each 9 to 30 feet (3 to 10 meters) in diameter and last only about ten seconds. The hurricane winds combine with the tornado winds, so the vortices produce winds of around 200 miles (320 kilometers) per hour.

Ranking hurricanes by strength As with tornadoes, hurricanes are ranked according to their strength. However, there is one main difference: Tornadoes are classified *after* they have struck an area based on the *actual* damage they have created, while hurricanes are categorized *before* they strike land based on their *potential* damage to coastal areas.

Each hurricane is placed into one of five categories according to its strength, described in the Saffir-Simpson Hurricane Damage Potential Scale. This scale was developed in the early 1970s by Robert Simpson, then director of the National Hurricane Center, and Herbert Saffir, an engineer who designed Miami's hurricane-proof building code.

According to the Saffir-Simpson scale, hurricanes in Category 1 are the weakest and hurricanes in Category 5 are the strongest. The factors that determine a hurricane's strength include: air pressure at the eye of the storm; range of wind speeds; potential height of the storm surge; and the potential damage caused. The categories of potential damage are defined as follows: 1) minimal; 2) moderate; 3) extensive; 4) extreme; and 5) catastrophic. A hurricane's ranking is upgraded or downgraded as it goes through its stages of development.

Saffir-Simpson hurricane intensity scale Most of the hurricanes that strike the United States are Category 1 or 2. Only two hurricanes ranked as Category 3 or higher strike the United States every three years, on average.

Theodore Fujita works with his tornado simulator. © BETTMANN/CORBIS.

Of the 126 tropical storms or hurricanes that hit the United States between the years 1949 and 1990, only 25 were Category 3 or higher. Those twenty-five storms, however, caused three-quarters of all property damage done by tropical storms or hurricanes during that period.

Category 5 hurricanes are the rarest kind—the United States only experienced three of them during the entire twentieth century. The first was a hurricane on Labor Day, 1935 (the practice of hurricane naming did not begin until 1953), the second was Hurricane Camille in 1969, and the third was Hurricane Allen in 1980. (The hurricane that leveled Galveston, for example, would have been listed as a Category 4.)

The human factor

People have always settled in hurricane-prone regions. This creates great risk for property damage when hurricanes strike. The effects of global warming, reportedly made worse by pollution, may be having an effect on hurricanes. The world—including the oceans—has been warming at a dramatic rate in recent years. Many scientists claim that as temperatures continue to rise, we can expect hurricanes to increase in number and size.

For people who live in areas affected by hurricanes, it is essential to understand and follow safety procedures. That includes making preparations before the hurricane season begins, knowing what to do when a hurricane watch or warning is issued, and how to respond once a hurricane has passed.

To prepare for hurricane season, you must understand the risks that hurricanes pose to your area, learn the evacuation routes inland, and find out where emergency shelters are located. It is also crucial to develop a safety plan for your family and keep a disaster kit on hand. A kit should include the following for each person: nonperishable food; three gallons of bottled water; one change of clothing and footwear; one blanket or sleeping bag; first aid kit; flashlight, radio, and batteries; extra set of car keys; credit card or cash; and diapers for infants.

The U.S. government's failed Katrina response

The destruction caused by Hurricane Katrina shocked the world. Almost as surprising, though, was the state and federal government's slow and awkward response to the disaster. Thousands of people were stranded for days on rooftops and highway overpasses, and in homes, hospitals, the Superdome, and the convention center. Food, water, and basic supplies were delayed for days. Many people died while a horrified nation looked on.

The first failures in dealing with Hurricane Katrina were failures of prevention and readiness. Experts from the U.S. Army Corps of Engineers had long predicted that the New Orleans levee system would not withstand a "megahurricane." For years the Army Corps had been asking the federal government for money to bolster the levees, but they would have needed to have begun the work long before in order to prevent the Katrina breaches.

Once the storm neared land, the government urged evacuation. However, the evacuation plan left thousands behind. It is estimated that as many as one third of the citizens of New Orleans did not own a car, and thus many of those people were left without a way to flee.

The Federal Emergency Management Agency, or FEMA, which falls under the department of Homeland Security, is the primary agency responsible for handling a disaster like Katrina. In the days following the hurricane, President George W. Bush praised FEMA, saying they were doing a "heck of a job." However, the realities of the situation in New Orleans were bleak. People were desperate and starving, and the city began to descend into a state of civil unrest. President Bush decided to survey the area by airplane, flying low over the Gulf Coast Region so he could get a first hand look at the devastation. By Friday of that week, Bush declared that government response was "not acceptable." That same week Congress called for an investigation of the botched response to the disaster. Further investigation revealed that FEMA chief Michael Brown was possibly not qualified to lead such a major disaster relief effort.

Other parts of the relief efforts were troubled as well. On Thursday after the hurricane, Homeland Security Chief Michael Chertoff claimed on National Public Radio to be unaware of the sickness, hunger, and unrest at the Superdome. State and local agencies were at times reluctant to cooperate with FEMA, and communication failures abounded. One of the major lessons of Hurricane Katrina was that federal, state, and local government entities need to improve their cooperation and preparedness for major hurricanes like Katrina.

Hurricanes in the United States

The part of the United States that experiences the greatest number of hurricanes is the Florida Keys. Forty-three hurricanes have hit the Keys in the last one hundred years. The places where hurricanes pose the greatest threat to humans, however, are the barrier islands that exist along portions of the Atlantic Coast and Gulf Coast. In the United States, people place themselves in the path of danger by settling in those areas most vulnerable to hurricane damage—the barrier islands.

The barrier islands are long, narrow strips of sand that run parallel to a 2,000-mile-long (3,200-kilometer-long) Atlantic and Gulf coastline from New York to Texas. Examples of barrier islands include New York's Fire Island, Texas's Galveston Island, North Carolina's Outer Banks, and the Sea Islands off the coasts of South Carolina and Georgia. Barrier islands, which stand only 5 to 10 feet (1.5 to 3 meters) above sea level, bear the brunt of a hurricane's wind and waves and provide the mainland with a buffer from the storm. The islands respond to hurricane beatings by moving—the sand actually becomes redistributed by the waves.

Despite the fact that living on the islands is known to be dangerous, people continue to settle there. In fact, in recent years the islands have seen a huge increase in construction of housing, hotels, and businesses geared toward tourism. In some parts of the world, people have no choice but to live in hurricane-prone regions. Bangladesh, for instance, is a magnet for hurricanes (called cyclones in that region of the world). Its coastal region endured seven of the nine deadliest hurricanes of the twentieth century. Bangladesh is also a densely populated, desperately poor country. For residents of the coast, moving inland would mean squeezing into already overflowing urban slums. But in the United States, people happily choose to settle on hurricane-prone barrier islands. Drawn by the beauty of the ocean, they pay top dollar for beach residences and flock to the islands for their vacations.

Before 1940, only 10 percent of Atlantic and Gulf Coast barrier islands held houses or hotels. Development steadily increased from that time. Many islands today are wholly buried under concrete and buildings.

Hurricane Fran, in 1996, battered North Carolina's southeastern barrier islands. Houses, cottages, condominiums, and cars were strewn across the beach and washed out to sea. Twenty-four people died in the storm, and property damage totaled $2 billion. The following week, people began rebuilding on those islands. Barrier island development is such an attractive business proposition, in part, because U.S. taxpayers—through the National Flood Insurance Program, the Federal Emergency Management Agency's Disaster Relief Program, and the Army Corps of Engineers' shoreline stabilization projects—regularly pay for storm damage.

Another danger specific to barrier islands is that once a hurricane warning has been issued, evacuation is difficult. Since construction of evacuation routes has not kept pace with the islands' population growth, bridges connecting the islands to the mainland become choked with traffic.

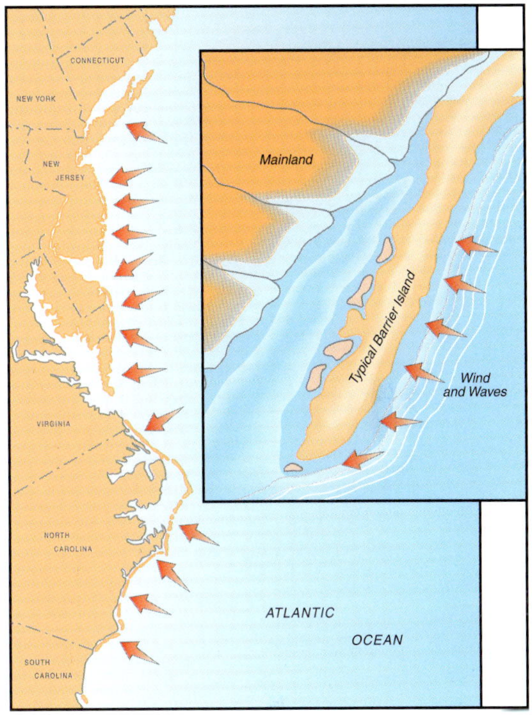

Atlantic coast barrier islands.

Hurricane watches and warnings The ability of weather forecasters to warn the public of potential hurricane strikes has greatly increased in recent decades. Some of the sophisticated technologies that are now used to detect and track tropical cyclones include radar, weather satellites, and weather aircraft. Although the erratic nature of hurricanes makes it impossible to predict exactly when and where they will strike, forecasters can now guess at the answers to these questions with a fair degree of certainty.

When a hurricane threatens a coastal area, hurricane watches and warnings are issued. If the hurricane is predicted to be life threatening, the residents of that area are evacuated. Hurricane watches and warnings are issued by the Tropical Prediction Center (formerly the National Hurricane Center), a branch of the National Weather Service.

A hurricane watch is issued when a hurricane is headed in the general direction of an area. It means that hurricane conditions are *possible* in the area. Hurricane watches are announced at least thirty-six hours, and sometimes several days, in advance.

If a hurricane is poised to strike an area within twenty-four hours, a hurricane warning is issued. It means that hurricane conditions are *expected* in the area. For each community within the warning area, meteorologists will also issue the probability of the hurricane's center coming within 65 miles (105 kilometers) of that community. The probability is intended to give residents an idea of the type of damage likely to occur in their area. It is also considered in the decision as to whether or not evacuation is necessary.

This distance is about three times the area that will actually be affected once a hurricane comes onshore. The reason the warning area is so large is that

Hurricane Andrew: The costliest natural disaster of the twentieth century

In August 1992, Hurricane Andrew struck Florida and Louisiana, causing fifty-eight deaths and $30 billion in damage. Over 200,000 homes and business were damaged or destroyed, and 160,000 people became homeless. Andrew, which made landfall as a Category 4 hurricane, was the costliest natural disaster of the twentieth century in the United States.

On August 21, Andrew, which was then classified as a tropical storm in the Atlantic, appeared to be weakening. However, it then moved over warmer waters and rapidly gained strength. On August 21, its winds were only 52 miles (84 kilometers) per hour. Two days later, its winds had increased to 140 miles (225 kilometers) per hour, and Andrew had developed into an intense hurricane.

Andrew came on shore at Homestead, on the southern tip of Florida, on August 24. With winds that peaked at about 200 miles (320 kilometers) per hour and a storm surge 16.9 feet (5.1 meters) tall—a record for Florida—Andrew devastated the town. It leveled trees, utility poles, and fifty thousand homes.

Andrew then traveled westward, over land, and into the Gulf of Mexico. While Andrew had weakened during its journey across the land, it regained strength over the Gulf's warm waters. On August 25, Andrew blew into Louisiana with winds of 138 miles (222 kilometers) per hour. There, Andrew continued its relentless destruction of property.

Andrew's death toll was relatively low due to the efficiency of prediction and warning systems. Over 1 million people in Florida and 1.7 million people in Louisiana and Mississippi were evacuated from areas in the storm's path. Had Andrew occurred in the first half of the 20th century, before the development of sophisticated hurricane-detecting technology, the death toll would have certainly been much higher.

it is possible for a hurricane to change course at any time, making it impossible to predict the exact point at which the hurricane will make landfall.

For people who live in areas affected by hurricanes, it is crucial to know and follow certain safety procedures. These procedures include making preparations before the hurricane season begins; knowing what to do when a hurricane is in progress; and taking certain steps after the hurricane has passed.

For more information about the dangers hurricanes pose to your area and hurricane preparedness, contact your local office of the National Weather Service, American Red Cross, or Federal Emergency Management Agency.

What to do when you are within a hurricane watch area:

- Stay tuned to radio or television reports of the storm's progress.
- Fill your car with gas and get cash, if needed.

- If you live in a mobile home, make sure it's securely fastened, then evacuate.
- Cover all windows and doors with shutters or plywood.
- Check your supply of nonperishable food and water.
- Gather first aid materials and medications.
- Bring lawn furniture, garbage cans, garden hoses, and other lightweight items inside.
- If you have a boat, be sure it is properly secured.
- Evacuate if you live in a mobile home or high-rise, on the coastline, on an offshore island, or near a river or flood plain.

What to do when you are within a hurricane warning area:

- Stay tuned to radio or television reports of the storm's progress.
- Finish covering your windows and doors and prepare your home for evacuation.
- Evacuate immediately upon the orders of local officials and travel inland, to the home of a friend or relative, a low-rise motel, or an emergency shelter.
- Notify someone outside of the hurricane warning area of your evacuation plans.
- If you have pets that you are unable to take with you, leave them plenty of food and water.

If you are staying at home:

- Fill the bathtub and containers with drinking water, unplug small appliances, turn off propane tanks, and turn your refrigerator to its coldest possible setting.
- In case of strong winds, close all outside and inside doors and go into a small interior room or hallway on the first floor, away from windows and doors. If possible, crouch beneath a sturdy piece of furniture.

What to do after the hurricane:

- Stay tuned to the radio or television for information.
- Don't return home until your area has been declared safe.
- Don't attempt to drive around a barricade; if you encounter one, turn around and take a different route.
- Don't drive on roads or bridges in flooded areas or on washed out roads.

- Inspect your gas, water, and electrical lines for damage before using.
- Be sure that your tap water is not contaminated before drinking or cooking with it.
- Make as few calls as possible so you don't tie up phone lines.

Naming hurricanes Before 1950, hurricanes were identified primarily by their latitude and longitude. This practice became confusing as hurricanes moved about, especially if there was more than one hurricane at the same time on the same ocean.

In 1950, meteorologists began the practice of assigning names to all hurricanes and tropical storms that formed in the western North Atlantic, Caribbean, and Gulf of Mexico. They began naming eastern Pacific storms in 1959. From 1950–53, names were taken from the international radio codes words that corresponded with letters of the alphabet. For instance, the first three letters—"a," "b," and "c"—had the names Able, Baker, and Charlie.

In 1953, meteorologists began giving the storms female names. The names were assigned in alphabetical order, starting with the "As" for each new season. Since 1978 in the eastern Pacific, and 1979 in the northern Atlantic, male names, as well as names in French and Spanish, have also been used.

Names are now assigned in advance for six-year cycles. The names are submitted by countries that lie in the path of hurricanes and must be approved by the Region 4 Hurricane Committee of the World Meteorological Organization, which is made up of representatives of countries affected by hurricanes.

After the six-year cycle has ended, the names are reused, except for names that are retired. The names of hurricanes that cause extensive damage or loss of life, such as Gilbert, Isabel, and Andrew, are removed from the list for at least ten years. Katrina was retired from the list after the 2005 season and was replaced by Katia. A total of five names—Dennis, Katrina, Rita, Stan, and Wilma—retired in 2005 breaks the previous single-season record of four retired names, reached in 1955, 1995, and 2004.

The list for the tropical North Atlantic normally includes twenty-one names. The letters Q, U, X, Y, and Z are not used. In a typical year, twenty-one names are more than enough. But 2005 set a record for the

Names for Hurricanes Through the Year 2011

Eastern Pacific Hurricane Names

2007	2008	2009	2010	2011
Alvin	Ima	Andres	Agatha	Adrian
Barbara	Boris	Blanca	Blas	Beatriz
Cosme	Cristina	Carlos	Celia	Calvin
Dalila	Douglas	Dolores	Darby	Dora
Erick	Elida	Enrique	Estelle	Eugene
Flossie	Fausto	Felicia	Frank	Fernanda
Gil	Genevieve	Guillermo	Georgette	Greg
Henriette	Hernan	Hilda	Howard	Hilary
Ivo	Iselle	Ignacio	Isis	Irwin
Juliette	Julio	Jimena	Javier	Jova
Kiko	Karina	Kevin	Kay	Kenneth
Lorena	Lowell	Linda	Lester	Lidia
Manuel	Marie	Marty	Madeline	Max
Narda	Norbert	Nora	Newton	Norma
Octave	Odile	Olaf	Orlene	Otis
Priscilla	Polo	Patricia	Paine	Pilar
Raymond	Rachel	Rick	Roslyn	Ramon
Sonia	Simon	Sandra	Seymour	Selma
Tico	Trudy	Terry	Tina	Todd
Velma	Vance	Vivian	Virgil	Veronica
Wallis	Winnie	Waldo	Winifred	Wiley
Xina	Xavier	Xina	Xavier	Xina
York	Yolanda	York	Yolanda	York
Zelda	Zeke	Zelda	Zeke	Zelda

North Atlantic Hurricane Names

2007	2008	2009	2010	2011
Andrea	Arthur	Ana	Alex	Arlene
Barry	Bertha	Bill	Bonnie	Bret
Chantal	Cristobal	Claudette	Colin	Cindy
Dean	Dolly	Danny	Danielle	Don
Erin	Edouard	Erika	Earl	Emily
Felix	Fay	Fred	Fiona	Franklin
Gabrielle	Gustav	Grace	Gaston	Gert
Humberto	Hanna	Henri	Hermine	Harvey
Ingrid	Ike	Ida	Igor	Irene
Jerry	Josephine	Joaquin	Julia	Jose
Karen	Kyle	Kate	Karl	Katia
Lorenzo	Laura	Larry	Lisa	Lee
Melissa	Marco	Mindy	Matthew	Maria
Noel	Nana	Nicholas	Nicole	Nate
Olga	Omar	Odette	Otto	Ophelia
Pablo	Paloma	Peter	Paula	Philippe
Rebekah	Rene	Rose	Richard	Rina
Sebastien	Sally	Sam	Shary	Sean
Tanya	Teddy	Teresa	Tomas	Tammy
Van	Vicky	Victor	Virginie	Vince
Wendy	Wilfred	Wanda	Walter	Whitney

Watch this: *When the Levees Broke: A Requiem in Four Acts*

Director Spike Lee created this wrenching 2006 HBO (Home Box Office) documentary about Hurricane Katrina and its aftermath using new footage and interviews with government official and survivors. The documentary includes very little narration. Instead, Lee lets the images and the people tell the story themselves.

number of named storms. The letters V and W were used for the first time (for Hurricanes Vince and Wilma). Even those were not enough. When the names in a list are exhausted, the World Meteorological Organization specifies that letters of the Greek alphabet be used. For the 2005 season, six letters were necessary. The twenty-eighth and last named storm of 2005 was Tropical Storm Zeta, which formed on December 29, well past the normal end of the hurricane season.

Presently, each hurricane-producing region of the world (except the northern Indian Ocean, where cyclones are not named) has its own lists of names, drawn up years in advance. Each storm is automatically assigned the next name on the alphabetical list.

Technology connection

The ability of weather forecasters to warn the public of potential hurricane danger has greatly increased in recent years. Forecasters are presently able to predict, within 200 to 250 miles (320 to 400 kilometers), where a storm will be three days in the future. Forecasters at the National Hurricane Center in Miami issued their most accurate prediction yet in September 1999, when they stated that Hurricane Floyd would spare Florida and head north before striking North Carolina. As it was, Floyd missed the Florida coast by a mere 50 miles (80 kilometers).

Predictions of where a hurricane will hit land are used by public officials when calling for evacuations. Forecasters want to be as certain as possible in their predictions before recommending evacuations. If an area is evacuated only to be spared by the hurricane, residents become less likely to heed evacuation notices in the future. That attitude is perilous, since the next evacuation could be a matter of life and death. Forecasters also wish to avoid unnecessary evacuations because they are very costly. Each day of evacuation represents $1 million of lost business revenues for every mile of coastline.

Two of the most useful instruments used by hurricane researchers to detect and track tropical storms are weather aircraft and weather satellites.

Gulfstream II flies over Los Angeles, California. © TECMAP CORPORATION/ERIC CURRY/CORBIS.

Weather aircraft Weather aircraft determine the intensity of hurricanes by probing storm clouds in upper levels of the atmosphere. They measure temperature, air pressure, and wind speed and direction. These planes have reinforced wings and bodies, in order to withstand the hail, ice, and strong winds they encounter within the clouds. The weather instruments are carried in pods beneath the plane's wings or attached to its nose cone.

In 1996, the U.S. National Oceanic and Atmospheric Association (NOAA) acquired a hurricane research jet, called the Gulfstream IV-SP. The jet can cruise right through these storms at heights of up to 45,000 feet (13,725 meters). It contains sensors that measure air pressure, temperature, humidity, and wind speed at the edges and the core of the storm. It also releases hundreds of dropwindsondes, also called dropsondes, which are instruments that transmit data on atmospheric conditions as they fall through the storm. The information collected by the jet is combined with readings taken at ground stations in order to better determine where a hurricane is headed.

Weather satellites Weather satellites, which circle the globe in space, provide meteorologists with pictures and other information about hurricanes and tropical storms. The first weather satellite, launched in April 1960, was TIROS 1—Television InfraRed Observation Satellite. In September 1961 weather satellites proved their value when they broadcast images of Hurricane Carla. Information from these images resulted in the nation's first widespread evacuation when 350,000 people along the Gulf Coast were removed from the path of the killer hurricane.

For most people, the words "weather satellite pictures" conjure up images of swirling clouds that are seen on television newscasts. While weather satellites do produce those photos, their function is far more extensive than that. Weather satellites determine the temperature at various atmospheric levels—from the cloud tops down to the land and oceans. They also measure humidity and wind speeds in the upper air and even track plumes of invisible water vapor and relay information from one ground station to another and pick up and transmit distress signals from vessels in the air and at sea. Today, several nations operate satellites that continuously monitor global weather.

[*See Also* **Clouds; Forecasting; Thunderstorm; Tornado; Weather: An Introduction**]

For More Information

BOOKS

Brinkley, Douglas. *The Great Deluge: Hurricane Katrina, New Orleans, and the Mississippi Gulf Coast.* New York: William Morrow, 2006.

Robinson, Andrew. *Earth Shock: Hurricanes, Volcanoes, Earthquakes, Tornadoes and Other Forces of Nature.* New York: W. W. Norton & Company, 2002.

Simon, Seymour. *Hurricanes.* New York: Harper Trophy, 2003.

PERIODICALS

Trenberth, Kevin. "Uncertainty in Hurricanes and Global Warming." *Science.* (17 Jun 2005): pp. 1753–1754.

WEB SITES

"Hurricanes." *FEMA for Kids.* <http://www.fema.gov/kids/hurr.htm> (accessed March 9, 2007).

"Hurricanes." *National Oceanic and Atmospheric Administration.* <http://hurricanes.noaa.gov/>(accessed March 9, 2007).

National Hurricane Center. <http://www.nhc.noaa.gov/> (accessed March 8, 2007).

Landslide

A landslide is the movement of large amounts of soil, rocks, mud, and other debris downward along a slope. The movement is caused by the pull of gravity and occurs when a mountainside or hillside weakens and is unable to support its own weight. The amount of material that falls in a landslide can be as small as the size of a refrigerator or as large as an entire mountainside. The falling material can move slowly or quickly, and may travel a few feet (meters) or several miles (kilometers) before it stops. Some landslides move only a little each year. Such movement may be irregular, or it may happen at the same time each year, such as in the spring, when the snow melts.

The most common cause of landslides is excessive moisture in the ground, because of heavy rains or melting snow. When the ground becomes so full of water it cannot hold any more, the soil loses its ability to stick together. It also becomes heavier, which hastens its movement down the slope. Not all landslides are caused by water. Earthquakes, the sudden movements of earth which release huge amounts of energy, trigger the largest and most devastating landslides. Other events that cause landslides include volcanoes and vibrations from explosions or heavy traffic. Human activities, such as mountainside development and mining, also contribute to instability on slopes. Forest fires are indirect causes of landslides, since they remove the vegetation and roots that hold the soil in place.

While rapid landslides cause the greatest loss of life and property, even slow landslides can cause structural damage to buildings and rupture underground power lines and water mains. Each year in the United States, landslides cause between twenty-five and fifty deaths and up to $2 billion in damage. In less developed nations, where there are often less strict zoning laws (allowing construction in landslide-prone areas), higher population densities, and a lack of protective structures, the death tolls and amount of property damage are much higher.

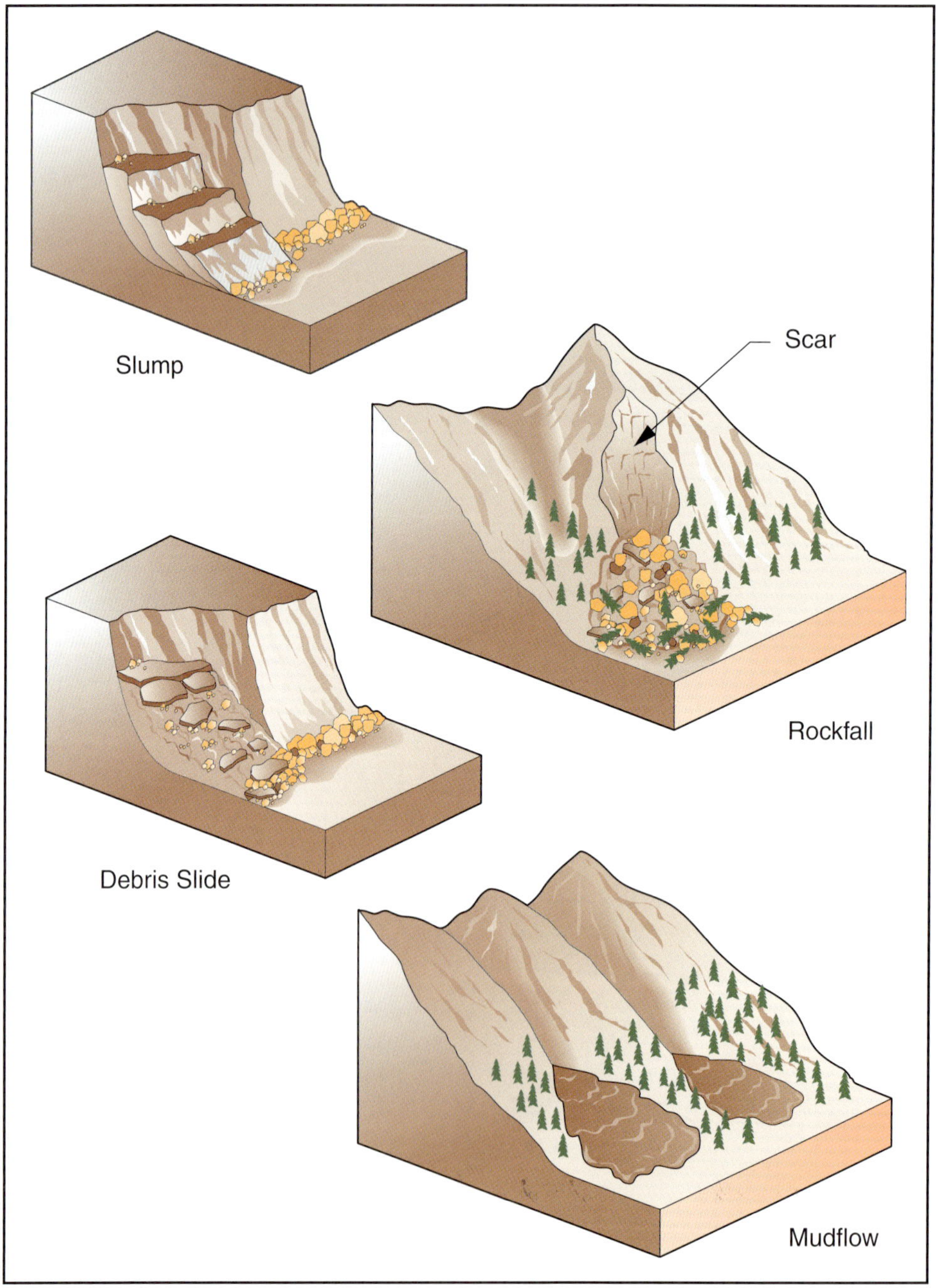

Four different types of landslides.

WORDS TO KNOW

debris avalanche: a downward slide of loose, earthen material (soil, mud, and small rocks) that begins suddenly and travels at great speeds; similar to a snow avalanche. It builds into a fearsome mass of mud, trees, and rocks that can cause much damage.

debris slide: a slide of small rocks and shallow layers of loose soil that commonly follows volcanic eruptions.

deforestation: the removal of all or most of the trees from a region.

earthflow: a landslide that consists of material that is moist and full of clay, yet drier than the material in mudflows.

earthquake: a sudden shifting of masses of rock beneath Earth's surface, which releases enormous amounts of energy and sends out shock waves that cause the ground to shake.

erosion: the removal of soil by water or wind. This is especially harmful when the uppermost layer of soil, called the topsoil, is stripped away, because this is the layer where plants grow.

fall: the downward motion of rock or soil through the air or along the surface of a steep slope.

lahar: a mudflow composed of volcanic ash and water that occurs in the wake of a volcanic eruption.

landslide: the movement of large amounts of soil, rocks, mud, and other debris downward and outward along a slope.

mudflow: a landslide consisting of soil mixed with water. It is wetter than the material in an earthflow.

rock slide: a cascade of rocks (of any size) down a steep slope at high speeds.

saturated: containing the maximum amount of water a material can hold.

slump: the slow downhill movement of large portions (called blocks) of a slope. Each block rotates backward toward the slope in a series of curving movements.

solifluction: the most rapid type of earthflow, occurring when snow or ice thaws or when earthquakes produce shocks that turn the soil into a fluid-like mass.

volcano: an opening in Earth's surface through which gases, hot rocks, and ash are ejected from the heated inner portion of the planet.

The Frank slide

In the early morning hours of April 29, 1903, a block of limestone approximately 0.5 square miles (0.8 square kilometers) in area cascaded onto the coal mining village of Frank in south-central Alberta, Canada. The limestone, which weighed 50 million to 90 million tons (45 million to 82 million metric tons) and was 500 feet (152 meters) thick, came hurtling down from a height of 3,100 feet (945 meters) between two peaks of Turtle Mountain. Seventy-six people were killed instantly in the

The Frank Slide Interpretive Center near the site of a 1903 rock slide that buried the town of Frank in Alberta, Canada. ©DAVE G. HOUSER/CORBIS.

landslide, although some records place the number as high as ninety. In addition to burying part of the town, the fallen rock dammed the Crowsnest River and created a new lake.

Native inhabitants feared the mountain The native people, who were the original inhabitants of the region, recognized the dangers of Turtle Mountain. The mountain had been named for its shape, which resembled a turtle's shell and had a slab of limestone sticking out like a turtle's head. To the Indians, it was "the mountain that walked." Fearing a rock slide, the native people shunned the idea of settling, or even so much as camping, at the base of the mountain.

Turtle Mountain was indeed geologically unstable, meaning it had little resistance to sliding or collapsing. The twin-peaked mountain was composed of weather-worn limestone near its peak and soft stone laced with veins of coal at lower altitudes. The angle of the mountain was especially steep on the eastern slope, and the face had developed cracks. Along the cracks, the rock was fragmented. An earthquake two years prior to the rock slide had made the rock fragmentation worse. Further weakening of the rock foundation was brought about by the tunneling of coal mining shafts, which were dug about 1 mile (1.3 kilometers) into the mountain.

Frank established as a mining town The town of Frank was incorporated on September 10, 1901, just eleven months after a coal deposit had been discovered at the base of the mountain. It was named after H. L. Frank, a banker from Montana who had funded a mining operation to extract the coal. He persuaded adventurous frontiersmen, many of them recent arrivals from Europe, to travel to Turtle Mountain and work in the mine. He also paid the Canadian Pacific Railway to run railroad tracks from the main line to the mine entrance. By the time the town of Frank was established, miners were extracting hundreds of tons of coal each day.

The town of Frank looked just like a Hollywood set for a Western movie. Among the company buildings—miners' cabins, office buildings, and a boarding house—sprang up hotels, saloons, and casinos. The miners spent a significant portion of their earnings on drinking and gambling. By the spring of 1903, Frank had a population of approximately six hundred people.

The mountain tumbles down In the months prior to the landslide, miners had reported numerous sounds that should have been taken as warnings of the mountain's instability. The wooden supports in the tunnels groaned loudly and the tunnel walls shook. The vibrations had become so violent that coal literally dropped from the ceiling, forming piles that the miners merely had to shovel into cars. The night before the landslide, the mountain emitted a rumble that could be heard throughout the valley. Area residents ignored the noise and went to sleep.

Disaster struck at 4:10 AM the next morning. According to Sid Choquette, a brakeman on the railroad who had been walking alongside a slow-moving train, the mountain began to creak and groan loudly, then emitted an eerie whistling roar. Next Choquette heard a sound like cannon fire and saw a huge slab of rock racing down the slope, right toward the town. Choquette jumped aboard the train and the engineer set the controls on full-throttle. The train raced for the bridge that spanned the Crowsnest River and made it across just moments before the avalanche of rocks wiped out the bridge. The railroad crew watched, stunned, as millions of tons of limestone plowed through the south side of Frank, continued 2.5 miles (3.2 kilometers) across the valley floor, and then climbed 400 feet (122 meters) up the opposite slope.

In a little more than a minute the rock slide, plus a wall of cold air that forcefully thrust ahead of it, leveled much of the town of Frank, killing many of its residents. Three-quarters of the houses were destroyed, as were the electric power plant, the livery stable, the shoe store, the miners' temporary quarters, the construction camp, the cemetery, and more than 1 mile (1.6 kilometers) of the Canadian Pacific Railroad. The debris tumbled into the river, blocking the flow of water, and portions of the railroad tracks were covered by rocks 100 feet (30 meters) deep. Structures were ripped apart, flung across the valley, and then buried forever by the massive limestone boulders. Only twelve bodies were recovered, and the exact number of dead was never determined. Because there were no accurate records of the number of inhabitants at the time, it was impossible to compile a list of the missing.

Trapped miners dig themselves out When the rocks fell, seventeen workers were inside the mine and three others were taking a lunch break outside the entrance. The rock slide fell on the entrance, killing the three men outside and trapping the others inside. The miner most familiar with the mine's layout informed his trapped co-workers that they were at least 295 feet (90 meters) from the edge of the mountain. The miners knew they had to act quickly if they were going to get out alive. They realized the airshafts were probably blocked, meaning that breathable air would be in short supply. They were also concerned that explosive and lethal gases might be escaping from cracks in the rock walls.

The miners first tried to tunnel outward, but made little progress. Every time they dug into the wall, more rock tumbled down to fill in the space. After a few hours they tried a new strategy: digging upward, along a vein of coal. The coal was softer and easier to remove than the limestone. Three men dug at a time. They worked in shifts, making slow but steady progress. About thirteen hours after the rock slide, the miners reached the surface. They climbed out onto the mountainside and looked in horror upon the devastation below.

Rescue efforts People in Frank not directly in the rock slide's path were shaken from their slumber by the loud roar. Stunned, they staggered into the streets to see what had happened. Seeing fires and hearing screams for help, some people grabbed their lanterns and rushed toward the wreckage. The avalanche, however, spared few of those it touched. Rescuers only found twenty-three people alive in the landslide's path.

At one ruined home, merchant Alex Leitch and his wife and four sons were found dead. At another home, Sam Ennis had dug himself out of the rubble and worked with rescuers to free his wife, Lucy, from a beam that had fallen on her. Even while trapped, Lucy Ennis had managed to save their baby daughter, Gladys, who was choking on a clod of dirt. Sam

Ennis' brother-in-law, James Warrington, was also buried beneath a pile of rocks. Warrington warned rescuers to dig gingerly, since he felt something soft beneath him. It turned out that Warrington had landed on top of his next-door neighbor, Mrs. Watkins, who had been thrown from her own house.

On the railroad tracks, brakeman Sid Choquette, still shaken from his brush with death, turned his attention to the passenger train that was due to arrive in an hour. If it wasn't warned, the train would crash into the rock-covered tracks. He made his way through the cloud of dust that hung in the air and across rocks the size of small buildings until he arrived at the tracks on the east side of the rockpile. With only minutes to spare, he was able to flag down the train and prevent a second disaster.

The aftermath of the slide It was later determined that the slide had been set in motion when a sudden cold spell caused water from melting snow to freeze within the cracks. The freezing water had expanded as it turned to ice and had forced the cracks to widen, sending the rocks tumbling down the slopes.

The mine reopened briefly after the landslide, only to be shut down by a fire in 1905. H. L. Frank suffered a nervous breakdown and was placed in a mental institution; he died there in 1908. The mine reopened one more time, but was permanently closed in 1918. Today, about two hundred people live in the town of Frank.

Recent devastating landslides

On February 17, 2006, a series of mud slides caused widespread damage and loss of life in the Philippine province of Southern Leyte. Over 80 inches (200 cm) of rain had fallen in ten days, loosening the soil. Deforestation, the removal of all or most of the trees, of mountain slopes may have contributed to the unstable conditions. The actual landslide was triggered by small earthquake of magnitude 2.6 on the Richter scale.

Devil's Slide is an area of California State Highway 1 that suffers from frequent blockage and damage due to slides and slumps, which are slower downhill movements. The most recent closure was in April of 2006, when longitudinal cracks appeared in the roadway. The highway was reopened for limited use in August 2006. Efforts to build a bypass around Devil's Slide that would have bisected a California state park were opposed by environmentalists concerned with loss of valuable and ecologically sensitive coastal habitat. Instead, California is constructing a tunnel, with completion set for 2011.

Mudflows strike southern Italy

Two days of heavy rains set off deadly mudflows in the Campania region of southern Italy on May 5, 1998. The rivers of mud that rushed down from the mountains flowed into several towns across a 35-mile (60-kilometer) stretch from Sarno to Naples. One week after the disaster the death toll was 139, with an estimated 146 people still missing. The majority of the fatalities occurred in Sarno.

The mudflows were so forceful that they inundated buildings, destroyed homes, and buried people. At least fifteen hundred people were left homeless. After the disaster, the streets of the affected towns were wastelands of mud, wood, boulders, and other debris. Telephone, electricity, and water service were cut off. The mudflows were among Italy's worst natural disasters of all time; they were nicknamed by the Italian media the "Pompeii of the Year 2000," after the famous volcanic eruption that took thousands of lives in 79 CE.

Several thousand soldiers, firefighters, and military personnel from a nearby U.S. Navy base searched for survivors. They freed several people trapped in homes or cars. Searchers found a man who, for three days, had been buried up to his neck in mud in his cellar. Rescue workers used bulldozers and shovels to clear streets of hardened mud, which in some places was 10 feet (3 meters) high.

The damage from the mud slide was blamed on lax construction codes, which allowed the building of houses in areas known to be vulnerable to mud slides. Another factor was the illegal building of houses in areas where construction had been off-limits. The intensity of the mud slides was due, in part, to recent forest fires that had stripped the slopes of vegetation.

Mud slides devastate the south of Naples in 1998. ©CORBIS SYGMA.

Experiment: What triggers a landslide?

You can trigger a landslide right in your own home or classroom. Here is what you will need:

- newspaper or plastic sheeting—this is a messy experiment!
- a cardboard milk carton with one side cut away
- "land" materials, like pebbles, sand, dirt, and clay
- small watering can or a soda bottle
- graduated cylinder or measuring cup

Remember, there are different variables—such as slope, type of earth, amount of water—that contribute to landslides. This experiment helps determine how landslides occur given different variables. To set it up, fill your milk carton half way with a mixture of your "land" material. Record what type of mixture you use. Next, prop one end of your carton up with a couple of books. You may have to place another book at the other end (under the plastic) to keep the whole thing from sliding. Pour a measured amount of water on the higher end of the soil mixture in the carton until it is soaked but not sliding. You will need to do this gently, so use your watering can and pour slowly. Once the material is soaked, you are ready to trigger the landslide. You can choose to do this in a couple of ways: make the angle of the slope steeper gradually, an inch or two at a time, until the land material slides or begin slowly pouring a measured amount of water over the land material until a slide begins. Record exactly the angle of the slope or the amount of water used to trigger the slide.

You can repeat this experiment with different variables and compare the results. For example, try using different mixtures of land materials and see how results differ. Try setting similar land mixtures at different slope angles and see how results differ. What type of land material is most prone to landslides?

The eruption of Mount St. Helens on May 18, 1980, produced a series of lahars, or volcanic mudflows. The lahars (pronounced LAH-hahrs) flowed many miles down the Toutle River and Cowlitz River, destroying bridges and lumber camps. A total of 3.9 million cubic yards (3.0 million cubic meters) of material was transported by the lahars.

Dangerous science: How landslides happen

Landslides are classified into three groups: slides, falls, and flows, depending upon the type of material involved, the amount of air and water they contain, and the speed with which they fall. Another group, called, slumps, are sometimes included in the definition of a landslide.

Slides A slide consists of rock, mud, soil, water, or debris—or any combination of those materials—that goes tumbling down a steep slope

Repairs are made to the Devil's Slide stretch of Pacific Coast Highway in Pacifica, California, after heavy rains caused it to crack and sink in 2006. AP IMAGES.

at high speeds. A slide typically destroys everything in its path before finally coming to rest on a plateau or in the valley below. Rock slides are common in the European Alps, the U.S. Appalachians, and the Canadian Rockies, especially on slopes with few trees. They are frequently triggered by heavy rains, but can occur at any time without an obvious cause. Debris slides, made up of small rocks and shallow layers of loose soil, commonly follow volcanic eruptions.

A debris avalanche, a particularly dangerous variety of slide, begins suddenly and travels at speeds as fast as hundreds of miles (kilometers) per hour. Debris avalanches, which resemble their snowy cousins, occur most frequently on mountains in humid climates. They begin when soil at the top of a slope becomes saturated with water. That material begins to slide downward, building into a fearsome mass of mud, trees, rocks, and anything else in its path. A debris avalanche that occurred in 1977 in the Peruvian Andes, for example, contained between 20 million and 45 million cubic yards (15 million and 34 million cubic meters) of material traveling at about 100 miles (160 kilometers) per hour. The debris fell upon a city in the foothills, killing some nineteen thousand people.

Falls A fall involves rock or soil dropping from an overhanging cliff or a steep slope. The most dangerous type of fall is a rockfall. Huge boulders may fall freely through the air or race down a mountainside, fragmenting into small pieces as they descend and becoming a raging current of debris.

Rockfalls typically occur where cliffs have become steepened by erosion, the removal of soil, by rivers, glaciers, or waves. The rocks may be pried loose from the cliff or mountain by the freezing and thawing of water in the slope's cracks. Evidence of rockfalls can be seen in the piles of rock and debris at the base of steep slopes.

Large rockfalls can cause terrific damage. In 1970, for instance, a rockfall from the peak of the Huascarán volcano in Peru, triggered by an earthquake, created a debris avalanche that buried villages at the base of the volcano and killed almost twenty thousand people.

A geologist who witnessed the 1970 rockfall reported:

> I heard a great roar coming from Huascarán. Looking up, I saw what appeared to be a great cloud of dust and it looked as though a large mass of rock and ice was breaking loose from the north peak.... The crest of the wave [of rock and ice] had a curl, like a huge breaker coming in from the ocean. I estimated the wave to be at least 80 meters [260 feet] high. I observed hundreds of people in Yungay running in all directions and many of them towards Cemetery Hill. All the while, there was a continuous loud roar and rumble. I reached the upper level of the cemetery near the top just as the debris flow struck the base of the hill and I was probably only ten seconds ahead of it.... It was the most horrible thing I have ever experienced and I will never forget it.

Flows A flow is a landslide of wet material, which may contain rock, soil, and debris, combined with water. Mudflows are the most common, most liquid, and fastest type of flow. They contain water and soil, with a consistency somewhere between soup and freshly poured concrete.

Mudflows frequently occur in dry or semidry mountains and on steep-sided volcanoes that receive sudden, heavy rainfall. Loose, weathered rock and steep slopes with little or no vegetation are prone to mudflows. Mudflows can travel as fast as 55 miles (88 kilometers) per hour and have enough force to pick up and carry along debris the size of boulders, cars, trees, and houses. They typically spread out across great distances on valley floors, depositing a thin layer of mud mixed with boulders. In the United States, mudflows do millions of dollars of damage every year. One region vulnerable to mudflow damage is Southern California, especially the hilly suburban communities.

Another type of flow, called an earthflow, consists of material that is moist and full of clay, yet drier than the material in mudflows. Earthflows

Heavy rains loosened a mountain of garbage in a dump in the Philippines, causing a massive landslide that killed hundreds of people in 2000. AP IMAGES.

are most often set in motion by heavy rains and move at a variety of speeds and distances, yet are generally slower and travel shorter distances than mudflows. Slow earthflows creep along, stopping and starting, moving sometimes just several feet per year. They are common on hillsides on the California coast where the soil has a high clay content.

A type of earthflow that occurs on slopes at high elevations and in polar regions is solifluction (pronounced so-lih-FLUK-shun; also called soil fluction); this action is not included in narrow definitions of landslide. Solifluction involves sensitive layers of silt and clay that underlie level terraces. It takes place, at speeds ranging from very slow to very fast, when snow or ice thaws or when earthquakes produce shocks that turn the soil into a fluid mass. This flow of watery sediment is common in Scandinavia and on the slopes above the St. Lawrence River valley in Quebec, Canada. In 1971, a solifluction earthflow at St.-Jean Vianney in the St. Lawrence River valley swept away thirty-eight homes and took thirty-one lives.

There are also earthflows of dry material that move very quickly, sometimes for great distances, over gentle slopes. Dry-material earthflows can be triggered by earthquakes or the falling of rock from steep slopes above. An earthquake in 1920 in the Gansu (formerly Kansu) province in China set into motion the massive flow of dry loess (pronounced LOW-ess; wind-deposited silt), which resulted in the deaths of tens of thousands of people.

Slumps A slump, which is included in broad definitions of landslide, is the slow, downhill movement—7 feet (2 meters) per day or slower—of portions of a slope. Slumps take place on slopes where there is a strong surface layer of rock or sediment and a weaker layer of material underneath. When the lower layer is no longer able to support the surface material, both layers slip downward together. A slump may range in size from a few square yards (square meters) to thousands of square yards (square meters). As the ground moves, it tilts, or rotates, backward toward the slope in a series of curving downward and outward movements. On a slope on which slump is occurring, steplike depressions are created, and a bulge of earth forms at the base of the slope. A curved scar is left in the area where the material existed before the slump.

Slumps often occur on sea cliffs, the bases of which have been cut away by currents or waves. They can also be seen on slopes that have been eroded by a stream or glacier, as well as those that have been made steeper by construction, such as along roads and highways. They are usually triggered by heavy, prolonged rains or earthquakes.

Garbage landslide in the Philippines

One of the strangest and most tragic landslides happened on July 10, 2000, in Manila, capital of the Philippines. A mountain of garbage in the metropolitan dump, saturated (filled with water to the absolute maximum) from monsoon rains, collapsed and swept away hundreds of shacks and huts used by locals who scavenged the dump for usable materials and food. The shanty town was nicknamed "Promised Land" because of the opportunity it offered to make a little money. Estimates of the number of lives lost range from two hundred to more than eight hundred.

Landslides prompted by heavy rains One cause of landslides is the saturation of soil on steep slopes, caused by prolonged or heavy rainfall (such as from severe storms) or the melting of large quantities of snow or ice. Once the soil on the surface becomes saturated, the water makes its way down to lower layers. Those layers become slippery at the same time that the surface material is made heavier by the water. At some point the soil, pulled downward by gravity and lubricated by the water underneath, slides away from the slope. On January 11–13, 1966, for instance, heavy rains gave way to landslides on the mountainsides above Rio de Janeiro, Brazil. The cascading mud and debris killed some 550 people and brought transportation and communication systems to a halt.

Similarly, on April 26, 1974, driving rains caused a landslide on a mountain above the Mantaro River in Huancavelica Province, Peru. The

A landslide approaching farm buildings in California. JLM VISUALS.

falling debris landed on twelve small villages, causing the deaths of two hundred to three hundred people. It also blocked the river, backing up the water into a natural reservoir 8 miles (13 kilometers) long, 200 yards (183 meters) wide, and 10 to 20 yards (9 to 18 meters) deep. The landslide caused about $5 million in damages. The greatest cost was for the repair of the Huancayo-Ayacucho Highway. In 1990 a rain-induced landslide again occurred in Peru, this time in the village of San Miguel de Río Mayo, some 500 miles (800 kilometers) north of the capital city of Lima. About two hundred people were unaccounted for and presumed dead after mud flooded the town.

In the low, rolling mountains capped with red sandstone above the Gros Ventre River in northwestern Wyoming (just south of Grand Teton National Park), several days of heavy rain, coupled with melting snow, caused the largest landslide in U.S. history on June 23, 1925. Some 50 million cubic yards (38 million cubic meters) of rock and debris fell into the

Gros Ventre River, creating a natural dam 350 feet (107 meters) in height. The 5-mile-long (8-kilometer-long) and 225-foot-deep (68-meter-deep) body of water created behind the dam was named Slide Lake by local residents. On May 18, 1927, almost two years after the landslide, melting snow flooded the river and the dam broke loose. Luckily there had been plenty of advance warning, and most of those living in the area evacuated before floodwaters destroyed their downriver settlement.

Intense rainfall from hurricanes can cause multiple landslides. In August 1969, for instance, Hurricane Camille dumped 27 inches (68 centimeters) of rain on the Appalachian Mountains in central Virginia over an eight-hour period. The soil at the top of steep slopes became saturated and set in motion dozens of debris avalanches. About 150 people were killed by the flowing material. Throughout the region, houses were destroyed and roads and bridges were buried or washed out.

Earthquake-generated landslides Earthquakes that occur in areas with steep slopes can cause the slipping of surface soil and rock, and the collapse of cliffs. The shock waves produced by earthquakes send material hurtling downward in violent landslides. Earthquake-induced landslides happen in mountainous regions such as China, parts of Southern California, Alaska, Turkey, and Iran.

One landslide produced by a severe earthquake occurred in Montana, west of Yellowstone Park, on August 17, 1959. In that case, 40 million cubic yards (30 million cubic meters) of rock tore off the wall of the Madison River Canyon and slid into the river below at a speed of about 100 miles (160 kilometers) per hour. The rocks killed twenty-six people and blocked the river. A lake 6 miles (9.7 kilometers) long and 180 feet (55 meters) deep was formed in the process. After the landslide, a spillway (a passageway near the top of a dam through which water from the reservoir travels when the water level becomes high) was carved out of the natural dam and lined with large blocks of rock, creating sufficient drainage to handle heavy rains and keep the dam from collapsing.

In Kashmir (a region in southwest Asia adjacent to India and Pakistan) in 1840, an earthquake sparked a landslide that dammed the Indus River, forming a lake about 40 miles (64 kilometers) long and 1,000 feet (300 meters) deep. In 1949 in Tajikistan (then part of the Soviet Union), earthquakes in the Pamir Mountains set off landslides that buried the town of Khait, killing all of its twelve thousand residents. Today, Russian

Sinkholes

The movement of Earth's surface sometimes takes the form of a vertical drop, in which case a sinkhole is formed. A sinkhole is a large depression in the ground, often shaped like a bowl or a funnel. Sinkholes vary greatly in diameter from several feet to several miles, and may attain depths of 100 feet (30 meters) or more. Some sinkholes become clogged with clay and then collect water, forming small lakes.

One cause of sinkholes is that the underlying layer of water-soluble rock, such as limestone, marble, or dolomite, is dissolved by groundwater. As the rock dissolves, underground spaces form and the support for the ground is reduced. When the spaces grow large or numerous and the remaining rock can no longer hold the land above it, the surface collapses.

Large sinkholes form when cave ceilings weaken, become unable to support the weight of the ground above them, and collapse. Another cause of sinkholes is the depletion of aquifers, which are underground layers of spongy rock, gravel, or sand in which water collects. Aquifers become depleted when the underground water is pumped out of the ground faster than it can be replenished by rainwater. A sinkhole may also be formed when pockets of underground gas escape, such as during an earthquake.

In the United States, sinkholes have caused the greatest damage in Florida, Texas, Alabama, Missouri, Kentucky, Tennessee, and Pennsylvania. The country's largest sinkhole on record, called the "December Giant," formed in the woods near Montevallo, Alabama, in Shelby County, on December 2, 1972. The sinkhole, discovered by hunters, was 425 feet (130 meters) long, 350 feet (107 meters) wide, and 150 feet (45 meters) deep. Two days prior to the discovery, a resident in the vicinity had reported that his house shook, trees broke, and he heard a roaring noise.

seismologists (scientists who study earthquakes) operate a laboratory for earthquake prediction research near Khait.

Landslides triggered by volcanic eruptions Volcanic eruptions often produce a type of mudflow called a lahar. The material in a lahar is created when volcanic ash mixes with water; the water comes from the melting of snow and glaciers around the volcanic crater. The lahar may be very hot and can travel down the steep sides of a volcano at speeds of 100 miles (160 kilometers) per hour. It can flow for great distances, sweeping up houses and cars, uprooting trees, and burying entire communities.

In May 1980, with the eruption of Mount St. Helens in southern Washington State, came one of the largest landslides in U.S. history. Part of the north face of the mountain blew out and the volcanic ash combined with water from lakes and rivers to form colossal mudflows. The mud blocked rivers and ruined bridges and roads. (Fortunately, the area had been evacuated

In 1981 a large sinkhole formed in Winter Park, Florida. As the ground gave way, a three-bedroom house and three cars were swallowed up. The formation of sinkholes is a growing problem in urban areas of central Florida, as the population grows and underground aquifers become depleted at an alarming rate.

Heavy rains from an El Nino-driven storm caused this 65 foot sinkhole in Balboa Avenue in San Diego, California.

in advance.) Mud even stopped up the Columbia River, a main thoroughfare to the Pacific Ocean, trapping thirty ocean-going ships downstream.

Lahars resulting from the 1985 eruption of the Nevado del Ruiz volcano in the Colombian Andes struck an area that had not been evacuated, despite warnings from geologists (scientists who study the origin, history, and structure of the Earth). The largest of the mudflows overtook the city of Armero, where it claimed at least twenty-three thousand lives and left another twenty thousand people homeless. In some places, the mud was 12 feet (3.7 meters) deep. About 15 square miles (39 square kilometers) of land, including rich farmlands where coffee and rice were grown, were covered by the lahar.

Where landslides occur Landslides occur throughout the world. They are serious problems in several nations, however, particularly in Italy and Japan. More than one thousand urban areas in Italy are in danger zones

Garage and contents damaged by a 1982 mud slide in California. ©JIM SUGAR/CORBIS.

for landslides. In Japan, thousands of homes are lost and more than one hundred people are killed by landslides each year.

In the United States, landslides take place in all fifty states. Across the country, they kill between twenty-five and fifty people and cause up to $2 billion in damage each year. Landslides are the most prevalent in the Appalachians and Rocky Mountains, as well as along the Pacific Coast. It is estimated that more than two million landslides have occurred in the Appalachians, and evidence of past landslides exists on more than 30 percent of the area of West Virginia. In Colorado that figure is 8 percent. More than six hundred landslides have been distinguished in Utah. Coastal slides are a constant menace in California; the San Gabriel Mountains frequently unleash debris flows that ruin homes in the northern Los Angeles area.

Consequences of landslides

Each year, landslides take hundreds of lives and cause billions of dollars in damage throughout the world. Landslides engulf villages and kill people and animals. Falling and sliding rock, soil, and debris flatten houses and cars and uproot trees. Material that spills onto a roadway or railroad tracks halts traffic and causes accidents and sometimes fatalities.

House damaged by a volcanic mud slide (lahar) in Japan. ©ROGER RUSSMEYER/CORBIS.

When rocks fall into a lake from high above, they create waves that threaten coastal settlements.

When a large quantity of material falls, it forces a wall of air ahead of it. That wind may be strong enough to knock down trees and houses. When the material strikes the ground it sends up a cloud of dust that may darken the sky and spread over a large area. Landslides also knock down utility poles and wires, and the region loses power and communication with the outside world. Landslides also scar the face of a hill or mountain, stripping it of soil, trees, and other vegetation.

Rock or soil that flows into a valley often blocks the flow of rivers, thus disrupting ecosystems and shipping routes and sometimes contaminating drinking water. The natural dam may later give way, causing floods.

The human factor

Most of the destructive impacts of landslides are due, in some part, to human activity. Many landslides occur on slopes that have been altered by grading (leveling off) for road or building construction. When a portion of a mountainside is graded, material is cut out of the slope and removed. The slope directly above the graded area is made much steeper, reducing support for earth and rock higher up the slope. If the excavated material is

The Yosemite rockfall

On July 10, 1996, a tremendous rockfall shook the ground in Yosemite (pronounced yo-SEM-it-ee) National Park in California. Two slabs of an enormous boulder, balanced 2,600 feet (79 meters) above Yosemite Valley on a granite arch, suddenly broke loose. The rocks, weighing 68,000 tons (61,676 metric tons), slid down a steep slope for the first 500 feet (152 meters) and then took to the air and fell freely for the next 1,700 feet (518 meters) until smashing into a rocky slope near the base of the cliff. When the fragmented rocks struck the ground, they were traveling faster than 160 miles (257 kilometers) per hour.

On impact, the rockfall released a wind blast that knocked over hundreds of pine and oak trees and destroyed a nature center and snack bar nearby. The falling trees killed one park visitor and injured several others. The dust from the rockfall and blast of wind blotted out the sky and hung in the air for several hours before settling over an area of about 50 acres (20 hectares).

Rock slide in Yosemite National Park in California in 1983. ©JONATHAN BLAIR/CORBIS.

deposited beneath the graded area, it may overload the lower portion of the slope and cause a landslide.

Construction is especially dangerous on slopes that, due to their geologic composition, are unstable (prone to landslides) in their natural state.

Landslides in Southern California

The mountains of Southern California are prone to mudflows, placing communities on the slopes above and in the valleys below in the danger zone. The slopes are steep and unstable. Much of the soil is barren, since frequent wildfires remove vegetation. Some landslides are triggered by intense storms, which saturate the soil and start it moving downhill. Frequent earthquakes also set landslides in motion.

The deadliest landslide in the region's history occurred in February 1969. During the winter of 1968–69, about 44 inches (112 centimeters) of rain fell on the Los Angeles area over a forty-two-day period. As the record-setting rain (which came after forest fires had cleared the slopes of vegetation the previous summer) fell on the San Gabriel Mountains, it soaked layers of soil and gravel. That material eventually began traveling down the mountainsides, gathering debris as it went. The muddy torrent drowned or buried one hundred people and caused about $1 billion in damage. One of the hardest-hit places was the fashionable suburb of Glendora, where the mud slide damaged 160 homes and destroyed 5 others. Mud piled up on the major highway leading into Los Angeles and destroyed citrus groves as far north as the Ventura, Santa Barbara, and San Luis Obispo counties.

Another part of the Los Angeles area that has suffered from slides is Portuguese Bend on the Palos Verdes Peninsula. Portuguese Bend is an expensive clifftop housing development overlooking the Pacific Ocean. It was built despite warnings from geologists about the region's instability. The material on the top of the cliffs, on which the houses sit, is sandstone mixed with a clay material made of hardened volcanic ash—materials that readily absorb water. The layer of rock below is shale, which becomes slippery when wet. The bases of the cliffs are subject to erosion by waves.

In 1956, heavy rains caused the first movement of the cliff tops since the homes went up. From the 1960s through the 1980s the gradual slide was made worse by a series of earthquakes, plus the increased weight from additional homes. In 1969, houses on nearby Point Fermin went sliding into the ocean. By the end of the 1980s, the slide of the cliff top in Portuguese Bend had damaged or destroyed 150 homes for a total cost of $10 million. Thereafter, new development in Portuguese Bend was halted and a drainage system was put in place to keep the slide from slipping further and to protect the remaining houses.

For example, mountains or cliffs that have a layer of sandstone on the surface and a layer of shale beneath are geologically unstable. Water can seep into pores and cracks in the sandstone and collect on the shale. The shale surface then becomes slippery, allowing the sandstone layer to slide off.

Mining is another activity that weakens slopes and promotes landslides. The removal of coal, stone, or other natural resources from the ground makes the remaining slope unstable and vulnerable to collapse.

Another contribution people make to landslides is cutting down trees on slopes, for use as fuel and lumber or to clear the land for farming. Trees

World's deadliest landslide: Gansu, China

On December 16, 1920, the deadliest landslide in recorded history struck Gansu (formerly Kansu), China, resulting in 180,000 deaths. The cause of the landslide was an earthquake centered near the border with Tibet. The hills and cliffs in the region were treeless and covered with a layer of loess (pronounced LOW-ess or LUSS), a soft, loosely packed material formed from the yellowish dust of the Gobi Desert. The combination of the bare slopes and the fine dust made the soil highly susceptible to slides.

The shock of the earthquake caused the sides of 100-foot (30-meter) cliffs to collapse. Falling material barricaded the entrances of mountainside caves, in which many peasants made their homes. The landslide laid waste to ten cities and numerous villages in the valleys.

In one village, the only survivors were a farmer and his two sons. Their plot of land had broken loose from a mountaintop and slid down the slope intact, atop a stream of flowing debris. The day of the Gansu landslides is known in China as *Shan Tso-liao*, or "When the mountains walked."

protect slopes by trapping rain on their leaves and reducing the erosive impact of wind and water on the soil. The roots of trees and other forms of vegetation absorb rainwater like a sponge and release it slowly into the soil. Roots also act as anchors, holding the soil together. Soil with no vegetative cover erodes quickly. It glides more easily over the rocky subsurface than does compact, cohesive soil. Landslides on deforested slopes, once set in motion, have no natural barriers to slow or stop them. Foot traffic on mountains, from sightseers or hikers, also tramples vegetation and increases the slopes' vulnerability to landslides.

Technology connection

Technology is of limited usefulness in predicting and preventing landslides. Most large slides occur without warning and are more powerful than any barrier that can be erected. A California engineer, at a conference in 1980, likened landslide prevention to "trying to hold back the storm tides of the ocean." Nonetheless, numerous measures are used to lessen the impact of landslides, as well as to predict certain kinds of landslides.

Limiting landscape damage Many methods are used to protect populated areas from material that may fall or slide down a slope. For instance, water drainage systems are employed to keep water from saturating ground that is vulnerable to landslides. Wells are pumped in the potential slide area to keep the rain from overflowing aquifers and soaking the ground. (An aquifer is an underground layer of spongy rock, gravel, or sand in which water collects.)

Trees, shrubs, or grasses are planted on bare slopes to hold the soil in place and to stop material that begins to slide. Terraces (broad, steplike cuts) are constructed on steep slopes, so that falling material or water is only able to travel short distances before landing on a plateau and losing its energy. Loose material is removed from high elevations before it begins rolling down a slope. The bases of slopes on which bulges of material, called "toes," have formed due to slump are immobilized with walls of rock, concrete, or soil. Strong wire-mesh fences are secured to some cliff faces above roadways to prevent rocks from falling. Railroads can be protected by electric fences that detect rock falls and communicate the need to halt trains in that section of track.

Another measure undertaken to prevent landslides is the filling-in of cracks that develop in the faces of mountains or hills. An option for protecting structures in landslide-prone areas is to build retaining walls or earth buttresses along slope bottoms. In some valleys, basins are constructed to trap landslide material. In Southern California, for instance, a series of 120 football-stadium-sized basins have been excavated along the base of the San Gabriel Mountains to catch rocks and debris. They must be emptied frequently in order to continue catching the falling material.

In Japan, which is home to 10 percent of the world's active volcanoes, walls of steel and concrete—as well as drainage systems—have been constructed on mountainsides to protect valley-dwellers from lahars. Television cameras are employed on some slopes to detect the start of landslides and provide advance warning to people in the path of danger.

Predicting landslides While most landslides occur without warning, certain types can be predicted. The U.S. Geological Survey, together with the National Weather Service, provides advance warning for landslides that are caused by heavy rains. Both organizations monitor rainfall data

Beams and wire netting form a rock slide fence near Bolungarvik, Iceland. © PATRICK BENNETT/CORBIS.

Housing development collapses in the Philippines

On August 3, 1999, following four days of heavy rains that caused widespread flooding throughout eastern Asia, a hillside collapsed in Antipolo City, a suburb of Manila. Thirty-one people were killed as the wall of earth crashed into a housing development; as many as forty others were missing and presumed dead. Twenty-five houses were buried by the landslide, and 378 others were damaged. During that same week in the central Philippines, sixty-one other people died in the flooding.

Filipino officials placed the blame for the landslide on a nearby rock and gravel quarry. They claimed that too much rock had been excavated from the slope too close to the houses, thereby allowing groundwater to reach the ground and soften it. The heavy rains proved to be the final straw that caused the earth to give way and collapse on the houses. Officials also noted that they had issued evacuation warnings when cracks appeared in houses and streets earlier that day, but most residents had ignored the warnings.

Rescuers move debris from collapsed houses in an attempt to rescue victims of a series of landslides in the Philippines in 1999.

and forecasts in areas prone to landslides and issue warnings when the ground is becoming saturated. Landslides that come in the wake of volcanic eruptions can also be predicted. Volcano early warning systems detect rumblings that precede eruptions and, quite likely, volcanic mudflows. People living in the vicinity of a volcano are given plenty of advance warning of the need to evacuate.

Assessing the danger of building When construction is proposed in hilly areas, an assessment is made of the hazards posed by landslides. To determine the stability of the slope and the suitability of the region for construction, researchers conduct geologic explorations to determine soil and rock properties and look at the history of landslides in the area. From that information they can predict the frequency with which landslides will occur, as well as the destructive potential of those landslides. Areas where landslides are likely to occur would then be placed off-limits to construction and possibly designated for parkland or other limited use.

[*See Also* **Avalanche; Drought; Earthquake; El Niño; Flood; Tsunami; Volcano; Weather: An Introduction**]

For More Information

BOOKS

Bishop, Amanda, and Vanessa Walker. *Avalanche and Landslide Alert (Disaster Alert!).* St. Catherines, Ontario: Crabtree Publishing Company, 2005.

Committee on the Review of the National Landslide Hazards Mitigation Strategy, Board on Earth Sciences and Resources, National Research Council. *Partnerships for Reducing Landslide Risk: Assessment of the National Landslide Hazards Mitigation Strategy.* Washington, DC: The National Academies Press, 2004.

Hyndman, Donald, and David Hyndman. *Natural Hazards and Disasters.* New York: Brooks Cole, 2006.

National Geographic Society and Ralph M. Feather Jr. *Earth Science.* New York: Glencoe/McGraw-Hill, 2002.

Robinson, Andrew. *Earth Shock: Hurricanes, Volcanoes, Earthquakes, Tornadoes and Other Forces of Nature.* New York: W. W. Norton, 2002.

PERIODICALS

Simpson, Sarah. "Raging Rivers of Rock." *Scientific American.* (July 2000): pp. 24–25.

WEB SITES

"Landslide and Debris Flow (Mudslide)." *Federal Emergency Management Agency: Disaster Information.* <http://www.fema.gov/hazard/landslide/index.shtm> (accessed March 22, 2007).

"Landslide Hazard Program." *United States Geological Survey.* <http://landslides.usgs.gov> (accessed March 22, 2007).

"Landslides in British Columbia." *British Columbia Geological Survey.* <http://www.em.gov.bc.ca/Mining/Geolsurv/Surficial/landslide> (accessed March 22, 2007).

"Slide!" *Open Learning Agency, British Columbia Knowledge Network.* <http://www.knowledgenetwork.ca/slide/splash.html> (accessed March 22, 2007).

La Niña

La Niña has traditionally received less attention than the more well-known El Niño. For example, during the years 1997 and 1998, El Niño (pronounced el NEE-nyo) was the weather phenomenon most in the news. However, from late 1998 through the first half of 2000 El Niño was succeeded by the less widely publicized La Niña (la NEE-nya) phenomenon. La Niña is the cold-water counterpart to El Niño. El Niño is a period of unusual warming in the Pacific near Peru and Ecuador, while La Niña is a period of abnormally cool water temperatures in the same region. La Niña sometimes follows in the wake of El Niño. La Niña's influence is typically felt in the form of colder-than-usual winters in the northern United States and warmer-than-usual winters in the southern United States. La Niña also promotes the formation of Atlantic Ocean hurricanes that can affect Caribbean islands and the U.S. East Coast.

The term "la niña" is Spanish for "little girl." It was named for its relation to El Niño. Two other terms that are sometimes used to describe this cold-water phenomenon are El Viejo (el vee-AY-hoe), which means "the old man"; and "cold-phase ENSO event" (in contrast to El Niño, the warm phase of the El Niño/Southern Oscillation). According to guidelines set forth by the Japanese Meteorological Association, a La Niña year is one in which average sea temperatures along the equator in the Pacific are more than 1°F (0.5°C) colder than usual, and the water remains cold for at least six months.

La Niña sometimes, but not always, follows El Niño. Since 1975 there have been half as many La Niñas as there have been El Niños. On average, La Niña is present one year in every four. Sometimes La Niñas occur as infrequently as once every ten years. La Niña conditions typically last from nine to twelve months, but may persist for up to two years.

WORDS TO KNOW

air pressure: the pressure exerted by the weight of air over a given area of Earth's surface. Also called atmospheric pressure or barometric pressure.

cold-phase ENSO (El Niño/Southern Oscillation): another name for La Niña; colder-than-normal eastern Pacific waters.

convective zone: the region of warm tropical water over which thunderstorms form; the ocean under the Intertropical Convergence Zone.

El Niño: a term that means "the Christ child" or "little boy" in Spanish. A period of unusual warming of the Pacific Ocean off the coast of Peru and Ecuador. It usually starts around Christmas, which is how it got its name.

El Niño/Southern Oscillation (ENSO): the simultaneous warming of the waters of the eastern Pacific and the accompanying shifts in air pressure over the eastern and western Pacific.

flooding: the inundation of water onto land that is normally dry.

gale-force wind: any wind whose sustained speed is between 39 and 54 mph (63 and 87 kph).

Intertropical Convergence Zone: a belt of warm, rising, unstable air formed from the inward-flowing trade winds from north and south of the equator.

jet stream: the world's fastest upper-air winds. Jet streams travel in a west-to-east direction, at speeds of 80 to 190 miles (130 to 300 kilometers) per hour, around 30,000 feet (9,150 meters) above the ground. Jet streams occur where the largest differences in air temperature and air pressure exist. In North America, jet streams are typically found over southern Canada and the northern United States, as well as over the southern United States and Mexico. The northern jet stream is called the polar jet stream, and the southern jet stream is called the subtropical jet stream.

La Niña: Spanish for "little girl," a period of cooler-than-normal water temperatures in the eastern Pacific near the coast of Peru and Ecuador. It often follows an El Niño.

monsoon: a name for seasonal winds that result in a rainy season during the summer on tropical continents, when the land becomes warmer than the sea beside it.

mud slide: a landslide of mostly mud mixed with debris, often caused by heavy rains on steep land with sparse vegetation.

polar jet stream: a North American jet stream, typically found over southern Canada or the northern United States.

precipitation: water in any form, such as rain, snow, ice pellets, or hail, that falls to Earth's surface.

pressure gradient: the difference in air pressure between a high and low pressure area relative to the distance separating them.

research buoy: a tethered or drifting buoy placed in the open ocean capable of recording atmospheric and ocean conditions and transmitting them to a satellite.

subtropical jet stream: a North American jet stream, typically found over the southern United States or northern Mexico.

thunderstorm: a storm resulting from strong rising air currents; characterized by heavy rain or hail along with thunder and lightning.

trade winds: an area near the equator of prevailing winds that blow from the northeast north of the equator and the southeast south of the equator.

upwelling: cold water flowing toward the surface, often caused by prevailing winds or pressure differences.

warm-phase ENSO (El Niño/Southern Oscillation): another name for El Niño; warmer-than-normal eastern Pacific waters.

Potential Temperature Impacts from La Niña Events (Cold Episodes)

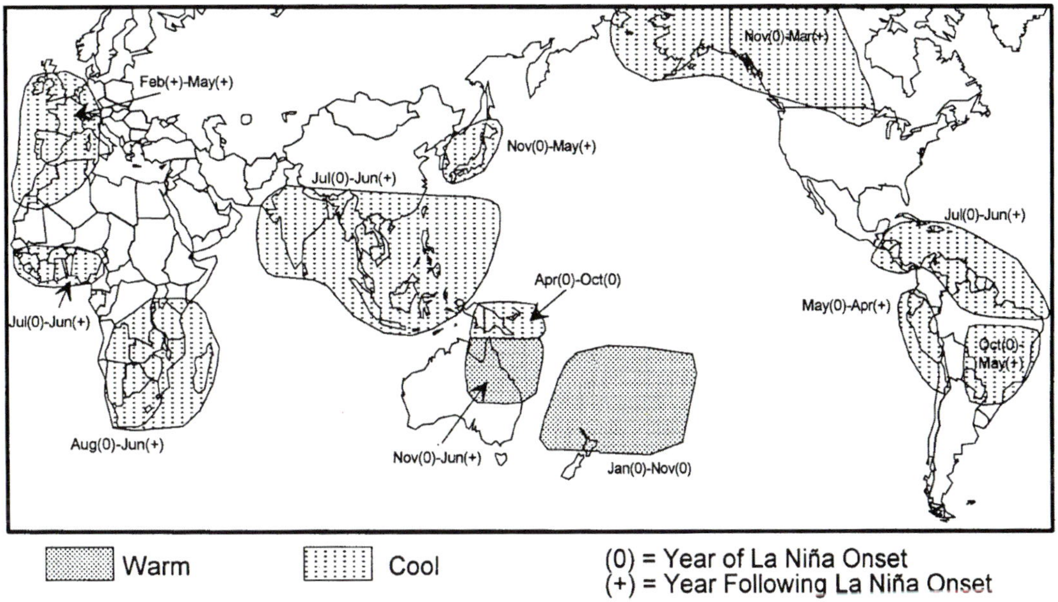

Source: Halpert and Ropelewski, 1990.

JOINT AGRICULTURAL WEATHER FACILITY (NOAA/USDA)

Global map showing potential cold episodes caused by a La Niña.

A cooling of the waters

The main characteristic of La Niña is a cooling of the waters in the tropical Pacific, from the coast of South America to the central equatorial region. Normally, the Pacific Ocean temperature off the coast of South America is around 68°F (20°C). During El Niño years the water temperature may be 10°F (6°C) warmer than normal. In contrast, the temperature of coastal waters falls as much as 15°F (8°C) below normal during La Niña years.

La Niña's cold surface waters are produced by a strong upwelling—a churning up of cold water from below. The upwelling during La Niña is intensified by a strong easterly (from the east) trade wind, which is a prevailing wind near the equator. As the trade wind blows warm surface water westward across the ocean, cold water upwells to take its place.

La Niña, El Niño, or normal?

Defining the condition of the tropical Pacific Ocean is tricky business. While some meteorologists assert that the ocean undergoes periods of "normalcy," others argue that El Niño or La Niña is always present to some degree. Weather expert Kevin Trenberth of the National Center for Atmospheric Research stated that in the tropical Pacific for the years 1950–1997: conditions were normal 46 percent of the time; El Niño was present 31 percent of the time; and La Niña was present 23 percent of the time.

The El Niño/La Niña connection

Like El Niño, La Niña is produced by shifts in water temperature and air pressure (also called atmospheric pressure) between the eastern and western portions of the southern tropical Pacific Ocean. While the shift in El Niño is toward warmer water and lower air pressure in the eastern Pacific, however, the shift in La Niña is toward colder water and higher air pressure in the eastern Pacific.

La Niña and El Niño can be thought of as extremes in the range of conditions that may exist in the tropical Pacific Ocean, or as bookends of the El Niño/Southern Oscillation (ENSO). Whereas El Niño is considered a warm-phase ENSO, La Niña is considered a cold-phase ENSO.

In normal conditions, trade winds blow from the eastern Pacific (from the coast of South America), where pressure is higher, to the western Pacific, where pressure is lower. During El Niño, the pressure over the western Pacific rises and the pressure over the eastern Pacific drops, causing the trade winds to weaken or reverse course. During La Niña, the pressure gradient, or the difference between the high and low pressure areas related to the distance between them, tilts more steeply toward the west than usual. This is primarily because of the presence of very cold water in the eastern Pacific, which increases the air pressure there. This steepening of the pressure gradient causes trade winds to blow strongly toward the west.

Meteorologists' understanding of La Niña is not as great as that of El Niño. Less effort has been spent researching La Niña, in part, because La Niña is not as powerful or potentially destructive a force as El Niño. Whereas El Niño provokes unusual weather patterns, La Niña merely intensifies typical weather patterns.

Scientists were driven to learn more about El Niño by the reduction of Peruvian fisheries in the 1970s. La Niña has no such obvious consequence. It was only in the 1980s, when the far-reaching impacts of La Niña (called teleconnections) were discovered, that research into La Niña began in earnest.

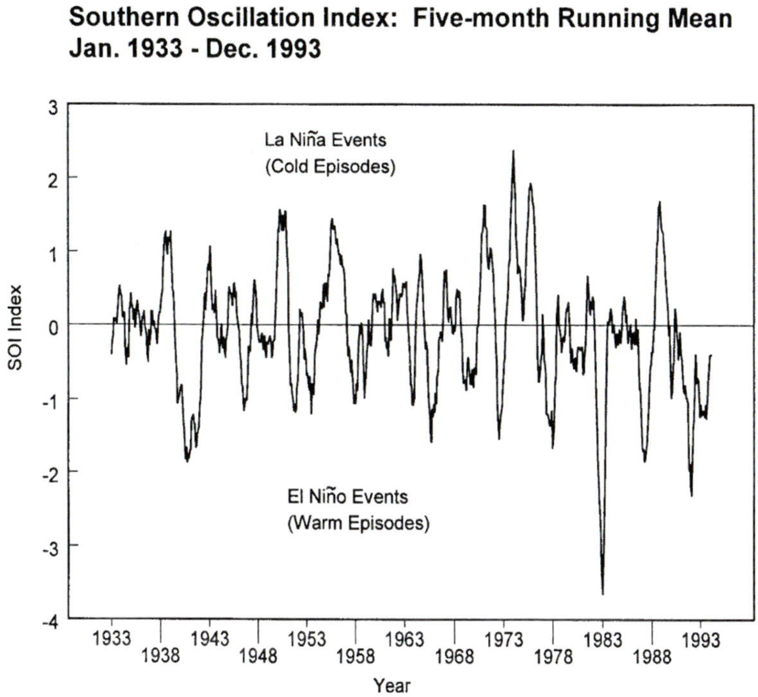

Chart of the Southern Oscillation Index: Five-month running mean (January 1933–December 1993).

La Niña and the jet stream

During La Niña, the "obstacles" that divert the jet stream during El Niño are removed. That is to say, the towering thunderstorms (storms caused by rising air currents) that form off the coast of South America during El Niño years shift to the western-central Pacific and weaken, due to cooler waters. With the displacement of the convective zone (the region of warm water over which thunderstorms form) comes a weakening of the subtropical jet stream found over the southern United States and northern Mexico.

Generally, during La Niña the subtropical jet stream occupies a region farther north than it does during El Niño. The area of strongest jet stream activity during La Niña is the central Rocky Mountains. It is there that the most severe weather can be expected. The jet stream also passes over the Great Lakes in the east. The polar jet stream, typically over the northern United States and southern Canada, is also weakened and pushed farther north, over Alaska and northern Canada.

Effects of La Niña

The effects of El Niño and La Niña are felt most intensely in the winter, when temperature contrasts between northern and southern states are greatest and the jet stream more directly influences the weather. The warming and cooling of the waters that characterize El Niño and La Niña also peak during the Northern Hemisphere winter.

In many ways, La Niña's effects on the weather are the opposite of El Niño's. For instance, La Niña brings cold winters to the northern Great Plains states, the Pacific Northwest, the Great Lakes states, and Canada, and warmer-than-usual winters to the Southeast. El Niño, in contrast, often spells warmer-than-usual winters for the northern United States. and colder-than-usual winters for the southern United States.

Whereas El Niño brings flooding (the inundation of normally dry land) to California, the Southwest, eastward across the states bordering the Gulf of Mexico, and Florida, La Niña brings drier-than-usual conditions to those locations. Also in contrast to El Niño, La Niña brings dry weather to the Central Plains states and the Southeast, and lots of precipitation to the Pacific Northwest. While El Niño brings unusually heavy rains to Peru and Ecuador, and drought to Southeast Asia and Australia, La Niña brings drought to the South American coast and flooding to the western Pacific region.

Another contrast between the two phenomena is that while El Niño hinders development of Atlantic hurricanes, La Niña seems to promote hurricane formation in the region. El Niño's westerly winds (from west to east) blow in the opposite direction of low-altitude winds in the Atlantic Ocean, lopping the tops off thunderclouds before they can come together into hurricanes. La Niña's winds, in contrast, which blow strongly from east to west, encourage the development of Atlantic hurricanes.

The effects of La Niña on weather patterns can be described as an exaggeration of normal conditions. For instance, while the northern United States typically has cold winters, La Niña makes them colder; and while coastal Peru and Ecuador are typically dry, La Niña makes them drier. Indonesia typically receives monsoon rains, caused by seasonal winds in the summer months, but La Niña makes the rains heavier.

However, it is it is misleading to label a specific rainstorm, hurricane, or other weather occurrence a "La Niña event" or an "El Niño event." La Niña and El Niño influence the position and intensity of weather patterns, but they are only two among many other factors that influence local weather.

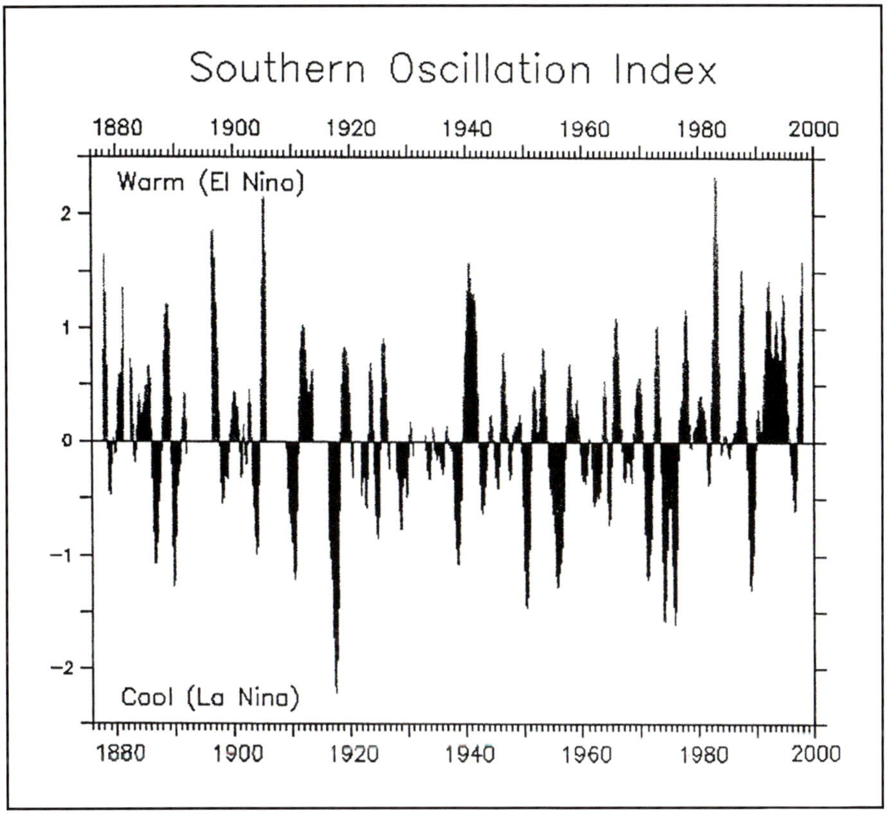

Chart of Southern Oscillation Index (1880–2000).

The 1998–2000 La Niña

In May 1998 a rapid cooling of the tropical Pacific waters began. This temperature drop signaled the end of El Niño and the start of La Niña. Over the next few months the cooling trend continued, after which temperatures varied. Ocean temperatures returned to normal at the end of June 1999, prompting some meteorologists to call a premature end to La Niña. The cooling resumed, however, leading to predictions that La Niña would continue through early 2000.

The first clue to the arrival of La Niña came in the fall of 1997. Scientists detected a drop in temperature of a large pool of ocean water in the western Pacific, 420 feet (128 meters) below the surface. Temperature readings over the next several months, taken by research buoys (floating devices containing weather instruments) indicated that the cool water was moving eastward and upward, toward the coast of South America.

A key reference to: The water cycle

The water cycle (also called the hydrologic cycle) is the continuous movement of water between the atmosphere and Earth's surface (oceans and landmasses). On one side of the equation is precipitation and on the other side is evaporation—the process by which liquid water at the surface converts to a gas and enters the atmosphere.

Eighty-five to ninety percent of the moisture that evaporates into the atmosphere comes from the oceans. The rest evaporates from the soil, lakes, and rivers that make up the continental landmasses. Plants lose water through tiny pores in the underside of their leaves in a process called transpiration.

Some of the moist air above oceans is carried over land by the wind. Clouds form and drop rain and snow on the ground. When precipitation hits the ground, it either sinks in or runs off, depending on the surface composition. On soft ground, most of the water sinks into the soil to be absorbed by plant roots or to seep down into underground aquifers, which are underground layers of spongy rock, gravel, or sand in which water collects. Some of it runs off into streams and rivers. If the water strikes a hard surface, like rock or pavement, most of it runs directly into streams or man-made drains. Eventually this water also flows into rivers.

The oceans lose water in this portion of the cycle. More water evaporates from them than returns as precipitation. The oceans get this water back when the rivers empty their water back into the oceans. Thus the global water budget—the volume of water coming and going from the oceans, atmosphere, and continental landmasses—is kept in balance.

If the water cycle is kept in balance, that means that global precipitation levels remain fairly constant. So why do droughts occur? The answer is that rain and snow do not consistently fall in equal amounts in any given place. Moisture may evaporate from one place, travel through the atmosphere, and fall to the ground as rain in another. It is possible, then, for a given location to get lots of rainfall one year and almost no rainfall the next.

Throughout May and June 1998, temperatures along a 5,000-mile (8,000 kilometer) strip of coastal water dropped more than 15°F (8°C), to about 65°F (18.4°C).

Drought and wildfire La Niña, as expected, produced dry conditions in the summers of 1998 and 1999 for the Southwest, the Southeast, the central Plains states, and even the mid-Atlantic states. In addition to drought, some of these areas faced extended heat waves. In many places, non-essential uses of water (such as watering lawns and washing cars) were banned. Perhaps the greatest consequence of the hot, dry conditions was the outbreak of wildfires. Hundreds of thousands of acres burned during these two summers.

In Florida, more than 500,000 acres were consumed by fire in the summer of 1998. In the first half of 1999, more than 35,000 acres

Figure 6

Potential Rainfall Impacts from La Niña Events (Cold Episodes)

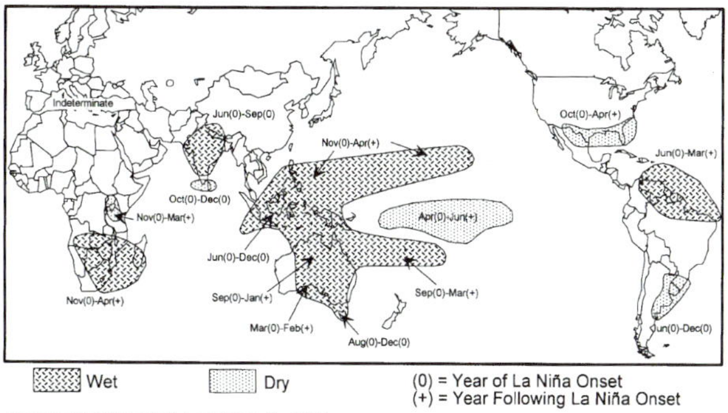

Source: Ropelewski and Halpert, 1989. Journal of Climate, (2) p. 268-284.

Global map of potential rainfall impacts of La Niña events.

burned. Several homes were lost to the blaze. A state of emergency for the entire state was declared in April 1999 and the National Guard was brought in to assist firefighters.

In March 1999, fire blackened seventy-eight thousand acres of Nebraska prairie—an area the size of Rhode Island—and killed hundreds of cattle. That fire came one month after an unusual wintertime grass fire near North Platte, Nebraska, that burned fifteen thousand acres.

For the first half of 1999, the mid-Atlantic region (New Jersey, New York, Pennsylvania, Delaware, Maryland, and Washington, D.C.) had precious few drops of precipitation. That spring wildfires raged in Georgia, eastern Tennessee, and western North Carolina, prompting the evacuation of hundreds of residents.

The Southwest rebounded from its wet El Niño years with extraordinarily dry conditions in late 1998. The desert wildflowers that bloomed in abundance in the spring of 1998 were noticeably absent in 1999. Precipitation was so scarce in the mountains that Arizona ski resorts took the unusual step of closing for the 1998–1999 season. Even desert oases dried up in Arizona, prompting mountain lions and other desert-dwellers to enter populated areas and drink water out of chlorinated swimming pools.

In some parts of Texas the drought began as early as August 1998. By April 1999, a state of emergency had been announced for 170 of the state's 254 counties.

Torrential rains caused by La Niña triggered a landslide in Sao Paulo, Brazil, in 1999. © MARIE HIPPENMEYER/ CORBIS.

The wet zone As predicted for La Niña, the Pacific Northwest received above average precipitation during the winter of 1998–99. In Washington State, Mount Baker logged more than 90 feet (27 meters) of snow, rivaling Mount Rainier's record for snowfall in a single season. Lowland communities in the Pacific Northwest and in the Sierra Nevada Mountains in California faced threats of flooding. Around Puget Sound, precipitation fell for ninety-one straight days during the first quarter of 1999.

In the early spring, the Midwest received heavy rains. The Midwest also experienced a series of tornadoes in early 1999; however, meteorologists are divided as to whether or not La Niña was responsible.

As predicted, India, China, Southeast Asia, and Australia experienced unusually heavy monsoon rains and flooding. In the summer of 1998 flood waters stood chest-high in parts of eastern India and Bangladesh. River flooding in China claimed the lives of 4,150 people.

In August 1999, several Asian countries were besieged by torrential downpours, and gale-force winds with speeds between 39 and 54 mph (63 and 87 kph). They also suffered from mud slides, landslides of mud caused by heavy rain, and flooding. Across South Korea, Thailand, the Philippines, and Vietnam tens of thousands of people were forced to evacuate their homes and at least fifty people perished in the floods.

Flooding in Thailand, 2005. PHOTODISC RED/GETTY IMAGES.

An active hurricane season A La Niña event began just in time for the 1998 hurricane season, which runs from June 1 through November 30. As predicted for a La Niña year, the Atlantic hurricane season was fast and furious. With a death toll of between twelve thousand and fifteen thousand, mostly in Central America and the Caribbean, 1998 was the deadliest Atlantic hurricane season 1780.

The year 1998 saw fourteen tropical storms, ten of which became hurricanes and three of which became major hurricanes. Seven of the 1998 storms made landfall in the United States (the third highest number on record), causing twenty-one deaths and more than 3.2 billion dollars in damage. The real story of the 1998 hurricane season was a pair of monster hurricanes, Georges and Mitch, that brought death and destruction to Central America.

A mild winter Predictions of an extra-cold winter of 1998–99 for the northern United States turned out to be wrong. The polar jet stream remained farther north than expected, trapping polar air north of the Canadian border. As a result, northerners enjoyed a relatively mild winter. The southern portion of the United States, south of the Rockies in the west and New York in the east, experienced spring-like conditions. Record high temperatures were set in many places.

The winter of 1999–2000 In July 1999, meteorologists at the National Centers for Environmental Prediction, the National Oceanic and Atmospheric Administration, and other agencies predicted a continuing, but weakened, La Niña for the winter of 1999–2000. Forecasts included wet conditions for the Pacific Northwest and dry conditions for the South. The predictions were at least partly accurate. The winter proved to be one of the warmest and driest on record. It was driest in the Southwest and Southeast with Louisiana recording abnormally dry conditions. The Northwest was average to wet, with Montana and Wyoming experiencing above-average precipitation.

Weather experts also predicted a lively hurricane season for autumn 1999, anticipating at least three major storms. This prediction proved accurate. There were twelve named storms, eight hurricanes, and five intense hurricanes during the season.

Predictions for winter of 2006–2007

Scientists continue to try and predict the effects of El Niño and La Niña. In the fall of 2006, the Climate Prediction Center/National Centers for Environmental Prediction (a branch of the National Weather Service) predicted El Niño conditions developing for the 2006–2007 winter season. These conditions included warmer-than-normal temperatures for western and central Canada, and the western and northern United States. Wetter-than-average conditions were predicted for portions of the U.S. Gulf Coast and Florida, while drier-than-average conditions were expected in the Ohio River Valley and the Pacific Northwest. As of February 2007 scientists saw a return to ENSO-neutral conditions with the possible development of La Niña conditions.

[*See Also* **Climate; El Niño; Flood; Forecasting; Hurricane; Weather: An Introduction**]

For More Information

BOOKS

D'Aleo, Joseph S. *The Oryx Resource Guide to El Niño and La Niña.* Phoenix, AZ: Oryx Press, 2002.

Philander, S. George. *El Niño, La Niña, and the Southern Oscillation.* San Diego, CA: Academic Press, 1990.

Rose, Sally. *El Niño! And La Niña.* New York: Simon and Schuster, 1999.

PERIODICALS

Trenberth, Kevin. "Uncertainty in Hurricanes and Global Warming." *Science.* (17 Jun 2005): pp. 1753–1754.

WEB SITES

"La Niña." *National Aeronautic and Space Administration: Earth Observatory.* <http://earthobservatory.nasa.gov/Library/LaNina/> (accessed March 8, 2007).

"La Niña." *National Oceanic and Atmospheric Administration.* <http://www.elnino.noaa.gov/lanina.html>(accessed March 9, 2007).

Local Winds

Mesoscale winds are winds that blow across areas of the surface ranging from a few miles to a hundred miles in width. Mesoscale winds are better known as local winds or regional winds. A local wind can persist anywhere from several minutes to several days. Local winds can be driven by temperature and pressure differences or by variations in topography, the shape and height of Earth's surface features. Regardless of their cause, local winds have certain general characteristics. In addition, local winds have many interesting and descriptive names.

Sea and land breezes

Sea breezes and land breezes are two familiar categories of local winds that are driven by differences in temperature and in air pressure, which is the pressure exerted by air on a given area. A sea breeze blows from the water to the shore. It comes as a welcome relief to coastal inhabitants on a hot day. A land breeze, in contrast, blows from the shore toward the water. Land breezes occur in the evening.

Sea breezes form on hot days because the land warms more rapidly than does the water. As a result, a low-pressure area develops over warm ground and a high-pressure area over the cooler water. A mild wind blows across the pressure gradient, from the high-pressure area (over the water) to the low-pressure area (over the land). At night, the process is reversed as the land loses heat more quickly than does the water. The resultant land breeze flows from the high-pressure area, over the shore, out to the low-pressure area, over the water.

Sea breezes and land breezes are strongest at the shoreline, where temperature and pressure differences are most pronounced. They lose intensity as they travel inland or out to sea. The time of day when temperature and pressure differences are greatest, and therefore the breezes are strongest, is midafternoon, when land reaches its maximum

WORDS TO KNOW

adiabatic process: a process by which the temperature of a moving air parcel changes, even though no heat is exchanged between the air parcel and the surrounding air.

air pressure: the pressure exerted by the weight of air over a given area of Earth's surface. Also called atmospheric pressure or barometric pressure.

anabatic wind: winds caused by warm air close to Earth's surface. The air is less dense than the surrounding air and travels upward along a slope.

anemometer: an instrument that measures wind speed.

barchan dune: a sand dune that, when viewed from above, resembles a crescent moon, with the tips of the crescent pointing downwind. Also called barchane dune, barkhan dune, or crescentic dune.

chinook wall cloud: a solid bank of wispy, white clouds which appears over the eastern edge of the Rocky Mountains in advance of a chinook wind.

cold front: the leading edge of a moving mass of cold air.

compressional warming: an adiabatic process by which an air parcel warms as it descends. The descending parcel is compressed by the increasing pressure of the surrounding air, which adds kinetic energy to the molecules. Also called compressional heating.

conduction: the transfer of heat from a substance at a higher temperature to a substance at a lower temperature through the transfer of kinetic energy from a faster-moving molecule to a slower-moving molecule.

cumuliform: a puffy, heaped-up cloud formation.

cyclone: a weather system characterized by air that flows inward and circulates around a low-pressure area.

desert pavement: hard, flat, dry ground and gravel that remain after all sand and dust has been eroded from a surface.

downburst: an extremely strong, localized downdraft beneath a thunderstorm that spreads horizontally when it hits the ground, destroying objects in its path.

heat stroke: a life-threatening condition that sets in when heat exhaustion is left untreated and the body has spent all its efforts to cool itself. Also called sunstroke.

hurricane-force wind: sustained winds greater than 74 mph (119 kph).

katabatic wind: a strong wind that travels down a mountain under the force of gravity, and is stronger than a valley breeze.

lake breeze: a wind similar to a sea breeze that can be felt at the edge of a large lake.

leeward slope: the slope of a mountain opposite to the direction of local or prevailing winds down which cold air descends, producing dry conditions.

lightning: a short-lived, bright flash of light during a thunderstorm that is produced by a 100-million-volt electrical discharge in the atmosphere.

local winds: winds that blow across surface areas ranging from a few miles to about 100 miles (about 160 kilometers) in width. Also known as mesoscale winds or regional winds.

mesoscale winds: winds that blow across surface areas ranging from a few miles to about 100 miles (about 160 kilometers) in width. Also known as local winds or regional winds.

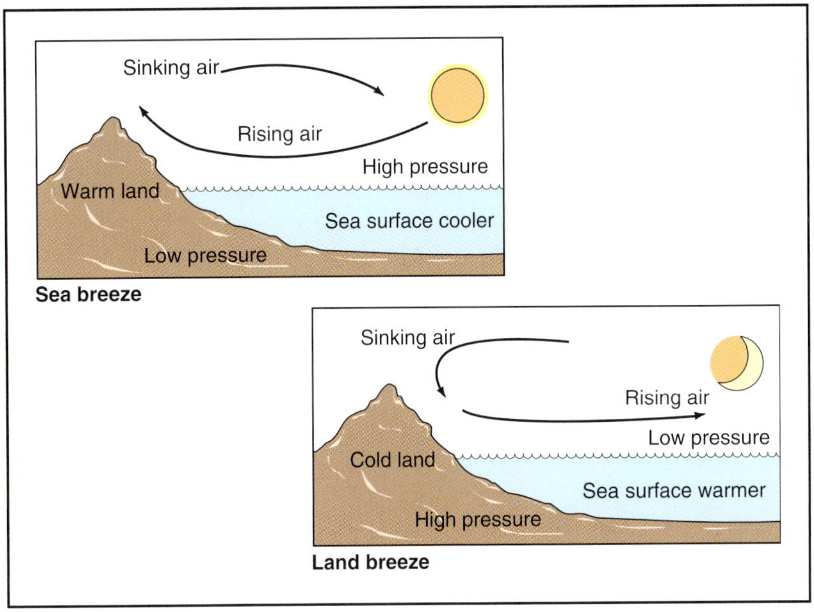

Sea and land breezes.

temperature. Sea breezes are generally stronger than land breezes, since temperature contrasts are greater during the day than at night.

While the strongest sea breezes blow in from over the ocean, sea breezes can also be felt on the edges of large lakes, such as the Great Lakes. They are called lake breezes. They form in the Northern Hemisphere, that is, north of the equator, between May and August on summer days when the land becomes warmer than the water. As a lake breeze or sea breeze travels over the land it acts like a cold front, or the leading edge of a moving cold air mass, thrusting the warm air above it. Vertical clouds, which are clouds developed upward to great heights, and rain showers are often produced over a stretch of land several miles (kilometers) inland.

Mountain and valley breezes

Mountain breezes and valley breezes arise from a mechanism similar to that of sea breezes and land breezes: different rates of surface heating and a resultant pressure differential. Valley breezes, also called anabatic (pronounced an-uh-BAT-ick; Greek for "climbing") winds are formed during the day. The sun warms air closest to the surface of a mountain most rapidly. Air that is farther from the surface, at the same altitude, warms more slowly. The warmer air hugging the surface, which is less dense than the surrounding

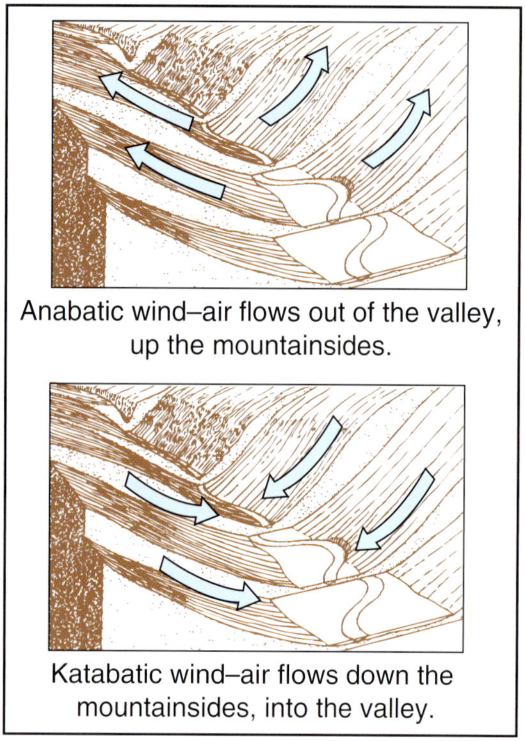

Anabatic and katabatic winds.

air, travels upward along the slope. This type of wind is called a "valley breeze" because the air is flowing upward, out of the valley.

A valley breeze typically begins shortly after sunrise. It is strongest on clear, sunny days, and first develops on slopes that face east, toward the rising sun. Since east-facing slopes are also the first ones during the day to end up in the shade, the valley wind there generally stops by late afternoon.

South-facing slopes receive the greatest amount of sunlight throughout the day. Hence it is on these slopes that the strongest valley winds are found. If a valley wind contains sufficient moisture, it will produce cumuliform clouds, which are puffy, piled-up formations, and possibly showers over the mountains in the early afternoon.

At night, the temperature gradient between the surface air and the layer of air above it is reversed, forming a mountain breeze that blows down the slope. Once the sun goes down, the mountain surface begins losing heat to the atmosphere by radiational cooling, which is the movement of heat from the ground upward. The layer of air just above the surface loses heat to the surface in a transfer process called conduction and also cools rapidly. This cold, dense surface air travels down the mountain and sinks into the valley. A mountain breeze is also called gravity wind or drainage wind.

Mountain breezes are usually stronger than valley winds, since at night the temperature difference is greatest between the layers of air next to and those farther away from the mountain. This is especially true in the winter, when the ground cools very quickly at night. A mountain breeze is one type of katabatic wind (pronounced kat-uh-BAT-ick; Greek for "going down"), a wind that blows downhill.

Katabatic winds

A katabatic wind is any wind that travels down a mountain under the force of gravity. However, the term is usually reserved for downhill winds which are considerably stronger than mountain breezes.

As a katabatic wind descends the mountainside, it is warmed by compressional warming. Compressional warming occurs as an air parcel descends and is compressed by the increasing pressure of the surrounding air. That compression leads to an increase in the kinetic energy of molecules and a resulting increase in the temperature of the air. In cases where the air is very cold when it begins its descent, it may still be colder than the surrounding air when it reaches the base of the mountain. However, where the air was somewhat less cold to start with, the wind that flows into the lowland may actually be warmer than the air mass it is replacing.

Katabatic winds range in strength from gentle to hurricane-force. Their speed depends largely on the terrain over which they travel. For instance, the wind accelerates when it travels down long, steep slopes or is squeezed through narrow canyons and valleys.

Cold katabatic winds Cold katabatic winds usually arise during winter or early spring on snow-capped mountains or high-elevation plateaus. The snow keeps the air above it exceedingly cold, forming a dome of high pressure just above the surface. The heavy, dense air descends along the mountainside and through the canyons. If a storm (a low-pressure system) moves into the area, the contrast in pressure between the cold surface air and the surrounding air increases, causing the wind to rush down the slopes even faster.

One of the most famous katabatic winds is the "mistral" of southern France. Its name comes from the Latin word *magistral,* which means "master wind." This cold, dry wind comes from the north or northwest in the winter. It originates in the snowy Alps and travels down to the Gulf of Lyons on the Mediterranean Sea.

As the mistral descends through the Rhône River Valley, it is squeezed through narrow passages and picks up speed. The gusts of a mistral can exceed 100 mph (160 kph), bringing a blast of frigid air to the otherwise warm French Riviera. The mistral sometimes lowers temperatures so much that frost forms and endangers vineyards.

A cold winter wind that occurs in eastern Europe is called the "bora." The bora blows from the Dinaric Alps down to the Adriatic Coast. This blustery wind travels from the north or northeast, like the mistral, and can also reach speeds greater than 100 mph (160 kph).

A "papagayo" (pronounced pa-puh-GUY-oh) is a strong, northeasterly wind that affects the Pacific coast of Central America, from Guatemala to the Gulf of Papagayo in Costa Rica. The papagayo winds

Experiment: How canyons affect wind speed

This experiment simulates how the wind accelerates as it squeezes through narrowing canyons or valleys. The only equipment needed is an electric fan, two pieces of cardboard or other material that can serve as walls, a pencil, and some string or yarn.

First, tape several 1-foot-long (30-centimeter-long) pieces of string or yarn to one end of the pencil. Then place the fan on a table and turn it on the lowest setting. Hold the pencil (by the end without the strings) a couple of feet (less than 1 meter) in front of the fan. Note how high the breeze blows the strings.

Now it's time to create your canyon walls. To do this, stand your pieces of cardboard on the table. Prop them up with bricks, heavy books, or other sturdy objects, if necessary. In order to "funnel" the wind, the distance between the walls must be greater at the end nearest the fan and smaller at the end farthest from the fan.

Turn the fan on the lowest setting again. Hold the pencil so that the end with the strings is just beyond the small opening between the "walls." The pencil should be about the same distance from the fan as it was the first time. Observe how high the strings are blown. Notice any difference in the intensity of the unobstructed breeze and the funneled breeze.

are produced by a cold air mass that travels down through the Central American mountains. It brings weather that is cold and blustery, yet clear.

The "Columbia Gorge wind" is the only cold katabatic wind native to the United States. Residents of Portland, Oregon, are all too familiar with this strong wind and the cold spell it introduces. The origin of the wind is cold air that settles over the Columbia Plateau. As it sinks, the air follows the Columbia River Gorge westward through the Cascade Mountains. Upon reaching the coast, the cold Columbia Gorge wind replaces the mild coastal air.

The world's fiercest katabatic winds occur in Antarctica. There, the cold, dense air roars down the mountainsides and along the ice sheets constantly, for days and months on end. The wind averages 50 mph (80 kph) in many parts of the continent. It sometimes rages to 100 mph (160 kph), generating intolerable windchill equivalent temperatures below –100°F (–75°C).

Warm katabatic winds Warm katabatic winds are generally set in motion by a larger-scale circulation pattern, for example the movement of strong upper-air westerlies across a mountain range. (Westerlies are global mid-latitude surface winds.) When a trough of low pressure is created over the mountain's leeward (opposite from the prevailing and local winds) slopes, it strengthens the high pressure system at the mountaintop and forces air down the mountains. Warm katabatic winds can also be drawn downhill by a strong cyclone (low-pressure system) or anticyclone (high-pressure system) located to the east of the mountains.

Chinook The best known warm katabatic wind in North America is the chinook, a dry wind that blows down the eastern side of the Rocky Mountains, from New Mexico to Canada, in winter or early spring. Chinooks are also common on the eastern side of the Cascade Mountains in Washington.

Chinook winds originate as cool, dry air at the top of a high mountain. The air is dry because it has released most of its moisture, forming clouds, when it ascended the mountains' windward side, which is the side of the local or prevailing winds. As the air descends the leeward, or opposite side, slopes, it undergoes compressional warming at the dry adiabatic lapse rate. The dry adiabatic lapse rate is the rate that the temperature of a parcel of unsaturated air—air that has less than 100 percent humidity—changes as it ascends or descends. Specifically, the air warms by 5.5°F for every 1,000 feet (10°C per 300 meters) it descends. Given that air can travel 9,000 feet or more (5,000 meters or more) down the slopes of the Rockies, the warming may be considerable.

"Chinook" is an Arapaho Indian word meaning "snow eater." This name is appropriate for this wind because chinook winds bring a dramatic warming to winter-weary regions and melt snow in their path. Chinooks are dry; they may have less than 5 percent relative humidity, that is, 5 percent of the amount of water vapor possible relative to temperature, so they rapidly vaporize melted snow. A chinook can erase all signs of a foot-deep cover of snow in just a few hours.

> ### Weather report: Chinooks to remember
>
> - On January 22, 1943, in Spearfish, South Dakota, the temperature rose 49°F (29°C) in just two minutes. At 7:30 AM the thermometer read –4°F (–20°C) and at 7:32 AM. It read 45°F (7°C)!
> - On January 27, 1962, in Pincher Creek, Alberta, Canada, the temperature rose by 57°F (14°C) within one hour. It was –20°F (–29°C) at midnight and 37°F (3°C) at 1 AM.
> - On January 6, 1966, also in Pincher Creek, the temperature rose by 38°F (23°C) within four minutes.
> - On January 7–8, 1969, outside of Boulder, Colorado, winds reached 130 mph (210 kph), with frequent gusts of more than 100 mph (160 kph). The greatest wind speed recorded within Boulder city limits was 97 mph (156 kph). That wind caused heavy property damage, including twenty-five roofs that were blown off.

Chinooks have been known to raise the temperature of an area by more than 35°F (20°C) in just one hour and by as much as 60°F (33°C) in a day. However, a chinook-induced warm spell does not mean that spring has come. The warm air can remain for several hours to days only to be displaced by cold winds from the west or the north. This can cause problems for plants that set buds or animals that start shedding winter coats too early.

While chinooks typically reach speeds of 25 to 50 mph (40 to 80 kph), they occasionally reach speeds greater than 100 mph (160 kph). The strongest chinook gust ever recorded was around 150 mph (230 kph) near Boulder, Colorado, on December 4, 1978. Violent chinooks can rip roofs off buildings and tear down trees and power lines. They whip up pebbles and debris, which can break windows and dent cars.

One warning sign of an approaching chinook is a chinook wall cloud. This solid bank of wispy, white clouds sometimes appears over the front range of the Rockies. A chinook wall cloud is formed as air rises along the windward slopes and moisture condenses. After this, air rapidly descends the leeward slopes.

Warm, dry winds similar to the chinook also occur in other parts of the world. Most notable is the foehn (or Fuhrn or fane), also spelled "föhn," that flows down from the Alps onto the plains of Austria and Germany. In Argentina this type of wind is called the zonda; in Romania it's called the austru; and in the Canterbury Plains of New Zealand it's called the nor'wester.

Santa Ana winds The Santa Ana winds are warm, dry, gusting katabatic winds from the east or northeast that create a major wildfire hazard in southern California. These winds occur between the months of October and February, peaking in intensity in December. In order to be classified as "Santa Anas" by the National Weather Service, the wind speed must be at least 30 mph (45 kph).

Smoke from massive forest fires in Southern California are fanned by dry Santa Ana winds. FMA, INC.

Santa Ana winds originate over the elevated plateau of the Mojave Desert and wind their way through the San Gabriel and San Bernardino mountains. They gain speed as they travel through the canyons and reach tremendous speeds in the Santa Ana Canyon, for which they are named. The winds then spill out into the foothills of the Los Angeles Basin and the San Fernando Valley.

The Santa Ana winds are generated by a high pressure system that sits above the Great Basin, the high-altitude plateau east of the Sierra Nevada Mountains and west of the Rockies. As this system turns clockwise, it pushes the air downward, over the edge of the high plateau, toward the lower pressure area at the coast.

Santa Ana winds blow with the force of about 40 mph (65 kph) on average, gusting to between 55 mph (90 kph) and 115 mph (185 kph). The strongest winds occur at night, in the absence of the sea breeze. The sea breeze blows in the opposite direction of the Santa Anas and acts as a counterforce.

As the air descends, it undergoes compressional warming in the same way as the chinooks. This air originates over the desert and, therefore, is dry from the start. Its relative humidity becomes even lower as it heats on descent. Santa Anas bring on heat waves throughout southern coastal California, with temperatures reaching 100°F (38°C) or higher.

Weather report: The losing battle against Mother Nature

Southern California's urban sprawl of recent decades has not stopped at the edge of wildfire- and mud slide–prone areas. Rather, homes have been and continue to be constructed in danger zones. Many foothill-dwellers have paid the price.

Since the start of southern California's building boom, Santa Ana wildfires and mud slides have caused billions of dollars in property damage and have claimed scores of lives. The following are some examples of Santa Ana–fueled disasters that have occurred in recent years:

- In October 1991, wildfire invaded Oakland and Berkeley. It burned down about 23,000 homes and killed 25 people.
- In October 1993, fifteen separate fires raged across the landscape from Ventura County to San Diego County. In all, the fires destroyed more than 1,200 buildings with damage totaling over $1 billion. One month later, fires fanned by 100 mph (160 kph) winds ravaged the outskirts of Malibu.
- In October 1996, fires in Malibu and Harmony Grove destroyed more than 150 homes and burned more than 41,000 acres.
- In 2003, California was beset by one of the worst wildfire seasons on record, prompting some to label it a "fire siege." Santa Ana–fueled fires raged across southern California, burned 750,000 acres, killed 24 people, and destroyed nearly 4,000 homes. Damage totaled $2 billion.

As the Santa Ana winds travel across the dry, scrubby southern California vegetation, they further dry it out and turn it into perfect brush-fire fuel. The Santa Anas create conditions such that a single spark can set off a fire. Once the fire begins, the winds fan the flames into an inferno. The Santa Anas are also known for changing direction rapidly, which spreads fire to new areas.

Mud slides are a secondary problem brought about by the Santa Ana winds. Mud slides often occur after wildfire has removed the vegetation and left the slopes bare. If heavy winter rains fall before seeds have germinated and new vegetation has taken hold, the top layer of soil and debris will be washed away. Mud slides occasionally inundate roadways and even destroy homes.

Desert winds

Deserts are windy places, primarily because of surface heating. The temperature of dry ground on a sunny day may be exceedingly hot, in some places over 130°F (55°C). Air rises from the hot surface in a powerful convection, which starts surface winds blowing. Wind speeds are greatest during the hottest part of the day and during the hottest time of year.

In addition to transporting scorching heat from one place to another, desert winds may produce sandstorms. As strong winds blow across a desert, they lift up and carry along sand and dust. Sandstorms may take the form of billowing walls or clouds, or spinning whirlwinds.

Sandstorms and dust storms One type of sandstorm that occurs frequently in the deserts of the Sudan region of north-central Africa and occasionally in the southwestern United States is the haboob. This word is taken from the Arabic word *habub,* which means "blowing furiously." A haboob is a tumbling, black wall of sand that has been stirred up by cold downdrafts along the leading edge of a thunderstorm or a cold front. These downdrafts strike the hot, dusty ground and force the surface air, as well as the top layer of sand and dust, upward. The sand wall may rise a mile or more above the ground, sometimes all the way to the base of the thunderstorm cloud. Haboobs sometimes travel across distances greater than 90 miles (145 kilometers), reducing visibility to near zero.

On the shelves: *Leaning on the Wind: Under the Spell of the Great Chinook*

Published in 1995, this widely acclaimed collection of essays by Canadian writer Sid Marty, a former park ranger, explores the folklore and realities surrounding the chinook winds. Marty takes readers on astonishing adventures through the retelling of his life in southwest Alberta, Canada.

A spinning vortex of sand and dust, called a dust devil, a whirlwind, or in Australia a willy-nilly, sometimes forms along the leading, cold air–warm air boundary of a haboob. More often, however, dust devils arise separately from haboobs, on clear, hot, relatively calm days. Fair-weather dust devils form over particularly warm areas, such as deserts, plowed fields, or flat expanses of dirt or pavement. Although dust devils bear a superficial resemblance to tornadoes, they form by different processes.

The first step in the formation of a dust devil is that hot air rises forcefully from the surface by convection, creating a low-pressure area at the surface. Next, surface winds converge to that point of low pressure. If there are horizontal layers of wind traveling at different speeds (a phenomenon called wind shear), rising air begins to spin around a vertical axis.

Dust devils are usually small and harmless, measuring less than 10 feet (3 meters) in diameter and less than 300 feet (90 meters) in height. They often last less than one minute. The largest dust devils reach a diameter of 100 feet (30 meters) and a height of 5,000 feet (1500 meters) and last for twenty minutes or more. The wind speed in dust devils may exceed 85 mph (135 kph).

While dust devils are generally harmless, they can sometimes cause significant damage, including overturning mobile homes and tearing roofs off buildings. A large and long-lived dust devil can toss over 50 tons (45 metric tons) of dust and debris into the sky.

Sand and dust storms are also common occurrences in western Africa, due to the "harmattan" (pronounced har-ma-TAHN). The harmattan—also

WORDS TO KNOW

monsoon: a name for shifting seasonal winds that result in a rainy season occurring in the summer on tropical continents, when the land becomes warmer than the sea beside it.

mountain breeze: a gentle downhill wind that forms at night as cold, dense, surface air travels down a mountainside and sinks into the valley. Also called gravity wind or drainage wind.

nor'easter: a strong northeasterly wind that brings cold air, often accompanied by heavy rain, snow, or sleet, to the coastal areas of New England and the mid-Atlantic states. Also called northeaster.

Northern Hemisphere: the half of the Earth that lies north of the equator.

precipitation: water in any form, such as rain, snow, ice pellets, or hail, that falls to Earth's surface.

pressure gradient: the difference in air pressure between a high and low pressure area relative to the distance separating them.

radiational cooling: the loss of heat from the ground upward into the atmosphere.

relative humidity: the amount of water vapor in an air mass relative to the amount of water in a saturated air mass of the same temperature.

sea breeze: the gentle wind that blows from over the sea to the shore during the day, due to differences in air pressure above each surface.

snow fence: a device placed in fields and along highways that slows the wind and reduces the blowing and drifting of snow.

squall line: a moving band of strong thunderstorms.

topography: the shape and height of Earth's surface features.

trade winds: an area of prevailing winds near the equator that blow from the northeast north of the equator and the southeast south of the equator.

transverse dune: a series of connected barchan dunes, which appear as tall, elongated crescents of sand running perpendicular to the prevailing wind.

tsunami: the largest type of water wave, generated by a submarine earthquake, landslide, or volcanic eruption.

unsaturated air: air that has less than 100 percent relative humidity.

valley breeze: an uphill wind that forms during the day as the valley air is heated and rises. Also called anabatic wind.

ventifact: a rock, boulder, or canyon wall that has been sculpted by wind and wind-blown sand.

vertical cloud: a cloud that develops upward to great heights. Vertical clouds are the products of sudden, forceful uplifts of small pockets of warm air.

westerlies: global mid-latitude surface winds that travel from the southwest to the northeast in the Northern Hemisphere, and from the northwest to the southeast in the Southern Hemisphere, between about 30 and 60 degrees latitude.

wind shear: a condition in which a vertical layer of air is sandwiched between two other vertical layers, each of which is traveling at a different speed and/or direction, causing the sandwiched air layer to roll.

windward: the slope of a mountain on the side of local or prevailing winds up which cooler air ascends producing moist, cloudy, or rainy conditions.

spelled "harmatan," "harmetan," or "hermitan"—is a mild, dry, and dusty wind. It is an easterly or northeasterly wind that originates over the Sahara during the cool winter months, from late November through mid-March. The harmattan blows across the continent to Africa's west coast, where, despite its dryness, it brings a welcome relief from the intense tropical heat and humidity.

The negative side of a harmattan is that it can create towering sand and dust storms, up to 20,000 feet (6,100 meters) high. Over 100 million tons (90 million metric tons) of dust are deposited into the Atlantic Ocean annually by harmattan dust storms.

Blowing sand and dust obscure a supermarket parking lot during a dust storm near Riverside, California. FMA, INC.

Winds of the Sahara In most cases, the winds that originate in the Sahara Desert in northern Africa are northerly winds, meaning they blow to the south. However, the presence of storm systems at certain locations may redirect these winds, turning them into southerly winds. In such cases, the winds blow across the Mediterranean Sea and into southern Europe or the Middle East. These patterns usually occur in spring or fall.

There are several names for the winds of the Sahara, depending on their point of origin and their destination.

The "leste" (pronounced LESS-tay) is a hot, dry wind that comes from Morocco or Algeria. When a storm system is present off the northwest tip of Africa, just southwest of Spain, this wind blows out over the Atlantic Ocean or the Mediterranean Sea. If the leste crosses the Mediterranean and blows onto southern Spanish shores, it is called the "leveche" (pronounced luh-VAY-chay). The leveche, like the leste, is hot and dry. The wind picks up only a very small amount of moisture during its short trip across the water.

The sirocco (pronounced suh-ROCK-oh), in contrast, has a longer journey across the Mediterranean. Hence, by the time this dry, dusty southeasterly wind out of North Africa reaches Sicily and southern Italy,

A dust devil—a spinning vortex of dust, dirt, and sand—in Kenya. JLM VISUALS.

it has become warm and humid. The sirocco is generated when a storm system is positioned to the southwest of Italy, over the Mediterranean.

The word "sirocco" (often spelled "scirocco") comes from the Arabic word *suruk,* which means "rising of the sun." In the central Sahara region, this wind is called "shahali" (pronounced SHA-ha-lee); in Tunisia it is called "chili" (pronounced SHILL-ee); and in southern Algeria it is called "chichili" (pronounced CHEE-chi-lee).

Another hot, dry, southerly wind originating on the Sahara, this one in Libya and Egypt, is the "khamsin" (pronounced kahm-SENE). When a storm is present to the north-northeast, over Turkey, the khamsin blows over the northern tip of the Red Sea and into Saudi Arabia, Jordan, and Israel. The khamsin is a strong wind that produces large sand and dust storms. The name for this wind in Israel is the "sharav" (pronounced shahr-AHV).

The khamsin reappears regularly each year. Its name is the Arabic word for "fifty" because it blows for about fifty days continuously, starting in mid-March. The air carried by the khamsin has a temperature greater than 120°F (50°C) and a relative humidity of 10 percent.

The "simoom" (pronounced si-MOOM) is a dry, blustery, dust-laden wind that blows across the Sahara and the deserts of Israel, Syria, and the Arabian peninsula. It often reaches temperatures of more than 130°F (55°C), with a relative humidity less than 10 percent. The simoom, which can cause the life-threatening condition heat stroke, is nicknamed the "poison wind." The word "simoom" comes from the Arabic word *semum,* which means "poisoning."

"Gharbi" (pronounced GAHR-bee) is the name of a wind that originates over the Atlantic Ocean, sweeps across Morocco, and travels over the Mediterranean. This wind picks up dust as it crosses the desert and moisture as it crosses the water. It then

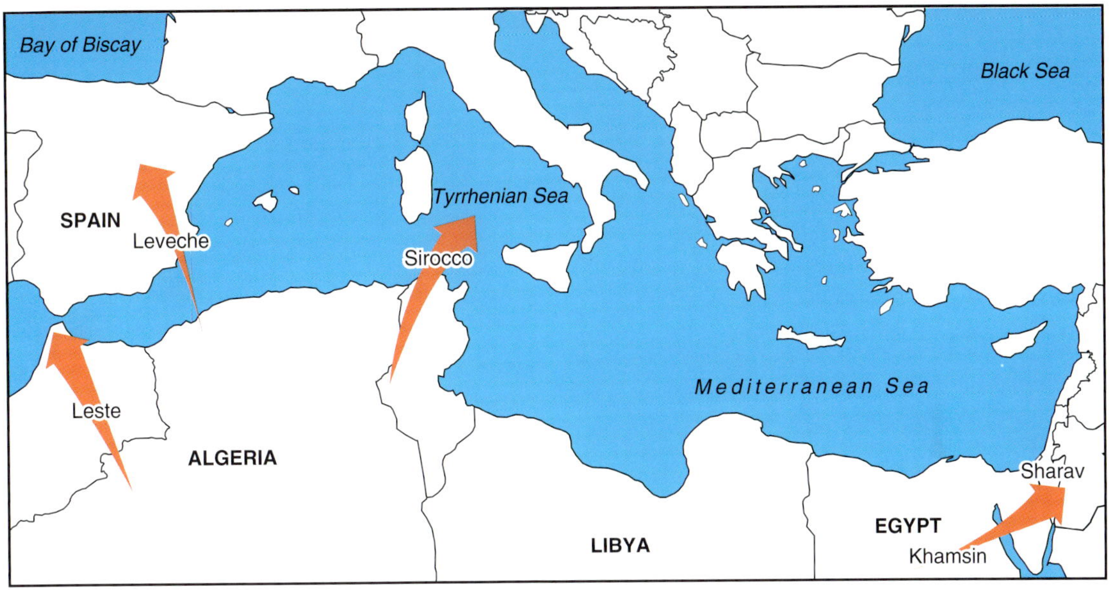

The migrating winds of the North African Sahara region.

deposits heavy rains on the lands of the north and east Mediterranean region. Due to the sand and dust, this precipitation is reddish and is called "red rain."

Other desert winds The "berg" wind originates in the interior of South Africa. It blows down the mountains and out to the coast. This wind is dry, dusty, and very hot. "Berg" is an Afrikaans word meaning "mountains."

The "brick fielder" is Australia's version of a dry, dusty, very hot wind. It comes from the central desert region in the summer months and blows heat, dust, and sand toward the southeastern coast.

The "shamal" (pronounced shah-MALL) is a northwesterly wind that blows throughout the Persian Gulf and the lower valley of the Tigris and Euphrates rivers in Iraq. This hot, dry, and dusty wind can begin to blow suddenly, at any time of year. It typically blows for forty days continuously in June and early July, in what is known as the "great shamal" or the "forty-day shamal." At all other times of year, it generally lasts from one to five days and becomes calm at night.

"Shamal" is the Arabic word for "left-hand" or "north." Another name for this wind is "barih" (pronounced BAR-ee).

Weather report: Daunting dust devils

One of the worst dust devils on record occurred in May 1995 near Minong, Wisconsin. It left a 300-yard-long (275-meter-long) path of destruction, including a damaged roof, a torn-up snow fence, and a downed power line that started a fire.

Another destructive dust devil rose up completely unannounced on a sunny day in March 1995 in upstate South Carolina. The whirlwind smashed the covered porch of a home and carried the wreckage hundreds of yards (meters) away.

In the spring of 1991, a dust devil passed right by the National Weather Service station at Albuquerque, New Mexico. The station's anemometer, a device that measures windspeed, measured the wind gusts at 70 mph (110 kph).

Cold winds

One of the more familiar examples of a regional cold wind is the "Texas norther." As its name implies, a Texas norther is a northerly wind that dips far south, bringing cold air into Texas. Texas northers (sometimes just called "northers") usually follow in the wake of an intense winter storm traveling eastward across the United States. A Texas norther can lower the temperature in Texas by dozens of degrees in just a few hours.

A Texas norther that causes a dramatic drop in temperature, possibly accompanied by sleet and snow, is called a "blue norther." A Texas norther that continues southward and brings cold air into Central America is called "el norte."

A nor'easter or "northeaster" is a strong, northeasterly wind that brings cold air to the coastal areas of New England and the mid-Atlantic states, occasionally as far south as Florida. Nor'easters are generated by extratropical cyclones in the Atlantic (cyclones that develop at high latitudes). These storms develop or intensify off the eastern seaboard of North America and move to the northeast along the coast. The gale-force wind that spins off the storm is often accompanied by heavy rain, snow, or sleet.

One of the most extreme cold winds is Australia's "southerly buster" (originally and properly called "southerly burster"). This violent, cold wind, which comes from the south, represents the leading edge of a strong cold front. A southerly buster can lower the temperature in southeastern Australia by as much as 36°F (20°C) in just a few minutes.

The strong cold wind of central Asia is called the "buran" (pronounced boo-RAN). This dreaded wind originates in Siberia and brings unbearably cold blasts into Russia and the central Asian republics. When the buran is accompanied by snow, which may be heavy, it is called "purga" (pronounced POOR-guh).

A cold, snowy wind similar to Russia's purga is Alaska's "burga" (pronounced BOOR-guh), also spelled "boorga." This wind comes from the northeast and may carry sleet as well as snow.

A cold, dry wind that comes from the north or northeast and invades southern Europe is called a "bise" (pronounced BEEZ, also spelled "bize"). This wind blows in the winter and early spring. It sometimes brings on frosts after the start of the growing season, thus endangering crops.

A "tehuantepecer" (pronounced te-WAHN-te-peck-er) is a cold, blustery, northerly wind that blows down from the Gulf of Mexico. This winter wind picks up speed as it crosses the mountains between Mexico and Guatemala. It then spills out into the Gulf of Tehuantepec, on the southern coast of Mexico, and can blow for 100 miles (160 kilometers) over the sea.

The "pampero" (pronounced pahm-PAIR-oh) is a South American wind. Similar to the Texas norther, the pampero descends from the plains and brings bitterly cold air to typically warm regions. This southwesterly wind originates in the Andes Mountains and blows across the grasslands (*pampas,* in Spanish) of Argentina and Uruguay and out to the Atlantic Coast of Brazil. The pampero is often accompanied by thunderstorms and brings about a rapid drop in temperature.

The coldest local wind of all is the "whirly." The whirly, sometimes classified as a storm, is a small, violent squall in Antarctica. It is a rapidly spinning wind that whips up snow across an area ranging from a few yards to hundreds of yards in diameter. This windstorm usually occurs during the transition periods between the light Antarctic summer and dark Antarctic winter.

Weather extremes: The Great Blue Norther of 11/11/11

On November 11, 1911, a weather event widely known as The Great Blue Norther of 11/11/11 produced the most dramatic temperature changes in U.S. history. The temperature in several places plunged over 60°F (30°C) in a few hours. By nightfall, several cities were dealing with single-digit temperatures. Kansas City, Missouri, had just established a record high temperature for the date of 76°F (25°C) in the late morning. By midnight, the temperature had dropped to 11°F (–12°C), setting a record low temperature for the same date.

Several cities broke high and low records that day. Springfield, Missouri, had set a record high of 80°F (27°C). Within two hours, the temperature had dropped to 40°F (4°C) and before midnight the temperature had plummeted to a record 13°F (–11°C). Oklahoma City also set record high and low temperatures on the same date, with a high of 83°F (28°C) and a low of 17°F (–8°C).

Other local winds

There are several other kinds of local winds that do not fall neatly into any of the categories listed above. They have been grouped together in this section.

Derechos A derecho (pronounced day-RAY-cho) is a destructive, hurricane-force wind that travels in a straight line. This wind was named in 1883 by

Weather extremes: Ravaging nor'easters

In February 1969, a storm with nor'easter winds dumped record-setting snowfalls throughout New England. In Rumford, Maine, snow accumulation totaled 70 inches (175 centimeters). There were 114 inches (290 centimeters) of snow in Mansfield, in the mountains of Vermont; and 164 inches (415 centimeters) at Pinkham Notch, in the mountains of New Hampshire.

In March 1984, a storm struck the Atlantic coast from Virginia to Maine. The shoreline was battered by waves that rose to heights of 20 feet (6 meters), along with 92 mph (148 kph) nor'-easter winds. This storm destroyed beaches, homes, boardwalks, and seawalls. The damage totaled over $1 billion.

the director of the Iowa Weather Service, Gustavus Hinrichs. Hinrichs decided on the name "derecho," a Spanish word meaning "straight ahead," to underscore the difference between this wind and a tornado, which spins. "Tornado" is from the Spanish word *tornar* meaning "to return" or "to change."

To be defined as a derecho, the winds must travel faster than 58 mph (93 kph) and the path of the damage must be at least 280 miles (450 kilometers) long. Derecho winds sometimes exceed 100 mph (160 kph) and cause damage across a 150-mile-wide (240-kilometer-wide) area. Derechos are relatively long-lived. Some have swept across several states in a period of sixteen hours.

A derecho is caused by a series of intense downbursts, which are extremely strong, localized downdrafts, from a squall line, or cluster of thunderstorms. These thunderstorms collectively cover an area that is 75 to 300 miles (120 to 480 kilometers) wide. They act as a single storm with tremendous force. The downbursts

Damage to a stand of trees and a home from the passage of derecho winds in the Midwest.
FMA, INC.

Weather extremes: Destructive derechos

Derechos occur most often at night, in the late spring and summer. They usually occur in the central and northern Great Plains states and the Midwest, and sometimes as far east as New York.

In July 1995, a derecho blasted through New York State and southern New England in just three and a half hours. It ravaged rural upstate New York with wind gusts of up to 106 mph (170 kph), and was accompanied by thousands of lightning strikes, each of which is produced by a 100 million-volt electrical discharge. The wind storm knocked down tens of millions of trees across the nearly one-million-acre (four-hundred-thousand-hectare) Adirondack State Park, piling felled trees 10 to 20 feet (3 to 6 meters) high. Four people who were camping in the park were killed by the falling trees.

In 1999, an unusually long-lived derecho hit the border area between the United States and Canada. The so-called "Boundary Waters-Canadian Derecho" began on July 4 and lasted twenty-two hours, with winds gusting above 100 mph (160 kph). The system traveled 1,300 miles (2,092 kilometers) from northen North Dakota to New England, injuring dozens, killing two, and causing property damage in excess of $100 million.

In June 2004, a derecho tore through northern Louisiana, southern Arkansas, east Texas, and Oklahoma, killing one person, uprooting trees, and overturning cars and trucks.

St. Louis, Missouri, was hit by two derechos in three days: one on July 21 and one on July 23, 2006. The winds, topping 80 mph (129 kph), knocked out power for more than 600,000 people and cut a swath of damage 400 miles long and several miles wide.

of a derecho form when a line of thunderstorms passes over a layer of dry air that is several thousand feet above ground. As precipitation, or water in any form, falls into this dry air, moisture rapidly evaporates, thus cooling the air. The cool, heavy air that is formed, assisted by the downward motion of the raindrops, then surges toward the ground. These forceful downbursts together form a derecho. They often spawn tornadoes as well.

Monsoons A "monsoon" is a seasonal wind that occurs throughout southeast Asia, along the Atlantic coastal regions of northern South America, and on the coasts of central Africa. The name "monsoon" comes from the Arabic word *mausim,* meaning "season." This wind blows throughout the summer months, bringing heavy rains and flooding to a region that is dry for most of the winter.

Throughout the winter, the region affected by monsoons is tilted away from the sun. As a result, the sea is warmer than the land during that time.

Commuters in Manila, the Philippines, wade through flood waters caused by monsoon rains when the passenger bus they were riding stalled. © REUTERS/CORBIS.

A land breeze forms, and hot, dry winds from far inland are blown out toward the sea.

When spring arrives, the monsoon area moves to a position almost directly beneath the sun and the winds shift direction. The land is heated intensely, which causes surface air to rise. This air is replaced by moist winds from over the ocean, similar to a sea breeze. The moisture from these winds forms clouds which yield heavy rains.

Levanters The "levanter" (pronounced li-VAN-ter, also spelled "levante") is the most pleasant wind in the Mediterranean region. The levanter is a fresh, mild easterly or northeasterly wind that blows across the southern coast of France, the eastern coast of Spain, and through the Straits of Gibraltar. It is named for Levant, a region along eastern shores of the Mediterranean Sea.

The levanter travels over the Mediterranean, which makes it humid. This often strong wind brings overcast skies and rain. It occurs most frequently in June through October.

Konas Hawaii is famous for its overall pleasant weather, which is largely influenced by the trade winds, which are the prevailing winds near the equator. The "kona" (pronounced KOH-nuh) winds, which usher in heavy rains and storms, stand in contrast to this trend. The konas are southwesterly winds that blow down leeward (the Hawaiian word for which is "kona") slopes of Hawaii's mountains, about five times each winter.

These warm, very humid winds are of moderate strength. They may produce intense storms with heavy rainfall or steady to light rainfall, lasting from several hours to several days.

The wind's effect on surfaces

Local winds are like sculptors, etching away at surfaces and objects standing in their path. The winds blow the sand, snow, and water, and even shape rock walls and trees. The effect of the winds can be gradual and long term, such as where it shapes the buttes of the American West and the sand dunes of the Sahara Desert. The effect of the winds can also be much more immediate and short term, such as where it whips water into waves and blows snow into drifts.

Sand formations Even a moderate desert wind can set sand in motion. A wind of about 15 mph (24 kph) is strong enough to move very small grains of sand, with diameters of about .008 inches (.2 millimeters). At speeds of 30 mph (48 kph), the wind can move grains with diameters of about .08 inches (2 millimeters). However, the tiniest particles of dust and sand can not be moved directly by the wind. The reason is that a very shallow layer of calm air, extending only about .004 inches (.1 millimeters) above the ground, is unaffected by the wind. The tiny particles are stirred only when they are struck by moving particles.

When the wind blows, it sets in motion a process called saltation, the migration of particles along the ground and through the air. When sand particles are set in motion by the wind, they first slide along the surface. Once these particles overtake and strike other particles, some of the particles bounce into the air and are carried along by the wind. These particles, in turn, fall back to the ground and kick other particles up, into

Weather report: Hot winds and human health

Numerous local winds are thought to be responsible for temporary declines in the mental and physical health of a region's inhabitants. While the health-wind connections in some cases are popularly accepted as fact, it remains a mystery as to whether or not scientific processes are involved. What follows are examples of winds and the alleged negative effects they have on human health.

- The chinooks are reported to cause irritability, depression, and illness.
- The sirocco winds are claimed to cause fatigue and mental weakness.
- The Santa Ana winds seem to make people nervous, anxious, and possibly even homicidal.
- The foehns are reported to increase the frequency of suicide attempts among people who have suicidal thoughts.

The statistical links between these various irritating winds and human psychological problems are weak and the effect, if any, is small. The frequency of suicide during a foehn event might increase by less than 10 percent. However, the alleged effect has been given the name "Föhnkrankheit" or "Föhn-sickness", and researchers are searching for a cause-and-effect relationship.

Desert winds blow sand particles in a process called saltation. FMA, INC.

the wind. Eventually, through this process, sand can be blown across great distances.

As sand is continually carried away from a particular location, the surface level becomes lower and lower. Eventually, if all the sand and dust is removed, all that remains is hard, flat, dry ground and gravel. This type of surface is called desert pavement. The bare, dry floor of the Gobi Desert in Mongolia is an example of desert pavement. Desert pavements can also be formed outside of deserts. Agricultural fields, for instance, may turn to desert pavement when soil erosion is accompanied by prolonged drought.

The wind may also sculpt the sand into sand dunes. Sand dunes form when billions of sand grains accumulate in a given location. A sand dune is a mound of sand that is produced over time by a strong wind blowing in a fairly constant direction. Blowing sand comes to a halt behind obstacles, such as rocks or plants. When an accumulation of sand becomes large enough, the sand pile itself acts as an obstacle behind which blowing sand continues to gather.

The angle of a sand dune is more gradual on the windward side, where the wind blows strongest, and steeper on the leeward side, where the wind is calm by comparison. The difference in angle of incline from one side of the dune to the other results because the wind blows the sand

Weather extremes: The windiest places in the world

Declaring a particular spot the windiest place is a bit tricky. For one thing, recorded wind speeds are probably not the highest speed winds that have ever happened on Earth. Faster winds have probably occurred at other locations, but were not recorded. The windiest spot on Earth is even more difficult to establish because the place with the highest average wind speed is not necessarily the place with the highest recorded wind speed.

Commonwealth Bay, Antarctica, is home to the world's highest recorded average wind speeds, so it is considered by many to be the world's windiest place. It was so named in 1912 by an early Australian explorer, Douglas Mawson (1882–1958), who spent two winters there. This bay is situated on the coast of Eastern Adelie Land and West King George Land. It is on the Indian Ocean side of the continent, opposite Australia.

The wind at Commonwealth Bay was measured in 1951 by a team of French scientists who established a base there. They clocked the cold katabatic winds at 40 mph (65 kph) on average, for the year. The highest monthly average winds were 65 mph (105 kph), in March. The highest average winds in a twenty-four-hour period were 108 mph (174 kph), on March 21–22. The winds regularly gusted to over 200 mph (320 kph).

Another candidate for windiest place on Earth, and certainly the windiest place in the United States, is Mount Washington, New Hampshire. The Mount Washington Observatory, located at an altitude of 6,288 feet (1,915 meters), recorded a wind gust of 231 mph (371 kph) on April 12, 1934. Subsequently, there have been frequent gusts up to 220 mph (355 kph) recorded there. Mount Washington also holds the U.S. record for the highest average wind speed in a twenty-four-hour period. On April 12, 1932, the wind blew at an average speed of 130 mph (210 kph).

up the windward face to the top of the dune. On reaching the top of the dune, the sand merely drops to the other side. By examining the shape of a sand dune, it is possible to tell the direction of the prevailing winds at the time the dune was formed.

Entire dunes are also nudged along by the wind. Sand dunes move as much as 50 feet (15 meters) a year.

Barchan (pronounced bar-KHAN) dunes, also called barchane, barkhan, or crescentic dunes, are formed by winds blowing in a nearly constant direction and moderate speed, across relatively flat land with only a shallow layer of sand. When viewed from above, these dunes resemble crescent moons, with the tips of the crescent pointing downwind.

Where sand is more plentiful, a series of connected barchan dunes may form. This structure, called transverse dunes, appears as tall, elongated crescents of sand running perpendicular to the prevailing winds.

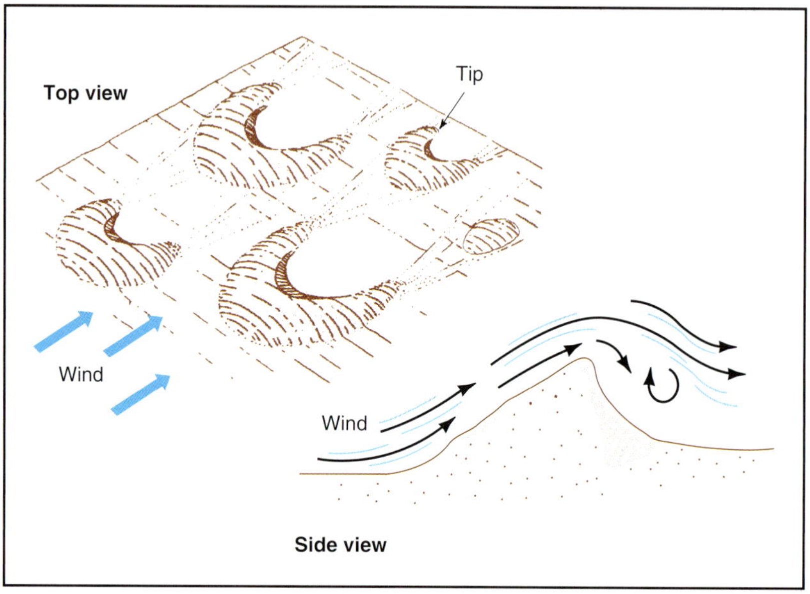

Barchan dunes.

Barchan dunes with very pronounced crescent shapes, that exist either singly or in connected lines, are called seif (pronounced safe) dunes. These dunes are very steep; the crest of a seif dune forms a sharp ridge.

"Seif" is an Arabic word meaning "sword." These dunes are so named because their shape resembles the curved blade of a sword. The seif dunes of Algeria and Iran reach up to 650 feet (197 meters) in height. When seifs exist in a series, they form a meandering pattern that is caused by shifting winds.

Sand ripples are wavy designs formed by the motion of sand along the surface of a sand dune. The ripples run in a direction perpendicular to the wind. Like the sand dune, sand ripples have a more gradual incline on the windward side of the dune and a steeper incline on the leeward side. The direction of the sand ripples changes whenever the wind changes direction.

Sculpted objects Another consequence of wind and wind-blown sand is the eroding and shaping of solid objects. Rocks that have been sculpted by these forces are called ventifacts. Ventifacts include not only rocks lying on the ground, but larger structures such as boulders and canyon walls. Surface rocks, however, constitute the bulk of ventifacts. The reason for this fact is that wind-borne sand generally travels close to the ground.

Ventifacts in Bryce Canyon National Park, Utah. FIELD MARK PUBLICATIONS.

Wind and blowing sand can also erode the bases of solid rock structures, such as boulders, canyons, and cliffs. The wind has the greatest effect on soft rock, such as sandstone. The windward side of a boulder may be rough and pitted, even notched, while its leeward side is relatively smooth. Sometimes wind-blown sand has the effect of polishing rocks. This effect occurs most often in areas prone to sandstorms, where billions of sand grains batter the rocky surfaces.

Ventifacts abound in Utah's Goblin Valley. The sandstone formations there, made of alternating hard and soft layers, have been sculpted into strange and beautiful shapes by the wind. One particular type of ventifact found in Goblin Valley is the "mushroom rock." Mushroom rocks form from boulders, the lower portions of which are made of soft sandstone and the upper portions of which are made of hard sandstone. The wind erodes the soft portion at a much faster rate than the hard portion. Thus, these rocks look like mushrooms, with large heads of hard sandstone sitting atop skinny stems of soft sandstone.

One of the world's largest and most magnificent collections of ventifacts is found in Bryce Canyon, Utah. There, the wind (as well as water) has battered the tops of tall, layered rock formations. The erosion of the outer layers has created a breathtaking array of stone spires.

Rock is not the only material to be shaped by wind-blown sand. Telephone poles, trees, and cars can also be sculpted in the desert. Because of the constant beating by wind-blown sand on lower portions of telephone poles, the poles become narrower at the base than they are higher up.

Snow formations Another medium sculpted by the wind is snow. Snow can be blown into large drifts called snow dunes that are similar to sand dunes. Snow dunes form when a strong wind comes along after snow has fallen on a flat landscape. The wind carries the snow until it meets a barrier, where it deposits the snow. In the Great Plains states, when snow falls on fields and is blown away, the first obstacles it meets are typically in populated areas. For this reason, snow accumulation may be negligible in the countryside at the same time that there are several inches (centimeters) in town.

Gentler winds form ripples in the snow, rather than blowing it away. Snow ripples, similar to sand ripples, are long wavelike patterns that run perpendicular to the direction of the wind.

Snow ripples in Antarctica and other very cold places are called sastrugi (pronounced SASS-truh-ghee). These patterns form when the wind blows from the same direction for several days. Sastrugi freeze solid and can

Did you know? Snow fences

Snow fences are devices that slow down winds and reduce the blowing and drifting of snow. They are erected in two areas: in fields and along highways. The purpose of snow fences in fields is to prevent the wind from stripping the ground of snow. A blanket of snow protects the soil by insulating it against bitter cold temperatures. The snow also provides much needed moisture when it melts.

The purpose of snow fences along a highway is to reduce the amount of snow that blows across or piles up on the road. As the wind whips across a clearing, it picks up snow. When this snow-laden wind hits a snow fence, its speed is reduced. A slower wind will deposit its snow, and at the same time will pick up very little new snow. The snow that's deposited forms a gradual drift on the other (downwind) side of the snow fence.

A snow fence must be placed far enough from the road so that most of the snow gets deposited between the fence and the road, with as little snow as possible reaching the road. The rule of thumb is that snow will accumulate downwind of the fence for a distance approximately ten times the height of the fence. Thus, if a fence is 10 feet (3 meters) high, it should be placed at least 100 feet (30 meters) from the road.

remain for a long time. The singular form of "sastrugi" is "sastruga," which comes from the Russian word *zastruga,* meaning "wind-made furrow."

Water formations In addition to sand and snow, the surface of water is also shaped by the winds. However, only one pattern can be created on the water's surface: waves. Wind-driven waves are technically known as wind waves. While the wind is the most common cause of surface waves, it is not the only cause. Some other forces that give rise to waves include: tides, volcanic activity, and earthquakes beneath the ocean floor.

Wave height is directly proportional to wind speed. To calculate the height of waves precisely, however, requires knowledge of the length of time the wind has been blowing, as well as the distance over water, or fetch, the wind is blowing. The longer the time and distance over which the wind blows, the taller the waves will be.

It stands to reason that the largest wind waves are generated by large, stationary storm systems. The tallest wind wave ever recorded was 112 feet (34 meters) high. This wave occurred during a storm on the Pacific Ocean, with winds of nearly 70 mph (112 kph), on February 7, 1933. This wave was not the tallest of all waves, however. That title is reserved for another class of waves called tsunamis, which are generated by submarine earthquakes.

[*See Also* **Climate; Monsoon; Tsunami; Weather: An Introduction**]

For More Information

BOOKS

Simpson, John E. *Sea Breeze and Local Winds.* New York: Cambridge University Press, 1994.

Van Sant, Bruce. *Tricks of the Trades.* St. Petersburg FL: Cruising Guide Publications, Inc., 2001.

Walker, Stuart H. *Sailor's Wind.* New York: W. W. Norton, 2006.

Watts, Allan. *Instant Wind Forecasting.* New York: Sheridan House, 2002.

WEB SITES

"Forces and Winds: Online Meteorology Guide." *University of Illinois: Weather World 2010 Project.* <http://ww2010.atmos.uiuc.edu/(Gh)/guides/mtr/fw/home.rxml> (accessed March 22, 2007).

"Local Winds: Mountain Breezes." *Danish Wind Industry Association.* <http://www.windpower.org/en/tour/wres/mount.htm> (accessed March 22, 2007).

"Local Winds: Sea Breezes." *Danish Wind Industry Association.* <http://www.windpower.org/en/tour/wres/localwin.htm> (accessed March 22, 2007).

"Names of Winds." *Golden Gate Weather Services.* <http://ggweather.com/winds.html> (accessed March 22, 2007).

Monsoon

A typical monsoon climate (climate is the weather experienced by a given location, averaged over several decades) is warm year-round with very rainy summers and relatively dry winters. The change from dry season to rainy season is abrupt, and the rainy season is marked by heavy rainfall. For many people, the monsoon represents only the anxiously awaited rains of summer, which provide a break from the oppressive heat and mark the beginning of the growing season.

While most people associate the term monsoon with seasonal rains, meteorologists (scientists who study weather and climate) use the term specifically to refer to a relatively abrupt seasonal wind shift: the wind blows from land to sea during the winter and from sea to land during the summer. The term "monsoon" comes from the Arabic word *mausim,* meaning "season."

The monsoon climate is most pronounced in India and in parts of Southeast Asia. Monsoon climates also exist along the Atlantic coastal regions of northern South America, on the coasts of central Africa, and in other warm regions of the world where large landmasses meet ocean basins.

Monsoon rains can mean salvation or disaster to the areas where they fall. Half the world's population relies on the seasonal rains to water their crops (principally rice, which requires very wet conditions) and support livestock, as well as to bring relief from the hot, dry winter and spring. If there isn't enough rain, crops will die and people may face food shortages and famine. Too much rainfall, on the other hand, may bring flooding, destruction, and death.

Bangladesh's monsoon floods of 1998

In the summer of 1998, monsoon rains in the south Asian republic of Bangladesh caused the worst flooding in that nation's history. While in an

WORDS TO KNOW

air pressure: the pressure exerted by the weight of air over a given area of Earth's surface.

climate: the weather experienced by a given location, averaged over several decades.

deforestation: the removal of all or most of the trees from a region.

drought: an extended period during which the amount of rain or snow that falls on an area is much lower than usual.

El Niño: Spanish for "the Christ child"; an extraordinarily strong episode (occurring every two to seven years) of the annual warming of the Pacific waters off the coast of Peru and Ecuador.

erosion: the wearing away of a surface by the action of wind, water, or ice.

flood: the overflow of water onto normally dry land.

meteorologist: a scientist who studies weather and climate.

monsoon: seasonal wind that blows from land to sea during the winter and from sea to land during the summer; also, more commonly, a seasonal period of heavy rainfall.

monsoon climate: a climate that is warm year-round with very rainy (flood-prone) summers and relatively dry winters. It encompasses much of southern and southeastern Asia, the Philippines, coastal regions of northern South America, and slices of central Africa.

orographic uplift: the forcing of air upward, caused bythe movement of air masses over mountains.

pressure gradient: the rate at which air pressure decreases with horizontal distance.

Southern Oscillation: shifting patterns of air pressure at sea level, between the eastern and western edges of the Pacific Ocean.

average rainy season Bangladesh has one-third of its land submerged, the rains of 1998 covered three-fourths of the country. While the flooding typically lasts one or two weeks, in 1998 it lasted two months (three times longer than the next longest flood in Bangladeshi history). The flooding began in late July, when the Ganges and other rivers overflowed their banks. The rivers continued to rise until mid-September, only starting to recede at the end of that month.

More than fifteen hundred people lost their lives in the floods, and about twenty-five million were left homeless. In many villages, residents spent two months living on the tin roofs of their homes. There was widespread loss of livestock and crops in this primarily agricultural nation. Countless roads, bridges, and power lines were damaged or destroyed, and half of the nation's rice seedlings, waiting to be planted, were washed away.

Families pass over a flooded highway in Kalaroa, Bangladesh, during the monsoon flood season. AP IMAGES.

Background on Bangladesh Bangladesh is a small, flood-prone country situated just east of India on the Bay of Bengal. It is the size of the state of Wisconsin, but holds more than 125 million people (about half the population of the United States), making it the most densely populated nation in the world. It is also one of the poorest nations in the world; its citizens earn an average of only $200 a year.

Bangladesh is in the path of waters that flow down the slopes of the Himalayas. Those waters course through India before entering Bangladesh. Since Bangladesh sits at a lower elevation than India, it receives the runoff from India's floods.

Most of the land of Bangladesh is in the flat, low-lying Plain of Bengal. Roughly 80 percent of Bangladesh is less than 30 feet (10 meters) in elevation. Near the coast, the land is practically at sea level with an elevation less than 3 feet (1 meter).

Bangladesh is crisscrossed by a complex and interconnected system of rivers and tributaries. The situation is further confused because the same river is known by different names in different portions of its course. The four major rivers are the Ganges, the Jamuna (also known as the Brahmaputra where it crosses India), the Padma, and the Meghna. These rivers also have hundreds of tributaries. The Ganges, Jamuna, and Padma combine to form the Meghna which enters the Bay of Bengal in a wide delta system. During the rainy season, the multiple channels of the Meghna merge to form a vast river of water and silt.

Much of the land exists as islands, called "chars" locally, that are constantly appearing and disappearing as the rivers change course. The chars' soil is made extremely fertile by the silt deposited by the rivers. Individual chars, however, rarely exist for more than ten years. Most homes in this fertile region are built on stilts to keep them above the flood waters.

Bangladesh has an extremely rainy climate, and flooding is common during the monsoon season. That flooding becomes disastrous if some or all of the major rivers flood, and worse yet if it coincides with high tides in the Bay of Bengal. The flooding can put nearly all of the country under water if a tropical cyclone strikes at the same time. The floodwaters run swiftly, sweeping away many homes—even those built on stilts. As dry ground disappears and villagers can no longer find safety from the floodwaters, the number of deaths from drowning increases. In the worst years, tens of thousands of people in Bangladesh have died, and millions have been made homeless.

Women trapped in flood waters, Bangladesh, 2000. © AFP/CORBIS.

Another consequence of flooding in Bangladesh is the spread of disease. Disease is common because of the mixing of sewage with drinking water and the increase of illness-spreading insects. In a country that has only one medical doctor for every forty-five hundred people, there is little chance that sick people will receive the necessary treatment.

Torrential rains swell rivers The primary source of Bangladesh's 1998 floods was torrential rains that pelted the nation every day for a month. Adding to the rising floods was runoff from rain in the Himalayas and India. Floodwaters took at least one thousand lives in India before continuing into Bangladesh. Bangladeshi rivers overflowed their banks and spread out over the land. In early September the Ganges River reached its highest level in recorded history.

Typically, Bangladesh's rivers empty into the Bay of Bengal. In the late summer of 1998, however, high sea levels blocked the seaward-flowing rivers. The high sea levels were believed to be the result of numerous minor undersea earthquakes in the region as well as runoff from melting glaciers in the Himalayas.

More than 10,000 miles (16,000 kilometers) of roads, fourteen thousand schools, and millions of homes were partially or totally submerged. Flooding was made worse by faulty levees (high walls built along the banks of a river to prevent flooding) that had been put in place in a failed attempt to tame the river. That effort, which was coordinated by

Flood victims line up outside a refugee camp in Bangladesh, 2000. © REUTERS/CORBIS.

the World Bank at a cost of $150 million and called the Flood Action Plan, was declared a failure in 1996.

"I can trace the orange clay lines of major roads, which are built on artificially raised ground . . . then, again and again, I see these roads disappear under water," wrote journalist Mark Levine in a November 1998 article in *Outside Magazine,* while surveying Bangladesh from an airplane. "I see floating clusters of trees and houses, isolated from one another like islands. I see the tips of power lines poking through the surface of the floodwater, and small herds of cattle—four or five heads apiece—huddling on tiny dots of land."

Crops destroyed by flooding More than 2 million tons (1.8 million metric tons) of rice crops were destroyed by the floods, reducing rice production in the nation by about 75 percent. Replanting of rice was impossible while the floods persisted and had to wait until the next year's growing season. In the winter months, some people were able to plant wheat, spices, and other dry-weather crops.

Some 80 percent of Bangladeshis make their living by farming. "I don't know how God will save us," stated Mohammad Harunuddin Sheik, a villager from Chor Shibola who was camped out on the roof of his shack with his wife and daughters, in a September 7, 1998, *New York Times* article. "All my crops were destroyed. Where will I get seeds to plant next year?"

Causes of death At the end of November 1998, the Bangladeshi death toll was estimated to be more than fifteen hundred people. The main causes of death were drowning, diarrhea, cobra bites, and being crushed by collapsing houses. Disease and hunger posed grave threats in a nation where two-thirds of children are seriously malnourished even in the best of times.

Sickness spread through the foul floodwaters, which served as both garbage dump and toilet in a nation where indoor plumbing is a rarity, and the landfills were now underwater. People living in slums had no choice but to use the thick, black water around them for cleaning, cooking, and in some cases for drinking.

By mid-October, more than one million people were suffering from diarrhea. While the government had ample supplies of anti-diarrheal medication, it was difficult to deliver the medicine to sufferers.

As the floods receded, they left in their wake a thick layer of black sludge. The sludge, like the floodwaters, contained contaminants that spread disease and provided a breeding ground for malaria-carrying mosquitoes.

Difficulties faced by relief missions The floods and resulting food shortages left Bangladeshis, especially those without grain reserves from the previous year's harvest, in desperate need of international aid. The United Nations responded to the crisis by raising about $200 million from international donors. The distribution of food was difficult, however, given that millions of hungry people were distributed on numerous strips of land that stood out in the rising water. Dropping supplies from airplanes was not feasible, since packages would likely fall into the water. Some aid agencies chartered boats to traverse the floodwaters, however many crews refused to work because they feared capsizing in the dangerously fast currents. As floodwaters receded, relief agencies faced new obstacles to food delivery: water was too shallow for boats yet the roads were too muddy for cars.

There were also political obstacles to aid distribution. Some residents of Dhaka, the capital of Bangladesh, accused the government of withholding food from people in regions known to be opposition-party strongholds.

As the fall wore on, food distribution became more reliable. According to the program set up by the government, each family in need received 31 pounds (14 kilograms) of rice and wheat every month. That quantity

Experiencing the monsoon: An eyewitness account

The following passages are from a book titled *Chasing the Monsoon* by English journalist Alexander Frater. Frater, who was in Trivandrum, India (at the country's southern tip), when the rains came, described the scene as he joined a group of Indians gathered on the seashore. His account demonstrates how quickly the monsoon season can start, and how its arrival is anxiously awaited by many people.

> A line of spectators had formed behind the Kovalam beach road. They were dressed with surprising formality, many of the men wearing ties and the women fine saris.... Their excitement was shared and sharply focused, like that of a committee preparing to greet a celebrated spiritual leader.... As I joined them they greeted me with smiles.... The sky was black, the sea white. Foaming like champagne it surged over the road to within a few feet of where we stood....
>
> More holiday-makers were joining the line. The imbroglio of inky cloud swirling overhead contained nimbostratus, cumulonimbus and Lord knows what else.... Thunder boomed. Lightning went zapping into the sea.... Then... we saw a broad, ragged ban of luminous indigo heading slowly inshore. Lesser clouds suspended beneath it like flapping curtains reached right down to the sea.
>
> 'The rains!' everyone sang.
>
> The wind struck us with a force that made our line bend and waver....
>
> The deluge began....
>
> The rain hissed on the sea and fell on us with a buzzing, swarming noise....
>
> Water sheeted off the hillside, a rippling red tide carrying the summer's dust down to the sea....

was said to be adequate for at least one meal a day. Programs were also initiated that paid Bangladeshis to rebuild roads, schools, and hospitals. In that way people were given the opportunity to buy their food rather than relying on handouts.

Moneylenders make it worse Many Bangladeshis, desperate to make ends meet, sold their farm animals for discouragingly low prices. Such a move meant they would have no animals with which to till their land the following year. Many were also left with no choice but to sell their chickens and milk cows—for about half of the pre-flood prices.

Even after selling their possessions, cash-strapped Bangladeshis had difficulty meeting their basic needs. Moneylenders took advantage of the situation. These businessmen lent villagers small amounts of money

Family returns home as floodwaters recede in Bangladesh, 2004. AP IMAGES.

(about $125 maximum per loan) at interest rates as high as 100 percent. For some borrowers, such an equation would leave them in debt the rest of their lives. "I borrowed 1,000 taka ($21.00) at 100 taka ($2.10) interest per month," stated one villager in a 1998 CNN report. "They (private lenders) squeeze us to the bones to get their money back."

Money matters were made worse by the financial crisis that struck Asia at the same time as Bangladesh's floods. Many Bangladeshis who had been working in other countries in Southeast Asia were sent home. Prior to the flooding, money sent to Bangladeshis by family members working abroad totaled almost $1.5 billion per year. That was second only to exports for the nation's largest source of foreign income.

Bangladesh floods in 2002 and 2004 Bangladesh suffered devastating floods again during the monsoon rains of 2002. While not as severe as the 1998 floods, 2.3 million people were left stranded or homeless from floodwaters and two hundred thousand homes were submerged. Fortunately, the death toll was relatively low. Official accounts place the toll at nineteen people dead, sixteen of them from waterborne diseases. Other news accounts place the death toll at around 157 people. Hundreds of homes and farms were destroyed.

Flood problems were worse in 2004 due to flooding caused by monsoon rains and high tides in the Bay of Bengal. Millions of people were left without adequate food or clean water as the floods submerged

A young street vendor is caught in a monsoon downpour in New Delhi, India, 2000. ©AFP/CORBIS.

two-thirds of the country. According to some news reports, the death toll was as high as one thousand persons. Annual floods during the monsoon rains are likely to continue to plague Bangladesh for years to come, especially when combined with high tides and tropical cyclones.

Dangerous science: Monsoon

A monsoon is a huge, natural weather event that exchanges heat and moisture between land and sea. It is driven by the temperature differences between the two environments.

The monsoon climate is most pronounced in the Indian subcontinent and southeast Asia—home to a full 50 percent of the world's population. The monsoon zone includes India, the Indus Valley of Pakistan, portions of Nepal, Bhutan, Bangladesh, Burma, Malaysia, Vietnam, Thailand, Laos, and the Philippines, and the southeast tip of China. Some Atlantic coastal regions of northern South America also experience monsoon climate, as do slices of central Africa. Recently monsoon winds have been shown to exist in the southwestern United States, Japan, and portions of southern Europe.

The monsoon-driven rainy season typically lasts for four months, from June through September. India, for instance, gets 80 percent of its yearly rainfall during that period. The start and end dates of the monsoon

Monsoon clouds over Nepal. ©GALEN ROWELL/CORBIS.

rains vary from place to place and from year to year, as do the rainfall amounts.

A seasonal wind pattern Throughout the winter, the region affected by the monsoon is tilted away from the sun. During that time the land is cooler than the ocean. (Land heats up and cools down more quickly than water. Water heats up more slowly than land in the summer—which is why we go swimming to cool off—but water retains its heat longer than land.) The cooler air, which is denser, sinks. As the air sinks, the moisture within it evaporates and prevents the formation of clouds. At the same time, the relatively warm air above the ocean expands and rises, because it is less dense. The air over the sea is replaced by cooler air from far inland, due to the difference in air pressure (the different pressures exerted by the weight of the air). The air travels from a region of higher air pressure, over land, to a region of lower air pressure, over sea.

When spring arrives, the monsoon-prone area moves to a position almost directly beneath the sun and the winds shift direction. The land heats up, becoming warmer than the ocean. The surface air over land expands and rises, thus lowering the air pressure. Relatively cool air from over the ocean, made moist by evaporated ocean water, flows in and equalizes the pressure. Once the ocean air is heated over the land, it also rises. As it rises, the moisture within it condenses and forms clouds. Those clouds yield heavy rains throughout the summer months. When temperatures on land in the summer are exceptionally hot, the rains are very strong and cause widespread flooding.

Experiment: Convection currents in the atmosphere

A monsoon is driven by solar energy working through convection. When air is heated, it becomes less dense and rises. Cooler air flows in to take its place. Likewise, cooler air is more dense and sinks, displacing warmer air.

For this experiment you will need a large clear, plastic box. A plastic shoe box works well. You will also need a cup full of ice cubes, a small candle in a candle holder (such as a tea-light), and some black or dark-colored construction paper. Ask a teacher or parent to help you with the lit candle.

First, attach black paper to the back side of the plastic box, so the convection currents will be visible. Next, place the cup of ice in one end of the shoe box. Then have your parent or a teacher carefully light the candle and place it at the opposite end of the shoe box. Allow the candle to sit for a few moments. Then gently blow out the candle and place the lid on the shoe box. The smoke from the candle will follow the convection current inside the box.

This experiment reproduces the circumstances under which monsoon winds are formed. Earth's surface is warmed by sunlight and the less dense air rises. Cooler, denser air from over the ocean flows in to take the place of the warmer, rising air. The cooler, denser air brings moisture from the ocean to the land and the rains come.

The monsoon climate In the monsoon climate, the year is divided into dry and rainy seasons. While monsoon regions generally receive as much total annual rainfall as do rain forests, the precipitation is concentrated in the summer months. It is typical for around 120 inches (300 centimeters) of rain to fall during the rainy season, causing destructive flooding. Rainfall in the spring and fall is moderate while the months of December, January, and February are dry. The official designation of a monsoon climate is one in which monthly precipitation drops below 2.3 inches (6 centimeters) for one or two months of the year.

The total annual rainfall in monsoon regions is generally sufficient to sustain forests, even through the dry period. In some areas this forest resembles a rain forest while in others it is less dense and merges into scrublands. The land is primarily cultivated with rice, a crop that thrives on flooding.

Monsoon in India The cycle of life in India is closely related to the seasonal rain pattern. In India, the shape of the land intensifies the monsoon; it strengthens the flow of the wind out to sea, as well as back to land. India is shaped like a huge triangle. It is surrounded by ocean on two sides and very tall mountains on the third. The Bay of Bengal lies to the east of India, the Arabian Sea lies to the west, and the Himalayan Mountains are situated to the north.

In the winter months, the land is at its coolest and the sea is warmer than the land. The relatively cool air sinks down from the mountains,

People caught in the monsoon rains, Simla, India. © BEN SPENCER; EYE UBIQUITOUS/ CORBIS.

pulled by the force of gravity, and moves across the land. It then moves out over the water. Precipitation during the winter months is scarce.

In the spring the land heats up. In May and June, daytime air temperatures are typically more than 104°F (40°C). By June the land becomes warmer than the sea and the wind reverses direction. Cool, moist air flows onto land from both the Indian Ocean and the Bay of Bengal, forming eastern and western arms of the monsoon. That humid air abruptly triggers torrential rainfalls. The air is forced upward, in a process called orographic uplift, by the hills that occupy the center of the Indian peninsula. This contributes to the rainfall along the coasts. In a typical year, most of India has rain every day in June.

The rainfall is particularly heavy in the foothills of the Himalayas. When the moist air reaches the mountains, it is forced upward sharply. That motion causes the formation of towering storm clouds that produce abundant rain. One of the wettest places on Earth is the town of Cherrapunji. This town sits on the slopes of the Himalayas, just north of the Bay of Bengal. Cherrapunji receives more than 400 inches (1,100 centimeters) of rain per year.

Consequences of monsoons

Monsoons are complex phenomena that, unlike tornadoes or avalanches, are not always disastrous. Yes, some monsoons, those that bring far too

The Arizona monsoon

In recent decades, meteorologists have recognized that the late summer thunderstorms that occur over the mountains of the southwestern United States are a monsoon, at least marginally. While the wind does seasonally shift from the west and northwest in winter to the south and southeast in late summer, the shift is not as strong or abrupt as that experienced in India and Southeast Asia.

The mechanics that drive the southwestern monsoon are similar to those that drive other monsoons. During the winter months the air pressure is higher over land than it is over bodies of water to the south. In the spring, as the air warms considerably and the pressure over land lowers, moist air from over the Pacific Ocean, the Sea of Cortez (the water separating the Baja Peninsula from the Mexican mainland), and the Gulf of Mexico flows northward. As a result, in mid-to-late summer and early fall the deserts and dry plateaus of Arizona and New Mexico experience numerous thunderstorms. The thunderstorms that accompany the monsoon are caused by a combination of orographic uplift, daytime heating from the sun, and weak upper-level disturbances moving across the region.

The summer rains supply a significant portion of the region's annual precipitation. Arizona, for instance, receives only 6 percent of its annual rainfall in April, May, and June. In July, August, and September—the period considered the wet monsoon—the state gets 32 percent of its annual rainfall.

A summer monsoon breaks over the desert sky in Tucson, Arizona. ©ANDREW BROWN; ECOSCENE/CORBIS.

A Sri Lankan farmer guides his oxen through a muddy rice paddy. ©TIM PAGE/CORBIS.

much or far too little rain, fit the definition of "natural disaster." In general however, monsoons are a seasonal rhythm. The billion people who live in monsoon climates have adapted their lives to the seasonal changes.

Flooding Many parts of India, Bangladesh, and certain Southeast Asian nations become flooded every rainy season. The poor generally feel the effects of the flooding the most, as their homes are built on land most prone to floods, especially in shantytowns surrounding major cities. Some people have standing water in their houses for weeks at a time every year. Particularly large floods cause drownings and carry away people's meager possessions—and sometimes even entire homes. Floodwaters often mix with sewage and other refuse, creating health hazards for people reliant on river water for drinking, cooking, and washing.

The collapse of the Manchu River Dam

On August 11, 1979, excessively heavy monsoon rains caused the collapse of the Manchu River Dam near Morvi, India. Morvi is located 300 miles (480 kilometers) northwest of Mumbai (formerly Bombay). Before the dambreak, Morvi was a thriving industrial town of seventy thousand people. The collapse of the dam unleashed a 20-foot (6-meter) wall of water that killed some fifteen thousand of Morvi's citizens, as well as countless others from thirty small villages between Morvi and the dam.

The Manchu River Dam, built in 1972, had been designed to withstand an average yearly rainfall of 22 inches (56 centimeters). The 197-foot-high (60-meter-high) dam protected Morvi and other downstream settlements from flooding. The heavy monsoon rains of the summer of 1979 had already been placing stress on the dam when a severe storm dumped 28 inches (71 centimeters) of rain on the region in just twenty-four hours. Engineers tried to open the sluice gates to allow more water to flow out of the dam and relieve the pressure, but they found the gates had been rusted shut. When water levels behind the dam had risen to 20 feet (6 meters) above normal, the dam gave way.

The concrete structure of the Manchu River Dam in Morvi, India. AP IMAGES.

The water rushed forward, destroying everything in its path within fifteen minutes. In Morvi, people were knocked over and drowned, and mud homes were washed away. The floodwaters reached the second stories of tall buildings. After the flood passed, bodies were strewn everywhere, and a thick layer of mud covered everything.

Drought For regions dependent on the monsoon rains for their livelihood, when a monsoon does not come it can be deadly as well. An example of this tragedy can be found in the African Sahel—the strip of semi-arid land south of the Sahara Desert. The Sahel depends on annual seasonal rains to support grasslands for grazing livestock and to grow crops. The monsoon was weak or virtually nonexistent in the Sahel from

Edmund Halley studies monsoons

English astronomer Edmund Halley (1656–1742) is best known for his calculations involving a comet that passed close to Earth in 1682, and which he (correctly) predicted would return again in 1758. Today, we know it as Halley's comet, and it crosses our skies about every seventy-five years. Halley was a friend of English physicist Isaac Newton (1642–1727), and it was Halley who provided the money to publish Newton's famous *Principia Mathematica* in 1687, which many people feel is the most important document in the history of science.

Edmund Halley.

What most people do not know is that Halley also made one of the first studies of monsoon wind patterns. He conducted his observations while at sea and during a two-year stay on the island of St. Helena in the Atlantic Ocean off the western coast of Africa. He combined his observations with information obtained from sailors who had traveled throughout the world. As a result of these studies, Halley established that the difference between the temperatures of the air over land and over the adjacent ocean produced different air densities, which were the driving force behind seasonal monsoon winds. He published his findings in 1686 along with one of the first meteorological maps, which showed wind patterns on the world's oceans.

1968 through 1973, and again during several periods throughout the 1970s, 1980s, and early 1990s. This caused extensive drought (pronounced DROWT), an extended period during which the amount of precipitation is much lower than usual. Due to the lack of rainfall, large portions of the Sahel have been turning to desert.

Positive aspects of monsoons Monsoon rains nourish crops and support people and livestock. For instance rice, the number-one crop in monsoon regions, requires very wet conditions to grow. There are even positive aspects of floods caused by the monsoon. The floodwaters deposit a layer of nutrient-rich soil on farmland, increasing its fertility. In some areas, along with the floodwaters come fish and other edible aquatic life. Fish provide a needed source of protein when crops are submerged and other food is scarce.

The effect of El Niño on India's monsoons

In recent years, scientists have discovered a link between El Niño and the failure of India's monsoon. El Niño is an extraordinarily strong episode (occurring every two to seven years) of the annual warming of the Pacific waters off the coast of Peru and Ecuador. In 1982–1983, in conjunction with one of history's strongest El Niños, India's monsoon rains never came.

Scientists linked El Niño and the monsoon by discovering that at the same time the waters grow warm off the coast of Peru, a warming also occurs in the Indian Ocean. That warming causes a reversal of the pressure gradient in the Indian Ocean. The surface winds that usually blow to the northwest, toward the coast of Africa and India, change direction. They blow toward the southeast, where temperatures are warmer and pressure is lower, bringing warmth and moisture to western Australia. At the same time they leave India and southern Africa drier than normal.

The human factor

The level of flooding caused by monsoon rains in India and Bangladesh is made worse by erosion (wearing away) of the Himalayan mountainsides. Massive deforestation, the removal of most or all of the trees, on the slopes, has left the soil exposed and vulnerable to being washed away by heavy rains. The sediments get swept downstream and are deposited in riverbeds and in the Bay of Bengal. The sediments raise the levels of the riverbeds, leaving less room for water and contributing to the incidence and severity of flooding.

Deforestation also contributes to the severity of drought when rainfall is scarce. The lack of plants reduces the soil's ability to retain moisture. Erosion creates hard-packed ground that is unable to absorb any rain that does fall.

Another way that human activity magnifies the negative effects of monsoons is through the concentration of settlements in monsoon regions. Indeed, the locations affected by monsoons have the highest population density in the world. This fact means that when natural disasters do occur there, large numbers of people suffer the consequences.

Another human factor when talking about monsoons is that aid meant for victims of floods or drought is often mishandled. Distribution of food, water and supplies may be hampered by inefficiency on the part of government officials or may be deliberately withheld from certain areas because of political considerations, such as support for an opposition political movement.

Technology connection

The behavior of monsoons has been the subject of intense study by meteorologists for the last century. Nonetheless, monsoons, and especially what causes them to vary from year to year, are not entirely understood. This lack of knowledge makes monsoon prediction very difficult.

Efforts at predicting the arrival dates of monsoons are largely based on readings of the Southern Oscillation—changes in patterns of air pressure at sea level between the eastern and western edges of the Pacific Ocean. The rising and falling of the pressure gradient (the rate at which air pressure changes with horizontal distance) across the ocean may foretell changing wind patterns and the arrival of monsoon rains. Attempts at predicting rainfall amounts for specific locations involve the imperfect method of searching for patterns in past rainfall records.

"Though the monsoon winds constitute one of the greatest weather systems on earth, and an enormous amount of research has been carried out . . . , many questions remain shrouded in mystery," stated Julius Joseph, Monsoon Officer of the Indian Meteorological Center, in the book *Chasing the Monsoon*. "It's like the human brain. We know it but we don't know it."

[*See Also* **Climate; Drought; El Niño; Flood; Weather: An Introduction**]

For More Information

BOOKS

De Villiers, Marq. *Windswept: The Story of Wind and Weather.* New York: Walker, 2006.

Frater, Alexander. *Chasing the Monsoon.* New York: Picador, 2005.

Hyndman, Donald, and David Hyndman. *Natural Hazards and Disasters.* New York: Brooks Cole, 2006.

WEB SITES

"The Monsoon." *National Weather Service.* <http://www.wrh.noaa.gov/fgz/science/monsoon.php?wfo=fgz> (accessed March 23, 2007).

"North American Monsoon Experiment (NAME)." *NASA Earth Observatory.* <http://earthobservatory.nasa.gov/Newsroom/Campaigns/NAME_Mission.html> (accessed March 23, 2007).

Where to Learn More

Books

Abbott, Patrick Leon, ed. *Natural Disasters.* 6th ed. Columbus, OH: McGraw-Hill Higher Education, 2008.

Aguado, Edward, and James Burt. *Understanding Weather and Climate.* 4th ed. Englewood Cliffs, NJ: Prentice Hall, 2006.

Ahrens, C. Donald. *Meteorology Today: An Introduction to Weather, Climate, and the Environment.* 7th ed. Belmont, CA: Thomson Brooks/Cole, 2006.

Allaby, Michael. *Blizzards.* 2nd ed. New York: Facts on File, 2003.

Allaby, Michael. *How the Weather Works: 100 Ways Parents and Kids Can Share the Secrets of the Atmosphere.* New York: Putnam Group, Inc., 1999.

Allen, Leslie, et. al. *Raging Forces: Earth in Upheaval.* Washington, DC: National Geographic Society, 1996.

Andryszewski, Tricia. *The Dust Bowl: Disaster on the Plains.* Brookfield, CT: The Millbrook Press, 1993.

Anthes, Richard A. *Meteorology,* 7th ed. New York: Prentice Hall, 1996.

Arnold, Caroline. *El Niño: Stormy Weather for People and Wildlife.* New York: Clarion Books, 2005.

Bair, Frank E.*Climates of States.* 5th ed. Farmington Hills, MI: Thomson Gale, 2007.

Binhua, Wang. *Sea Fog.* New York: Springer-Verlag, 1985.

Bolt, Bruce A. *Earthquakes.* 4th ed. Salt Lake City, UT: W. H. Freeman and Co., 1999.

Botkin, Daniel, and Edward Keller. *Environmental Science: Earth as a Living Planet.* 4th ed. Hoboken, NJ: John Wiley & Sons, Inc. 2004.

Breen, Mark, Kathleen Friestad, and Michael Kline. *The Kid's Book of Weather Forecasting: Build a Weather Station, "Read" the Sky & Make Predictions!* Charlotte, VT: Williamson Publishing Company, 2000.

Brinkley, Douglas. *The Great Deluge: Hurricane Katrina, New Orleans, and the Mississippi Gulf Coast.* New York: William Morrow, 2006.

Bronson, William. *The Earth Shook, the Sky Burned.* San Francisco, CA: Chronicle Books, 1997.

Burroughs, William J., Bob Crowder, et. al. *Nature Company Guides: Weather.* New York: Time Life Books, 2000.

Campbell, N. A. *Biology.* 4th ed. Menlo Park, CA: The Benjamin/Cummings Publishing Company, Inc., 1996.

Carr, Michael. *International Marine's Weather Predicting Simplified: How to Read Weather Charts and Satellite Images.* New York: McGraw-Hill, 1999.

Chambers, Catherine. *Thunderstorm.* 2nd ed. Portsmouth, NH: Heinemann, 2007.

Chernov, Y. I. *The Living Tundra.* West Nyack, NY: Cambridge University Press, 1988.

Christian, Spencer, and Antonia Felix. *Shake, Rattle, and Roll: The World's Most Amazing Earthquakes, Volcanoes, and Other Forces.* New York: John Wiley & Sons, Inc., 1997.

Colten, Craig E. *An Unnatural Metropolis: Wrestling New Orleans from Nature.* Baton Rouge: Louisiana State University Press, 2005.

Cotton, William R., and Roger A. Pielke, Sr. *Human Impacts on Weather and Climate.* 2nd ed. New York: Cambridge University Press, 2007.

Dasch, E. Julius, ed. *Encyclopedia of Earth Sciences.* New York: Macmillan Library Reference, 1996.

De Blij, Harm J., et al. *Nature on the Rampage.* Washington, DC: Smithsonian Institution, 1994.

De Blij, Harm J., et al. *Restless Earth.* Washington, DC: National Geographic Society, 1997.

De Villiers, Marq. *Windswept: The Story of Wind and Weather.* New York: Walker & Company, 2006.

DeMillo, Rob. *How Weather Works.* Emeryville, CA: Ziff-Davis Press, 1994.

Drake, Frances. *Global Warming: The Science of Climate Change.* New York: Oxford University Press, 2000.

Drohan, Michele Ingber. *Avalanches.* New York: Rosen Publishing and PowerKids Press, 1999.

Drohan, Michele Ingber. *Floods.* New York: Rosen Publishing and PowerKids Press, 1999.

Fagan, Brian. *Floods, Famines and Emperors: El Niño and the Fate of Civilizations.* New York: Basic Books, 2000.

Ferguson, Sue, and Edward R. LaChapelle. *The ABCs of Avalanche Safety.* 3rd ed. Seattle, WA: Mountaineers Books, 2003.

Fisher, David E. *The Scariest Place on Earth: Eye to Eye with Hurricanes. New York: Random House, 1994.*

Flannery, Tim. *The Weather Makers: How Man Is Changing the Climate and What It Means for Life on Earth.* New York: Atlantic Monthly Press, 2006.

Frater, Alexander. *Chasing the Monsoon.* New York: Picador, 2005.

Geiger, Rudolf. *The Climate Near the Ground,* Cambridge, MA: Harvard University Press, 1965.

Gemmell, Kathy. *Storms and Hurricanes.* London: Usborne Publishing Ltd., 1996.

Glantz, Michael H. *Currents of Change: El Niño's Impact on Climate and Society.* 2nd ed. New York: Cambridge University Press, 2001.

Gore, Al. *An Inconvenient Truth: The Planetary Emergency of Global Warming and What We Can Do About It.* 2nd ed. New York: Rodale Books, 2006.

Hamblyn, Richard. *The Invention of Clouds: How an Amateur Meteorologist Forged the Language of the Skies.* London: Pan MacMillan, 2001.

Hambrey, Michael, and Jürg Alean. *Glaciers.* 2nd ed. Cambridge, UK: Cambridge University Press, 2004.

Hamilton, Richard. *Avalanches: Nature's Fury.* Minneapolis, MN: Abdo and Daughters, 2005.

Hodgson, Michael. *Basic Essentials Weather Forecasting.* 3rd ed. Guilford, CT: Falcon, 2007.

Hopping, Lorraine Jean. *Wild Weather: Blizzards!* New York: Scholastic Inc., 1999.

Houghton, John. *Global Warming: The Complete Briefing.* Cambridge, UK: Cambridge University Press, 2004.

Houze, Robert A., Jr. *Cloud Dynamics.* San Diego, CA: Academic Press, Inc., 1994.

Hurt, R. Douglas. *The Dust Bowl: An Agricultural and Social History.* Chicago: Nelson-Hall, 1981.

Hyndman, Donald, and David Hyndman. *Natural Hazards and Disasters.* New York: Brooks Cole, 2005.

Kahl, Jonathan D. W. *Weather Watch: Forecasting the Weather.* Toronto: Monarch Books of Canada Limited, 2002.

Kolber, Elizabeth. *Field Notes from a Catastrophe: Man, Nature, and Climate Change.* New York: Bloomsbury USA, 2006.

Larsen, Erik. *Isaac's Storm.* New York: Vintage Books, 2000.

Lauber, Patricia. *Hurricanes: Earth's Mightiest Storms.* New York: Scholastic Press, 1996.

Libby, W. F. *Radiocarbon Dating.* 2nd ed. University of Chicago Press, 1955.

Linden, Eugene. *The Winds of Change: Climate, Weather, and the Destruction of Civilizations.* New York: Simon & Schuster, 2006.

Lydolph, Paul E. *The Climate of the Earth.* Lanham, MD: Rowman & Littlefield Publishers, Inc., 1985.

McPhee, John. *Annals of the Former World.* New York: Farrar, Straus & Giroux, 1999.

McPhee, John. *The Control of Nature.* New York: Farrar, Straus & Giroux, 1999.

Merrick, Patrick. *Avalanches.* Plymouth, MN: Child's World, 1998.

Mogil, H. Michael. *Tornadoes.* Saint Paul, MN: Voyageur Press, 2003.

Moran, Joseph M., and Lewis W. Morgan. *Essentials of Weather.* Englewood Cliffs, NJ: Prentice Hall, 1995.

Murck, Barbara W. *Dangerous Earth: An Introduction to Geologic Hazards.* New York: John Wiley & Sons, Inc., 1996.

Murphee, Tom, and Mary Miller, with the San Francisco Exploratorium. *Watching Weather: A Low Pressure Book about High Pressure Systems.* New York: Henry Holt and Company, 1998.

Nash, J. Madeleine. *El Niño: Unlocking the Secrets of the Master Weather-Maker.* New York: Warner Books, 2003.

National Geographic Society. *Restless Earth: Disasters of Nature.* Washington, DC: National Geographic Society, 1997.

The National Geographic Desk Reference. Washington, DC: National Geographic Society, 1999.

National Geographic Society and Ralph M. Feather, Jr. *Earth Science.* New York: Glencoe/McGraw-Hill, 2002.

O'Meara, Donna. *Into the Volcano: A Volcano Researcher at Work.* Tonawanda, NY: Kids Can Press, 2007.

Pearce, Fred. *When the Rivers Run Dry: Water—The Defining Crisis of the Twenty-First Century.* Boston, MA: Beacon Press, 2006.

Philander, S. George. *Our Affair with El Niño: How We Transformed an Enchanting Peruvian Current into a Global Climate Hazard.* Princeton, NJ: Princeton University Press, 2004.

Pretor-Pinney, Gavin. *The Cloudspotter's Guide.* New York: Perigee, 2006.

Reader's Digest Association, eds. *Great Disasters: Dramatic True Stories of Nature's Awesome Powers.* Pleasantville, NY: Reader's Digest, 1991.

Robinson, Andrew. *Earth Shock: Hurricanes, Volcanoes, Earthquakes, Tornadoes and Other Forces of Nature.* New York: W. W. Norton & Company, 2002.

Rosenfeld, Jeffrey P. *Eye of the Storm: Inside the World's Deadliest Hurricanes, Tornadoes, and Blizzards.* New York: Basic Books, 2005.

Rubin, Louis D., and Jim Duncan. *The Weather Wizard's Cloud Book.* Chapel Hill, NC: Algonquin Books of Chapel Hill, 1989.

Simon, Seymour. *Hurricanes.* New York: Harper Trophy, 2003.

Simon, Seymour. *Tornadoes.* New York: Harper Trophy, 2001.

Simon, Seymour. *Weather.* New York: Collins, 2006.

Stanley, Jerry. *Children of the Dust Bowl: The True Story of the School at Weedpatch Camp.* New York: Crown Publishers Inc., 1992.

Stewart, Gail. *Overview Series—Catastrophe in Southern Asia: The Tsunami of 2004.* San Diego, CA: Lucent Books, 2005.

Svobida, Lawrence. *Farming the Dust Bowl: A First-Hand Account from Kansas.* Lawrence, KS: University Press of Kansas, 1986. (Originally published in 1940 by The Caxton Printers, Ltd.)

Sweeney, Karen O'Connor. *Nature Runs Wild.* Danbury, CT: Franklin Watts Inc., 1979.

Tannenbaum, Beulah, and Harold E. Tannenbaum. *Making and Using Your own Weather Station.* New York: Franklin Watts, 1989.

Tibballs, Geoff. *Tsunami: The Most Terrifying Disaster.* London: Carlton Publishing Group, 2005.

Trewartha, Glenn T., and Lyle H. Horn. *An Introduction to Climate.* 5th ed. New York: McGraw-Hill, 1980.

VanCleave, Janice. *Earth Science for Every Kid: 101 Easy Experiments that Really Work.* New York: John Wiley, 1991.

Vasquez, Tim. *Weather Forecasting Handbook.* 5th ed. Garland, TX: Weather Graphics Technologies, 2002.

Verkaik, Jerrine, and Arjen Verkaik. *Under the Whirlwind: Everything You Need to Know About Tornadoes But Didn't Know Who to Ask.* 2nd ed., Elmwood, Ontario, Canada: Whirlwind Books, 2001.

Walker, Jane. *Avalanches and Landslides.* New York: Gloucester Press, 1992.

Walker, Jane. *Famine, Drought and Plagues.* New York: Gloucester Press, 1992.

Ward, Kaari, ed. *Great Disasters.* Pleasantville, NY: Reader's Digest Association, 1989.

Waterlow, Julia. *Violent Earth: Flood.* New York: Hodder Children's Books, 1994.

Watt, Fiona, and Francis Wilson. *Weather and Climate.* London: Usborne Publishing Ltd., 1992.

Williams, Jack. *The Weather Book: An Easy-to-Understand Guide to the USA's Weather.* New York: Vintage Books, 1997.

Worster, Donald. *Dust Bowl: The Southern Plains in the 1930s.* New York: Oxford University Press, 1979.

Wright, Richard T. *Environmental Science: Toward A Sustainable Future.* 10th ed. Upper Saddle River, NJ: Prentice Hall, 2007.

Zebrowski, Ernest, and Ernest Zebrowski Jr. *Perils of a Restless Planet: Scientific Perspectives on Natural Disasters.* Ann Arbor: University of Michigan Press, 2005.

Zebrowski, Ernest, and Judith A. Howard. *Category 5: The Story of Camille: Lessons Unlearned from America's Most Violent Hurricane.* Cambridge, UK: Cambridge University Press, 1999.

Periodicals

Ackerman, Jennifer. "Islands at the Edge." *National Geographic* (August 1997): pp. 2–31.

Akin, Wallace. "The Great Tri-State Tornado." *American Heritage* (May/June 2000): pp. 32–36.

Allen, Brian. "Capitol Hill Meltdown: While the Nation Sizzles, Congress Fiddles over Measures to Slow Down Future Climate Change." *Time* (August 9, 1999): p. 56+.

Annin, Peter. "Power on the Prairie: In Minnesota, They're Harvesting the Wind." *Newsweek* (October 26, 1998): p. 66.

Appenzeller, Tim. "The Case of the Missing Carbon." *National Geographic* (February, 2004): pp. 88–117.

Appenzeller, Tim. "Humans in the Hot Seat." *U.S. News & World Report* (November 6, 2000): p. 54.

Appenzeller, Tim, and Dennis R. Dimick. "Signs from Earth." *National Geographic* (September 2004): pp. 2–12.

"Avalanche!" *National Geographic World* (January 1997): pp. 2–6.

Baliunas, Sallie. "Full of Hot Air: A Climate Alarmist Takes on 'Criminals Against Humanity'." *Reason* (October 2005): p. 1.

Beardsley, Tim. "Dissecting a Hurricane." *Scientific American* (March 2000): pp. 80–85.

Begley, Sharon. "The Mercury's Rising." *Newsweek* (December 4, 2000): p. 52.

Bentley, Mace. "A Midsummer's Nightmare." *Weatherwise* (August/September 1996).

Bentley, Mace, and Steve Horstmeyer. "Monstrous Mitch." *Weatherwise* (March/April 1999).

Bishop, Ian D., and David R. Miller. "Visual Assessment Of Off-Shore Wind Turbines: The Influence of Distance, Contrast, Movement and Social Variables." *Renewable Energy: An International Journal* (April 2007): pp. 814–831.

Bond, Kathleen. "Church Backs Poor in Drought; Brazil's Leaders Slow to Respond." *National Catholic Reporter* (August 14, 1998): p. 11+.

Brenstein, Seth. "Hottest Years Ever Strengthen the Scientific Case for an Ever-Warming World." Knight-Ridder/Tribune News Service (January 13, 2000).

Brooks, Tim. "Fire and Rain: Forecasting the Chaos of Weather." *National Geographic* (June 2005): pp. 90–109.

Brown, Kathryn. "Invisible Energy." *Discover* (October 1999): p. 36.

Carroll, Chris. "In Hot Water." *National Geographic* (August 2005): pp. 72–85.

Chacon, Richard. "The Earth Calms, and Recovery Begins." *Boston Globe* (January 19, 2001): p. A13.

Coila, Bridget. "Changing the Weather." *Weatherwise* (May/June 2005): pp. 50–54.

Currie, Lloyd. "The Remarkable Metrological History of Radiocarbon Dating." *Journal of Research of the National Institute of Standards and Technology* (March/April 2004): pp. 185–217.

De Roy, Tui. "Caught in a Melting World." *International Wildlife* (November/December 2000): pp. 12–19.

Dick, Jason. "Global Warming." *Amicus Journal* (Summer 1999): p. 13.

"Drowning: Bangladesh." *The Economist* (September 12, 1998): p. 43.

Duffy, James A. "Administration Signs Global Warming Agreement." Knight-Ridder/Tribune News Service (November 12, 1998).

Dugger, Celia W. "2-Month Flood Breeds Havoc and Diseases in Bangladesh." *New York Times* (October 10, 1998): p. A9.

Dugger, Celia W. "Monsoon Hangs On, Swamping Bangladesh." *New York Times* (September 7, 1998): p. A1, A5.

Ehrlich, Gretel. "Last Days of the Ice Hunters." *National Geographic* (January 2006): pp. 79–101.

"Enviro-Cars: The Race Is On." *Business Week* (February 8, 1999): p. 74.

Favstovsky, D. E., and P. M. Sheehan. "The Extinction of the Dinosaurs in North America." *GSA Today* (March 2005): pp. 4–10.

"Fighting Global Warming with Iron at Sea." *Newsweek* (October 23, 2000): p. 54.

Findley, Rowe. "Mount St. Helens: Nature on Fast Forward." *National Geographic* (May 2000): pp. 106–125.

"Fire Forces 200 from Homes Near Boulder." *New York Times* (September 18, 2000): p. A22.

Fox, Stephen. "For a While... It Was Fun." *Smithsonian* (September 1999): pp. 128–130, 132, 134–140, 142.

Franklin, James L. "A Season of Devastation: Atlantic Hurricanes 2004." *Weatherwise* (March/April 2005): pp. 52–61.

Gaines, Ernest J. "Home No More." *National Geographic* (August 2006): pp. 42–53.

Glick, Daniel. "The Big Thaw." *National Geographic* (September 2004): pp. 13–33.

"Global Warming May Be Beneficial." *USA Today Magazine* (June 2000): p. 10.

Gonzalez, Frank I. "Tsumani!" *Scientific American* (May 1999): pp. 56–65.

Gore, Rick. "Andrew Aftermath." *National Geographic* (April 1993): pp. 2–37.

Griekspoor, Phyllis J. "Baked Kansas: La Niña Heralds a Possible Drought for State." *Wichita Eagle* (February 2006).

Grove, Noel. "Volcanoes: Crucibles of Creation." *National Geographic* (December 1992): pp. 5–41.

Halverson, Jeffrey B. "Chasing Hurricanes in Africa." *Weatherwise* (November/December 2006): pp. 62–64.

Halverson, Jeffrey B. "A Climate Conundrum." *Weatherwise* (March/April 2006): pp. 18–23.

Halverson, Jeffrey B. "A Hurricane Is Born." *Weatherwise* (November/December 2004): pp. 72–73.

Hanson-Harding, Alexandra. "Global Warming." *Junior Scholastic* (November 27, 2000): p. 6.

Hayden, Thomas. "Super Storms: No End in Sight." *National Geographic* (August 2006): pp. 66–77.

Hebert, H. Josef. "Scientists Paint Grim View of Impact on U.S. of Global Warming." Associated Press (June 9, 2000).

Helvarg, David. "Antarctica: The Ice Is Moving." *E* (September 2000): p. 33.

Henson, Robert. "Hot, Hotter, Hottest: 1998 Raised the Bar for Global Temperature Leaps." *Weatherwise* (March/April 1999): pp. 34–37.

Henson, Robert. "The Intensity Problem: How Strong Will a Hurricane Get?" *Weatherwise* (September/October 1998): pp. 20–26.

Hertsgaard, Mark. "Killer Weather Ahead." *Nation* (February 26, 2007): pp. 5–6.

Hodges, Glenn. "Russian Smokejumpers." *National Geographic* (August 2002): pp. 82–100.

"Hurricane Havoc in Central America." *The Economist* (November 7, 1998): p. 33.

"Hurricanes Rip Through Impoverished Caribbean, Central American Regions." *National Catholic Reporter* (November 20, 1998): p. 12.

"Iceland's Trial by Fire." *National Geographic* (May 1997): pp. 58–71.

Iocavelli, Debi. "Hurricanes: Eye Spy." *Weatherwise* (August/September 1996): pp. 10–11.

Keisterm, Edwin, Jr. " Battling the Orange Monster." *Smithsonian* (July 2000): pp. 32–42.

Klesius, Michael. "The Mystery of Snowflakes." *National Geographic* (January 2007): p. 22.

Lange, Karen. "Direct Hit: Inside a Tornado." *National Geographic* (June 2005): pp. 112–115.

Larsen, Josh. "The Emergence of the Weather Blog." *Weatherwise* (January/February 2007): pp. 10–11.

Lawless, Jill. "Global Warming Threatens a Third of World's Habitats." Associated Press (August 30, 2000).

Le Comte, Douglas. "Weather around the World." *Weatherwise* (March/April 2001): pp. 23–28.

Levine, Mark. "A Storm at the Bone: A Personal Exploration into Deep Weather." *Outside Magazine* (November 1998).

Libbrecht, Kenneth G. "The Formation of Snow Crystals." *American Scientist* (January/February 2007): pp. 52–59.

McDonald, Kim A. "Unearthing Earth's Ancient Atmosphere Beneath Two Miles of Greenland Ice." *Chronicle of Higher Education* (August 2, 1996): pp. A6+.

McKibbin, Warwick J., and Peter J. Wilcoxen. "Until We Know More About Global Warming, the Best Policy Is a Highly Flexible One." *Chronicle of Higher Education* (July 2, 1999): pp. B4+.

Mazza, Patrick. "Global Warming Is Here!" *Earth Island Journal* (Fall 1999): p. 14.

Mazza, Patrick. "The Invisible Hand: As Human Activity Warms the Earth, El Niño Grows More Violent." *Sierra* (May/June 1998): pp. 68+.

Miner, Todd, Peter J. Sousounis, James Wallman, and Greg Mann. "Hurricane Huron." *Bulletin of the American Meteorological Society* (February 2000): pp. 223–236.

Mitchell, Mitch. "Wind Gusts Cause Power Outages, Dust Storm." *Fort Worth Star-Telegram* (April 2006).

Montaigner, Fenck. "No Room to Run." *National Geographic* (September 2004): pp. 34–55.

Mulvaney, Kieran. "Alaska: The Big Meltdown." *E* (September 2000): p. 36.

Nielsen, Clifford H. "Hurd Willett: Forecaster Extraordinaire." *Weatherwise* (August/September 1993): pp. 38–44.

Nuttall, Nick. "Ganges Glacier Melting Fast." *The Times* (London). (July 20, 1999): p. 9.

Pearce, Fred. "Science: Meltdown in the Mountains." *The Independent* (London). (March 31, 2000): p. 8.

Perkins, S. "Greenland's Ice Is Thinner at the Margins." *Science News* (July 22, 2000): p. 54.

Peterson, Chester Jr. "Harvest the Wind: The Midwest Could Be the Saudi Arabia of Wind Powered Energy." *Successful Farming* (January 1999): p. 44+.

Pinna, Marco. "Etna Ignites." *National Geographic* (February, 2002): pp. 68–87.

Proctor, Paul. "Fire-Fighting Fleet Stretched to Limit as U.S. West Burns." *Aviation Week & Space Technology* (August 21, 2000): pp. 38–39.

"Rain, Rain, Go Away . . . ." *Time International* (September 14, 1998): p. 18.

Rasicot, Julie. "Locals Help Battle Fires in Montana." *The Washington Post* (August 17, 2000): p. 16.

"Renewable Energy Resources." *Current Health 2* (April 1999): p. S14.

Revkin, Andrew C. "Treaty Talks Fail to Find Consensus in Global Warming." *New York Times* (November 26, 2000).

Rosenfeld, Jeff. "Mr. Tornado: The Life and Career of Ted Fujita." *Weatherwise* (May/June 1999): p. 18.

Rosenfeld, Jeff. "Sentinels in the Sky." *Weatherwise* (January/February 2000): pp. 24–27.

Rosenfeld, Jeff. "Unearthing Climate." *Weatherwise* (May/June 2000): p. 12.

Santana, Sofia. "Remembering Andrew." *Weatherwise* (July/August 2002): pp. 14–19.

Shepherd, Marshall. "The big picture: Satellites have changed our view of the world." *Weatherwise.* (January/February 2003): pp. 24–37.

Shilts, Elizabeth. "Harnessing a Powerful Breeze." *Canadian Geographic* (May/June 1999): p. 20.

Simpson, Sarah. "Raging Rivers of Rock." *Scientific American* (July 2000): pp. 24–25.

"The State of U.S. Renewable Power." *Mother Earth News* (February 1999): p. 16.

Stevens, William K. "Catastrophic Melting of Ice Sheet Is Possible, Studies Hint." *New York Times* (July 7, 1998): p. B13.

Stevens, William K. "Human Imprint on Climate Change Grows Clearer." *New York Times* (June 29, 1999): p. 1+.

Sudetic, Chuck. "As the World Burns." *Rolling Stone* (September 2, 1999): p. 97+.

Suplee, Curt. "El Niño/La Niña." *National Geographic* (March 1999): pp. 72–95.

Taylor, Jeff. "Flood Convergence." *Reason* (December 2005).

"That Dreadful Smog Is Back." *The Economist* (March 18, 2000): p. 40.

Trenberth, Kevin. "Uncertainty in Hurricanes and Global Warming." *Science* (17 June 2005): pp. 1753–1754.

Vesilind, Priit J. "The Hard Science, Dumb Luck, and Cowboy Nerve of Chasing Tornadoes." *National Geographic* (April 2004): pp. 2–37.

"U.S. Signs Kyoto Pact." *Maclean's* (November 23, 1998): p. 93.

Williams, A. R. "After the Deluge." *National Geographic* (November 1999): pp. 108–129.

Williams, A. R. "Popocatepetl: Mexico's Smoking Mountain." *National Geographic* (January 1999): pp. 116–137.

Williams, A. R. "Montserrat: Under the Volcano." *National Geographic* (July 1997): pp. 58–75.

Williams, Jack. "Antarctica: A Land of Ice and Wind." *Weatherwise* (January/February 2000): pp. 14–22.

Wunsch, Carl. "Quantitative Estimate of the Milankovitch-forced Contribution to Observed Quaternary Climate Change." *Quaternary Science Reviews* (Vol. 23, 2004):1001–1012.

Zwingle, Erla. "Meltdown: The Alps under Pressure." *National Geographic* (February, 2006): pp. 96–115.

Web Sites

Allgeyer, Robert. "APPENDIX: The Fata Morgana Mirage over Monterey Bay." *View to the Horizon.* <http://www.icogitate.com/~ergosum/essays/vtth/viewtothehorizon.htm> (accessed June 14, 2007).

American Avalanche Association. <http://www.americanavalancheassociation.org/> (accessed June 14, 2007).

"Avalanche!" *NOVA Online.* <http://www.pbs.org/wgbh/nova/avalanche/> (accessed June 14, 2007).

"Avalanche Awareness." *National Snow and Ice Data Center.* <http://nsidc.org/snow/avalanche/> (accessed June 14, 2007).

"Cascades Volcano Observatory." *United States Geological Survey.* <http://vulcan.wr.usgs.gov/> (accessed June 14, 2007).

"Climate Change." *United States Environmental Protection Agency.* <http://www.epa.gov/climatechange/> (accessed June 14, 2007).

"Climate Change." *World Wildlife Fund.* <http://www.panda.org/about_wwf/what_we_do/climate_change/index.cfm> (accessed June 14, 2007).

"Climate Change Impacts: Feeling the Heat." *Nature Conservancy.* <http://www.nature.org/initiatives/climatechange/issues> (accessed June 14, 2007).

Cowley, Les. "Rainbows." *Atmosphere Optics.* <http://www.atoptics.co.uk/rayshad.htm> (accessed June 14, 2007).

"Do-It-Yourself Weather Forecasting." *Weather Michigan.* <http://www.weathermichigan.com/u_do_it.htm> (accessed June 14, 2007).

"Driving in Fog." *California Highway Patrol.* <http://www.chp.ca.gov/html/fog-tips.html> (accessed June 14, 2007).

"Drought." *National Weather Service: Hydrologic Information Center.* <http://www.nws.noaa.gov/oh/hic/current/drought/> (accessed June 14, 2007).

"Drought Watch." *U.S. Geological Survey.* <http://water.usgs.gov/waterwatch/?m=dryw> (accessed June 14, 2007).

"El Niño." *National Oceanic and Atmospheric Administration.* <http://www.elnino.noaa.gov/> (accessed June 14, 2007).

"Flood." *Federal Emergency Management Agency.* <http://www.fema.gov/hazard/flood/index.shtm> (accessed June 14, 2007).

"Flood Safety." *National Weather Service Flood Safety.* <http://www.floodsafety.noaa.gov/> (accessed June 14, 2007).

"Forces and Winds: Online Meteorology Guide." *University of Illinois: Weather World 2010 Project.* <http://ww2010.atmos.uiuc.edu/(Gh)/guides/mtr/fw/home.rxml> (accessed June 14, 2007).

Geist, Eric L., and Laura Zink Torresan. "Life of a Tsunami." *United States Geological Survey.* <http://walrus.wr.usgs.gov/tsunami/basics.html> (accessed June 14, 2007).

"Hawaiian Volcano Observatory." *United States Geological Survey.* <http://hvo.wr.usgs.gov/> (accessed June 14, 2007).

Helmuth, Laura. "Antarctica Erupts!" *Smithsonian Science and Technology.* <http://www.smithsonianmag.com/issues/2006/december/antarctica.php> (accessed June 14, 2007).

"Historical Winter Storms." *The Weather Channel.* <http://www.weather.com/encyclopedia/winter/history.html> (accessed June 14, 2007).

"Hurricanes." *FEMA for Kids.* <http://www.fema.gov/kids/hurr.htm> (accessed June 14, 2007).

"Hurricanes." *National Oceanic and Atmospheric Administration.* <http://hurricanes.noaa.gov/>(accessed June 14, 2007).

Jaffe, Eric. "Volcanic Lightning." *Smithsonian Science and Technology.* <http://www.smithsonianmag.com/issues/2007/february/augustine.php> (accessed June 14, 2007).

"La Niña." *National Aeronautic and Space Administration: Earth Observatory.* <http://earthobservatory.nasa.gov/Library/LaNina/> (accessed June 14, 2007).

"La Niña." *National Oceanic and Atmospheric Administration.* <http://www.elnino.noaa.gov/lanina.html>(accessed June 14, 2007).

"Local Winds: Mountain Breezes." *Danish Wind Industry Association.* <http://www.windpower.org/en/tour/wres/mount.htm> (accessed June 14, 2007).

"The Monsoon." *National Weather Service.* <http://www.wrh.noaa.gov/fgz/science/monsoon.php?wfo=fgz> (accessed June 14, 2007).

"Names of Winds." *Golden Gate Weather Services.* <http://ggweather.com/winds.html> (accessed June 14, 2007).

"National Avalanche Center." *U.S. Forest Service.* <http://www.avalanche.org/%7enac/> (accessed June 14, 2007).

"National Hurricane Center Home Page." *National Hurricane Center.* <http://www.nhc.noaa.gov/> (accessed June 14, 2007).

"National Oceanic and Atmospheric Administration Home Page." *National Oceanic and Atmospheric Administration.* <http://www.noaa.org> (accessed June 14, 2007).

"Natural Hazards—Wildfires." *United States Geological Survey.* <http://www.usgs.gov/hazards/wildfires/> (accessed June 14, 2007).

"North American Monsoon Experiment (NAME)." *NASA Earth Observatory.* <http://earthobservatory.nasa.gov/Newsroom/Campaigns/NAME_Mission.html> (accessed June 14, 2007).

"NCAR/UCAR/UOP Home." *National Center for Atmospheric Research.* <http://www.ucar.edu/> (accessed June 14, 2007).

"Official Weather Forecasts and Warnings." *The World Meteorological Organization.* <http://www.wmo.int/> (accessed June 14, 2007).

Pacific Tsunami Museum. <http://www.tsunami.org/> (accessed June 14, 2007).

"Planet Earth." *NASA's Observatorium.* <http://observe.arc.nasa.gov/nasa/earth/earth_index.shtml.html> (accessed June 14, 2007).

"Thunderstorms and Lightning." *Federal Emergency Management Administration.* <http://www.fema.gov/hazard/thunderstorm/index.shtm> (accessed June 14, 2007).

"Tornado." *Federal Emergency Management Administration.* <http://www.fema.gov/hazard/tornado/index.shtm> (accessed June 14, 2007).

"Tsunamis." *Coastal Ocean Institute.* <http://www.whoi.edu/institutes/coi/viewTopic.do?o=readid=281> (accessed June 14, 2007).

"U.S. Drought Monitor." *University of Nebraska, Lincoln.* <http://www.drought.unl.edu/dm/monitor.html> (accessed June 14, 2007).

"Wave that Shook the World." *NOVA.* <http://www.pbs.org/wgbh/nova/tsunami/> (accessed June 14, 2007).

"Weather." *National Oceanic and Atmospheric Administration.* <http://www.noaa.gov/wx.html> (accessed June 14, 2007).

"Weather Office." *Environment Canada.* <http://weatheroffice.ec.gc.ca/canada_e.html> (accessed June 14, 2007).

"Welcome to the Weather Underground." *Weather Underground.* <http://www.wunderground.com/> (accessed June 14, 2007).

"Wildfire." *Federal Emergency Management Administration.* <http://www.fema.gov/hazard/wildfire/index.shtm> (accessed June 14, 2007).

Wilhelmson, Bob, et al. "Types of Thunderstorms." *University of Illinois: Weather World 2010 Project.* <http://ww2010.atmos.uiuc.edu/(Gh)/guides/mtr/svr/type/home.rxml> (accessed June 14, 2007).

"World Meteorological Organization Homepage." *World Meteorological Organization: A United Nations Specialized Agency.* <http://www.wmo.> (accessed June 14, 2007).

Index

Numerals in *italic type* indicate volume number. Items in **boldface** indicate main entries. Graphic elements (photos, graphs, illustrations) are denoted by (ill.). Tables are denoted by *t*.

A

B

D

E

F

G

H

I

J

K

M

N

O

P

T

U

Y

Z